wxPython Application Development Cookbook

Over 80 step-by-step recipes to get you up to speed with building your own wxPython applications

Cody Precord

[PACKT] open source*
community experience distilled
PUBLISHING

BIRMINGHAM – MUMBAI

wxPython Application Development Cookbook

First published: December 2015

Production reference: 1171215

Published by Packt Publishing Ltd.

Livery Place

35 Livery Street

Birmingham B3 2PB, UK.

ISBN 978-1-78528-773-2

www.packtpub.com

Credits

Author
Cody Precord

Reviewers
Joran Beasley
Jens Göpfert

Acquisition Editor
Usha Iyer

Content Development Editor
Neeshma Ramakrishnan
Deepti Thore

Technical Editor
Vijin Boricha

Copy Editor
Shruti Iyer

Project Coordinator
Shweta H Birwatkar

Proofreader
Safis Editing

Indexer
Mariammal Chettiyar

Production Coordinator
Nilesh Mohite

Cover Work
Nilesh Mohite

About the Author

Cody Precord is a software engineer based in Minneapolis, MN, USA. He designs and writes systems and application software for Windows, AIX, Linux, and Macintosh OS X using primarily C++, C#, C, Perl, Bash, and Python. The constant need for working on multiple platforms naturally led Cody to the wxPython toolkit, which he has used for several years. He is the author of *wxPython 2.8 Application Development Cookbook, Packt Publishing* and has also contributed to the development of the wxPython library. Cody is interested in promoting cross platform development practices and improving usability in software.

About the Reviewers

Joran Beasley received his degree in computer science from the University of Idaho. He has programmed desktop applications in wxPython professionally to monitor large-scale sensor networks that can be used in agriculture for the last 7 years. Joran currently lives in Moscow, Idaho, and works for Decagon Devices, Inc. as a software engineer.

> I would like to thank my wife, Nicole, for putting up with my long hours hunched over a keyboard and her constant support and help in raising our two wonderful children.

Jens Göpfert started developing applications with wxPyton in 2003, as a student assistant first and later on during his professional career. He is known and considered by peers as a wxPython expert. Jens has developed applications for engineers in the automotive domain, where he further gained invaluable experience in working with complex and easily operable user interfaces. With this knowledge, he started using wxPython for various projects in his spare time as well. Also, as a user of the underlying C++ implementation, Jens applies his analytical skills to better understand the wxPython functionality and address problems or make enhancements.

> Special thanks go to my wife, Marlene, and my two children, Melinda and Julius, for supporting me and my passion for developing while I spent a lot of time working on the computer.

www.PacktPub.com

Support files, eBooks, discount offers, and more

For support files and downloads related to your book, please visit www.PacktPub.com.

Did you know that Packt offers eBook versions of every book published, with PDF and ePub files available? You can upgrade to the eBook version at www.PacktPub.com and as a print book customer, you are entitled to a discount on the eBook copy. Get in touch with us at service@packtpub.com for more details.

At www.PacktPub.com, you can also read a collection of free technical articles, sign up for a range of free newsletters and receive exclusive discounts and offers on Packt books and eBooks.

https://www2.packtpub.com/books/subscription/packtlib

Do you need instant solutions to your IT questions? PacktLib is Packt's online digital book library. Here, you can search, access, and read Packt's entire library of books.

Why Subscribe?

- Fully searchable across every book published by Packt
- Copy and paste, print, and bookmark content
- On demand and accessible via a web browser

Free Access for Packt account holders

If you have an account with Packt at www.PacktPub.com, you can use this to access PacktLib today and view 9 entirely free books. Simply use your login credentials for immediate access.

Table of Contents

Preface

In today's world of desktop applications, there is a great amount of incentive in being able to develop applications that can run in more than one environment. Currently, there are a handful of options available for cross platform frameworks to develop desktop applications in Python; wxPython is one such cross platform GUI toolkit for the Python programming language. It allows Python programmers to simply and easily create programs with a complete, highly functional graphical user interface. The wxPython code style has changed quite a bit over the years and has become much more Pythonic. The examples that you will find in this book are fully up to date and reflect this change in style. This cookbook provides you with the latest recipes to quickly create robust, reliable, and reusable wxPython applications. These recipes will guide you right from writing simple, basic wxPython scripts all the way through complex concepts and also feature various design approaches and techniques in wxPython.

This book starts off by covering a variety of topics, from the most basic requirements of a wxPython application to some of the more in-depth details of the inner workings of the framework, thus laying a foundation for any wxPython application. It then explains event handling, basic and advanced user interface controls, interface design and layout, creating dialogs, components, extending functionality, and so on. We will conclude by learning how to build and manage applications for distribution.

For each of the recipes, there is first an introductory and then more advanced examples along with plenty of example code that shows you how to develop and manage user-friendly applications. For more experienced developers, most recipes also include an additional discussion of the solution, allowing you to further customize and enhance the component.

What this book covers

Chapter 1, *wxPython Starting Points*, teaches the basics of getting started with building applications with wxPython.

Chapter 2, *Common User Controls*, introduces you to the commonly used UI components and how use them in wxPython.

Chapter 3, *UI Layout and Organization*, shows you how to lay out and present user controls on screen using Sizers.

Chapter 4, *Containers and Advanced Controls*, introduces you to various container-type and specialized controls, such as web browsers.

Chapter 5, *Data Displays and Grids*, shows you how to display and work with data using the Grids, Lists, and DataView controls.

Chapter 6, *Ways to Notify and Alert*, teaches you the techniques of alerting and notifying users with information.

Chapter 7, *Requesting and Retrieving Information*, shows you how to prompt users for information and input.

Chapter 8, *User Interface Primitives*, shows you how to use DeviceContexts to draw and customize your own UI components.

Chapter 9, *Creating and Customizing Components*, teaches you the techniques of designing and creating your own custom controls.

Chapter 10, *Getting Your Application Ready for Release*, shows you how to manage application configuration and build packages for release.

What you need for this book

All the recipes in this book were written using the following software:

- ▸ wxPython 3.0.2.0
- ▸ Python 2.7.9

A small selection of recipes requires some additional external Python packages, which are described in the recipe.

In addition to these tools, you will just need a good text editor that can work with Python files.

Who this book is for

This book is written for Python programmers wanting to develop user interfaces for their applications. An understanding of the Python language and basic object-oriented programming concepts is required to get the most out of this book.

Sections

In this book, you will find several headings that appear frequently (Getting ready, How to do it, How it works, There's more, and See also).

To give clear instructions on how to complete a recipe, we use these sections as follows:

Getting ready

This section tells you what to expect in the recipe, and describes how to set up any software or any preliminary settings required for the recipe.

How to do it...

This section contains the steps required to follow the recipe.

How it works...

This section usually consists of a detailed explanation of what happened in the previous section.

There's more...

This section consists of additional information about the recipe in order to make the reader more knowledgeable about the recipe.

See also

This section provides helpful links to other useful information for the recipe.

Conventions

In this book, you will find a number of text styles that distinguish between different kinds of information. Here are some examples of these styles and an explanation of their meaning.

Code words in text, database table names, folder names, filenames, file extensions, pathnames, dummy URLs, user input, and Twitter handles are shown as follows: "To make the control visible to the user we call the `Show` method."

A block of code is set as follows:

```
class MyPanel(sized.SizedScrolledPanel):
    def __init__(self, parent):
        super(MyPanel, self).__init__(parent)

        self.SetSizerType("form")
```

When we wish to draw your attention to a particular part of a code block, the relevant lines or items are set in bold:

```
class MyPanel(sized.SizedScrolledPanel):
    def __init__(self, parent):
        super(MyPanel, self).__init__(parent)

        self.SetSizerType("form")
```

Any command-line input or output is written as follows:

```
python main.py
```

New terms and **important words** are shown in bold. Words that you see on the screen, for example, in menus or dialog boxes, appear in the text like this: "So now, it's time to add this method in to build up a simple **File** and **Edit** menu."

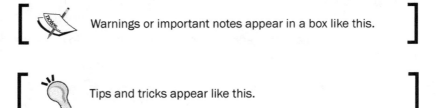

Warnings or important notes appear in a box like this.

Tips and tricks appear like this.

Reader feedback

Feedback from our readers is always welcome. Let us know what you think about this book—what you liked or disliked. Reader feedback is important for us as it helps us develop titles that you will really get the most out of.

To send us general feedback, simply e-mail feedback@packtpub.com, and mention the book's title in the subject of your message.

If there is a topic that you have expertise in and you are interested in either writing or contributing to a book, see our author guide at www.packtpub.com/authors.

Customer support

Now that you are the proud owner of a Packt book, we have a number of things to help you to get the most from your purchase.

Downloading the example code

You can download the example code files from your account at `http://www.packtpub.com` for all the Packt Publishing books you have purchased. If you purchased this book elsewhere, you can visit `http://www.packtpub.com/support` and register to have the files e-mailed directly to you.

Errata

Although we have taken every care to ensure the accuracy of our content, mistakes do happen. If you find a mistake in one of our books—maybe a mistake in the text or the code—we would be grateful if you could report this to us. By doing so, you can save other readers from frustration and help us improve subsequent versions of this book. If you find any errata, please report them by visiting `http://www.packtpub.com/submit-errata`, selecting your book, clicking on the **Errata Submission Form** link, and entering the details of your errata. Once your errata are verified, your submission will be accepted and the errata will be uploaded to our website or added to any list of existing errata under the Errata section of that title.

To view the previously submitted errata, go to `https://www.packtpub.com/books/content/support` and enter the name of the book in the search field. The required information will appear under the **Errata** section.

Piracy

Piracy of copyrighted material on the Internet is an ongoing problem across all media. At Packt, we take the protection of our copyright and licenses very seriously. If you come across any illegal copies of our works in any form on the Internet, please provide us with the location address or website name immediately so that we can pursue a remedy.

Please contact us at `copyright@packtpub.com` with a link to the suspected pirated material.

We appreciate your help in protecting our authors and our ability to bring you valuable content.

Questions

If you have a problem with any aspect of this book, you can contact us at `questions@packtpub.com`, and we will do our best to address the problem.

1
wxPython Starting Points

In this chapter, we will cover:

- ▶ Creating an application object
- ▶ Adding the main frame
- ▶ Using bitmaps
- ▶ Binding to events
- ▶ Understanding the hierarchy of the UI
- ▶ Controlling the propagation of events
- ▶ Accessing the clipboard
- ▶ Supporting drag and drop
- ▶ Handling AppleEvents

Introduction

In this chapter, we will take a quick overview on getting started with wxPython, including how to get an app started as well as handling events and supporting basic integration with various operating system features for the environments that the application may be operated in. These concepts are used throughout the recipes in this book as well as in any wxPython application you may develop. The recipes throughout this book target wxPython 3.0 running on Python 2.7. Many features exist and work in earlier versions of wxPython as well, but your mileage may vary with the recipes in this book when using a version earlier than 3.0.

Creating an application object

The `App` object is an object that all wxPython applications must create before any other GUI object. This object creates the application and provides its main event loop, which is used to dispatch events and connect actions in the UI with the actions in your programs.

This recipe will introduce how to create a minimal wxPython application, which will be used as foundation for every other recipe in this book.

How to do it...

Perform the following steps:

1. Make the script as follows:

   ```
   import wx

   class MyApp(wx.App):
       def OnInit(self):
           wx.MessageBox("Hello wxPython", "wxApp")
           return True

   if __name__ == "__main__":
       app = MyApp(False)
       app.MainLoop()
   ```

2. Run the script and take a look at the result:

How it works...

There are three things to take note of in this simple application: the first, we created a subclass of the `wx.App` object; the second, we overrode the `OnInit` method; and the third, we called the `MainLoop` method of the application object. These simple steps set up the base for any application.

The `OnInit` method is called by the application's `MainLoop` method when it is started and provides an entry point to start up the main logic and user interface of your application. In this example, we just used it to show a simple pop-up dialog box. The application's `MainLoop` method continues to run until the last window associated with the application is closed. The `OnInit` method must return `true` in order to continue the initialization of the `MainLoop` applications.

The `MainLoop` method processes and dispatches all the messages that are needed to present the UI and direct messages for user actions initiated with button clicks. When the **OK** button is clicked on the dialog, it sends a message that is dispatched by the `MainLoop` method to close the dialog. In this example, once the dialog has returned, `OnInit` will also return, and there will be no window objects remaining. So, the application's `MainLoop` method will return as well, and this script will exit.

There's more...

Though generally the `wx.App` object is created as we did in this example, the class constructor also has four optional keyword arguments that can be used to modify some of its behavior:

```
wx.App(redirect=False, filename=None, useBestVisual=False,
clearSigInt=True)
```

The four optional keyword arguments are as follows:

- `redirect`: If set to `True`, `stdout` is redirected to a debug window
- `filename`: If redirect is `True` and this is not `None`, then `stdout` can be redirected to a file specified by this argument
- `useBestVisual`: This specifies whether the application should try to use the best visuals provided by the underlying toolkit. (This has no effect on most systems.)
- `clearSigInt`: Setting this to `True` will allow the application to be terminated by pressing *Ctrl+C* from the command line.

See also

- The *Handling errors gracefully* recipe in *Chapter 10, Getting Your Application Ready for Release*, provides additional information on methods that can be overridden in `wx.App`.

Adding the main frame

Most applications have some sort of main window that they want to show to allow their users to interact with the software. In wxPython, this window is called a frame. The frame is the main top-level container and the base for building most user interfaces in wxPython. This recipe will show how to create a frame and add it to an application.

How to do it...

You can do this by performing the following steps:

1. Start by making a subclass of `wx.Frame` with the following code:

```python
class MyFrame(wx.Frame):
    def __init__(self, parent, title=""):
        super(MyFrame, self).__init__(parent, title=title)

        # Set an application icon
        self.SetIcon(wx.Icon("appIcon.png"))

        # Set the panel
        self.panel = wx.Panel(self)
```

2. Next, create an instance of the frame and show it using the following code:

```python
class MyApp(wx.App):
    def OnInit(self):
        self.frame = MyFrame(None, title="Main Frame")
        self.frame.Show()
        return True
```

3. Run the script and take a look at what we made:

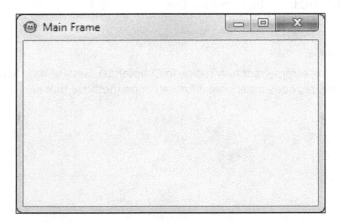

How it works...

The `Frame` class creates a top-level window that can be used to present any number of other controls. A frame can be created without any parent window and will remain in the application until it is dismissed by the user.

In this recipe, we set up a couple of items on the `MyFrame` class:

1. We called `SetIcon` to set the custom application icon on the title bar of the frame. This icon was created from the `appIcon.png` file, which exists in the same directory as the script.

2. We created a `Panel` object and set the frame as its parent object. A panel is a plain rectangular control used to contain other controls and is shown as the rectangular area inside the frame's borders. A panel must have a parent window in order to be created.

Finally, in the `App` object's `OnInit` method, we created an instance of the frame specifying the title that we wanted to show in the frame's title bar and then called its `Show` method to display it on the screen. This recipe can be used as the preparation to create any wxPython application.

There's more...

The `wx.Frame` constructor has several style flags that can be specified in its constructor to modify its behavior and appearance.

Style flag	Description
`wx.DEFAULT_FRAME_STYLE`	This flag is a bit mask of all the other flags described in the following sections
`wx.MINIMIZE_BOX`	This displays the minimize button on the title bar
`wx.MAXIMIZE_BOX`	This displays the maximize button on the title bar
`wx.RESIZE_BORDER`	This allows the frame to be resized by the user
`wx.CAPTION`	This displays a title caption on the frames title bar
`wx.CLOSE_BOX`	This displays the close button on the title bar
`wx.SYSTEM_MENU`	This displays a system menu (the menu that appears when clicking on the frame icon on Windows)
`wx.CLIP_CHILDREN`	This eliminates the flicker caused by background repainting (Windows only)

These style flags can be passed in any combination using a bitwise operator to turn off any of the features that you may not want to provide on all frames. Multiple flags can be combined using a bitwise or operation.

Using bitmaps

Bitmaps are the basic data type used to represent images in an application. The `wx.Bitmap` object can seamlessly load and decompress most common image file formats into a common representation that is usable by many UI controls. Adding bitmaps to the controls can make a UI more intuitive and easier to use.

How to do it...

Perform the following steps:

1. Let's start this time by making a subclass of `wx.Panel` to use as the container for the control that will show our bitmap on the screen, as follows:

```
class ImagePanel(wx.Panel):
    def __init__(self, parent):
        super(ImagePanel, self).__init__(parent)

        # Load the image data into a Bitmap
        theBitmap = wx.Bitmap("usingBitmaps.png")

        # Create a control that can display the
        # bitmap on the screen.
        self.bitmap = wx.StaticBitmap(self, bitmap=theBitmap)
```

2. Next, we will create an instance of the panel in a frame:

```
class MyFrame(wx.Frame):
    def __init__(self, parent, title=""):
        super(MyFrame, self).__init__(parent, title=title)

        # Set the panel
        self.panel = ImagePanel(self)
```

3. Run it and see the image shown on the panel:

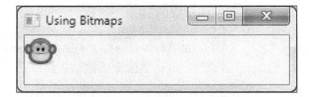

How it works...

The `Bitmap` class is used to load image data from the `usingBitmaps.png` file, which is located in the same directory as the script. This loads the PNG file data into a bitmap object, which can be used by the controls.

In this example, we used the `StaticBitmap` control, which is one of the easiest ways to display a bitmap in the UI. This control takes the bitmap data object and handles drawing it on the screen.

There's more...

In this recipe, we used a PNG file as the source for the bitmap, but `wx.Bitmap` also supports a wide range of other image formats, such as `BMP`, `GIF`, `ICO`, `ICON`, `JPEG`, `TIF`, `XBM`, `XPM`, and several others, depending on the build of wxWidgets used by wxPython.

Binding to events

wxPython is an event-driven framework; this means that all actions and the running of the UI is driven by events. Events are fired by objects to indicate that something has happened or needs to happen. `MainLoop` then dispatches these events to callback methods that are registered to be notified of the event. This recipe will show how to bind callback functions to events.

How to do it...

Perform the following functions:

1. First, start by creating a frame and binding to some of its events with the following code:

```python
class MyApp(wx.App):
    def OnInit(self):
        self.frame = wx.Frame(None, title="Binding Events")

        # Bind to events we are interested in
        self.frame.Bind(wx.EVT_SHOW, self.OnFrameShow)
        self.frame.Bind(wx.EVT_CLOSE, self.OnFrameExit)

        # Show the frame
        self.frame.Show()
        return True
```

2. Next, define the event handler callback methods we specified in the Bind calls. These will get executed when the bound event occurs, as follows:

```
def OnFrameShow(self, event):
    theFrame = event.EventObject
    print("Frame (%s) Shown!" % theFrame.Title)
    event.Skip()

def OnFrameExit(self, event):
    theFrame = event.EventObject
    print("Frame (%s) is closing!" % theFrame.Title)
    event.Skip()
```

How it works...

In the OnInit method, we created a frame object and then called Bind on it two times in order to bind our own two callback methods to these events that the frame emits. In this case, we bound to EVT_SHOW and EVT_CLOSE; these two events will be emitted by a window when the window transitions from being hidden to shown on screen and then when it is closed. Binding to events allows us to add some application-specific response when these two events occur. Now, our app's OnFrameShow and OnFrameExit callbacks will be executed by the framework in response to the event and allow us to print our log messages.

The first event, EVT_SHOW, happens as part of when the Show method is called on the frame in the app's OnInit method. The other event, EVT_CLOSE, occurs when the frame's close button is clicked on.

The event handler methods used in Bind always take one argument, which is an event object. This object is passed into the handler by the framework when it is called. The event object contains information about the event, such as a reference to the object that emitted it and other state information depending on what type of event was emitted.

There's more...

The Bind function can also take some additional optional parameters to set more fine-grain control on when the callback should be executed, as follows:

```
Bind(event, handler, source=None, id=-1, id2=-1)
```

The arguments to this function are described as follows:

- ▶ event: This is the event to bind to.
- ▶ handler: This is the event handler callback function to bind.

- source: This can be used to specify the window object that is the source of the event. If specified, then only when the source object generates the event will the handler be executed. By default, any event of the type that gets to the control will cause the handler to execute.

- id1: This is used to specify the source object's ID instead of using the instance.

- id2: When specified with id1, this can be used to specify a range of IDs to bind to.

There are many kinds of events that can be bound to depending on the type of control. The wxPython and wxWidgets online documentation provides a fairly complete list of events that are available for each control in the library. Note that the documentation is based on object hierarchy, so you may have to look to the base classes of an object to find the more general events that many controls share. You can find the documentation at http://wxpython.org/onlinedocs.php.

See also

- Take a look at the *Controlling the propagation of events* recipe section in this chapter for information on the behavior of events.

Understanding the hierarchy of the UI

There are certain rules and requirements to create a user interface; in its most fundamental form, the UI is just a collection of rectangles contained within other rectangles. This recipe will discuss how the hierarchy of controls is linked together.

How to do it...

You need to perform the following steps:

1. Let's start by defining the top-level window that resides at the top of the hierarchy:

```
class MyFrame(wx.Frame):
    def __init__(self, parent, title=""):
        super(MyFrame, self).__init__(parent, title=title)

        self.panel = MyPanel(self)
```

2. Next, let's define the Panel class, which will serve as the general container for user controls and give it a child control through the following code:

```
class MyPanel(wx.Panel):
    def __init__(self, parent):
        super(MyPanel, self).__init__(parent)

        self.button = wx.Button(self, label="Push Me")
```

How it works...

All controls have an argument for a parent in their constructor. The parent is the container that the child control belongs to; so, in the first snippet when the MyPanel object was created, it was passed into the Frame object as its parent. This caused the panel rectangle to be placed inside of the rectangle of the Frame object. Then again, inside of the MyPanel object, a Button object was created with Panel as the parent, which instructed the button rectangle to be positioned inside the area owned by Panel.

There are three layers of containment in the window hierarchy for different categories of control types:

- **Top-level Windows (Frames and Dialogs)**: These cannot be contained by any type of container when displayed on screen. They are always at the top of the visual hierarchy.

- **General Containers (Panels, Notebooks, and so on)**: These are general container windows that serve the purpose of grouping other controls together and providing layout. They can contain other general containers or controls.

- **Controls (Buttons, CheckBoxes, ComboBoxes, and so on)**: These are user controls that cannot contain any other controls. They are the leaves at the bottom of the tree.

There's more...

When building an application with a user interface, this hierarchy is important to remember as it plays a critical role in how the layout and design of the interface is performed. Most notably, in the middle general containers layer, the nesting and composition of the control layout in combination with event handling can lead to unexpected issues if this hierarchy is forgotten. So, just remember this tree structure when building out your application's interface:

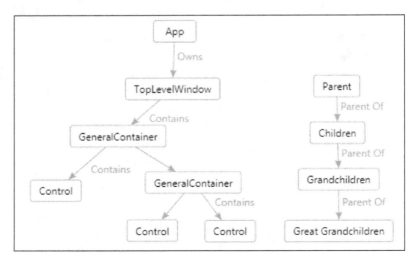

▸ The *Controlling the propagation of events* recipe in this chapter explains the way this hierarchy affects how events are reported.

Controlling the propagation of events

There are two main types of events in wxPython:

▸ Normal events

▸ Command events

Understanding how these events travel through the framework is important to understanding how to develop an application in this event-driven framework. This recipe will develop an example to show how to control the way an event is propagated.

How to do it...

The following steps can help us:

1. Let's start by creating a panel that has two buttons in it, by creating the following class:

```python
class MyPanel(wx.Panel):
    def __init__(self, parent):
        super(MyPanel, self).__init__(parent)

        sizer = wx.BoxSizer()
        self.button1 = wx.Button(self, label="Button 1")
        sizer.Add(self.button1)
        self.button2 = wx.Button(self, label="Button 2")
        sizer.Add(self.button2)
        self.SetSizer(sizer)

        self.Bind(wx.EVT_BUTTON, self.OnButton)
```

2. Next, let's define the event handler for the panel to handle the button events as follows:

```python
    def OnButton(self, event):
        button = event.EventObject
        print("Button (%s) event at Panel!" % button.Label)
        if button is self.button1:
            event.Skip()
```

3. In the next layer, let's make a frame to hold the panel and also set it up to catch button events through the following code:

```
class MyFrame(wx.Frame):
    def __init__(self, parent, title=""):
        super(MyFrame, self).__init__(parent, title=title)

        self.panel = MyPanel(self)

        self.Bind(wx.EVT_BUTTON, self.OnButton)

    def OnButton(self, event):
        button = event.EventObject
        print("Button (%s) event at Frame!" % button.Label)
        event.Skip()
```

4. Finally, let's do the same thing at the app level:

```
class MyApp(wx.App):
    def OnInit(self):
        self.frame = MyFrame(None, title="Event Propagation")
        self.frame.Show();

        self.Bind(wx.EVT_BUTTON, self.OnButton)
        return True

    def OnButton(self, event):
        button = event.EventObject
        print("Button (%s) event at App!" % button.Label)
        event.Skip()
```

Downloading the example code

You can download the example code files for all Packt books you have purchased from your account at http://www.packtpub.com. If you purchased this book elsewhere, you can visit http://www.packtpub.com/support and register to have the files e-mailed directly to you.

How it works...

When you run this application and click on each of the buttons, you should see two distinct differences in behavior between how the events propagate. When clicking on the first button, the event handlers from the panel to the frame and finally to the app will be executed, whereas when clicking the second button, only the event handler at the panel is executed.

The EVT_BUTTON object is a command event, meaning it will propagate upward until it is stopped or it reaches the app. In this example, the second button is only propagated to the Panel handler because we called event.Skip when the event originated from the first button. Calling the Skip method tells the framework to propagate the event to the next handler in the chain, whereas not calling the Skip method tells the framework that the event has been handled and does not require further processing. So, it's important to know when to call Skip and when not to as sometimes it is necessary for the event to propagate to the base default handler in order for additional processing to occur. Try going back to the *Binding to events* recipe and removing the call to Skip in OnFrameExit to ensure that it prevents the frame from closing.

There's more...

As discussed at the beginning of this recipe, there are two types of events. This recipe only explored the more common types of command events that were propagated. Normal events stay local to where they are generated and do not propagate.

You can also create your own custom events if you want to use the event loop to pass messages using the newevent module in wx.lib, as follows:

```
import wx
import wx.lib.newevent

# Create a special event
MyEvent, EVT_MYEVENT = wx.lib.newevent.NewCommandEvent();
```

This creates a new event object type and event binder object. The EVT_MYEVENT binder object can be bound to as any other event. Then, the MyEvent event object can be emitted through the use of the wx.PostEvent function, which sends the instance of the event through the event handler chain.

Accessing the clipboard

The clipboard is a system resource used to pass user data between applications in the operating system. This is most often associated with copying and pasting actions in an application. This recipe will show some basics on putting and getting data from the clipboard.

How to do it...

1. Let's first define a helper function to get some text from the clipboard, as follows:

```
def GetClipboardText():
    text_obj = wx.TextDataObject()
    rtext = ""
    if wx.TheClipboard.IsOpened() or wx.TheClipboard.Open():
```

```
        if wx.TheClipboard.GetData(text_obj):
          rtext = text_obj.GetText()
        wx.TheClipboard.Close()
        return rtext
```

2. Now, let's do the reverse and define a helper function to put text into the clipboard, as done with the following code:

```
def SetClipboardText(text):
    data_o = wx.TextDataObject()
    data_o.SetText(text)
    if wx.TheClipboard.IsOpened() or wx.TheClipboard.Open():
        wx.TheClipboard.SetData(data_o)
        wx.TheClipboard.Close()
```

How it works...

Both functions work by creating `TextDataObject`, which provides a platform-independent way to represent the systems' native data format. Then, `TheClipboard` object is opened, and it is used to either get data from the clipboard of the given type or put data in the clipboard from the application. This can be boiled down to a simple three step process for any clipboard interaction:

1. Open clipboard
2. Set or get `DataObject`
3. Close the clipboard

Closing the clipboard after using is very important; it may prevent other processes from accessing it. The clipboard should only be kept open momentarily.

There's more...

The clipboard supports many other datatypes besides plain text, which can be used based on the situation and needs of the application.

Datatypes	Description
wx.BitmapDataObject	This is a bitmap data from the clipboard (drag and drop)
wx.CustomDataObject	This is a base class to represent application-specific data
wx.DataObjectSimple	This is a base class to create other data object types
wx.DataObjectComposite	This is a base class to support multiple formats
wx.FileDataObject	This is the data object for filenames
wx.HTMLDataObject	This is the HTML-formatted text container
wx.URLDataObject	This is the URL container data object

See also

> ▸ Take a look at the next recipe in this chapter, *Supporting drag and drop*, for more on how clipboard data objects can be used to transfer data between controls.

Supporting drag and drop

Many applications allow users to open files by dragging a file from the operating system and dropping it in the application. wxPython, of course, provides support for this as well, through its controls using `DropTargets`. This recipe will show how to set up a `DropTarget` to allow handling the dragging and dropping of files in an application.

How to do it...

1. First, let's create a drop target object to accept files that are dragged over and dropped in the application with the following code:

```python
class MyFileDropTarget(wx.FileDropTarget):
    def __init__(self, target):
        super(MyFileDropTarget, self).__init__()
        self.target = target

    def OnDropFiles(self, x, y, filenames):
        for fname in filenames:
            self.target.AppendText(fname)
```

2. Next, all that is left is to connect the drop target to the window that should accept the dropped file(s). An example of this is shown in the following code:

```python
class MyFrame(wx.Frame):
    def __init__(self, parent, title=""):
        super(MyFrame, self).__init__(parent, title=title)

        # Set the panel
        self.text = wx.TextCtrl(self, style=wx.TE_MULTILINE)
        self.text.AppendText("Drag and drop some files here!")
        dropTarget = MyFileDropTarget(self.text)
        self.text.SetDropTarget(dropTarget)
```

How it works...

Drag and drop functions with the use of `DropSources` and `DropTargets`. In this case, we wanted to allow files to be dropped in the application, so `FileDropTarget` was created and associated with the `TextCtrl` window. `DropTargets` have several virtual callback functions that can be overridden to intercept different actions during the drag and drop events. As `FileDropTarget` is specialized for files, it only required overriding `OnDropFiles`, which is called with the list of filenames that were dropped in the application. It is necessary to subclass the drop target in order to intercept and handle the data it receives.

In order for a window to accept drag and drop actions, it must have a `DropTarget` set; the `DropTarget` then gives feedback on whether the data can be accepted or not as well as handling the reception of the data. Try out the example code with this recipe and you will see the mouse cursor change as you drag a file over; then, try again by dragging some text from another application to see the difference.

There's more...

It's also possible to create more application-specific drag and drop handling if needed for custom datatypes by deriving a custom drop target class from `PyDropTarget`. This class provides several more overridable methods to allow the handling of various events during the action. Here's a table explaining this:

Methods	Description
`OnEnter(x, y, dragResult)`	This is called when a drag object enters the window. The `dragResult` value returned from this method sets the custom cursor to provide feedback to the user (`wx.DragCancel`, `wx.DragCopy`, and so on).
`OnDragOver(x, y, dragResult)`	This is called while the object is dragged over the window. It returns a `dragResult` to give visual feedback.
`OnLeave()`	This is called when the drag object leaves the window.
`OnDrop(x, y)`	This is called when the drag object is dropped in the window. This method should return `True` if the data is accepted.
`OnData(x, y, dragResult)`	This is called after the data is accepted in `OnDrop`. The dropped data object is contained in drop targets data object (refer to `GetDataObject`). This should then typically just return the default passed in `dragResult`.

Handling AppleEvents

AppleEvents are special kinds of high-level system events used by the OS X operating system to pass information between processes. In order to handle system events, such as when a file is dropped in the application's Dock icon, it's necessary to handle AppleEvents. Implementing the handlers for these methods can allow your app to behave more natively when run on OS X.

 This recipe is specific to the OS X operating system and will have no effect on other operating systems.

How to do it...

Perform the following steps:

1. Define an app object in which we will override the available AppleEvent handlers through the following code:

```
class MyApp(wx.App):
    def OnInit(self):
        self.frame = MyFrame("Apple Events")
        self.frame.Show()
        return True
```

2. Override the handlers that are available to deal with the opening of files:

```
def MacNewFile(self):
    """Called in response to an open-application event"""
    self.frame.AddNewFile()

def MacOpenFiles(self, fileNames):
    """Called in response to an openFiles message in Cocoa
    or an open-document event in Carbon
    """
    self.frame.AddFiles(fileNames)
```

3. Finally, let's also override the remaining available AppleEvent handlers that are defined in wx.App and have them redirected to some actions with our application's main window. The following code can help us do this:

```
def MacOpenURL(self, url):
    """Called in response to get-url event"""
    self.frame.AddURL(url)
```

```
def MacPrintFile(self, fileName):
    """Called in response to a print-document event"""
    self.frame.PrintFile(fileName)

def MacReopenApp(self):
    """Called in response to a reopen-application event"""
    if self.frame.IsIconized():
        self.frame.Iconize(False)
    self.frame.Raise()
```

How it works...

In the Carbon and Cocoa builds of wxPython, these additional Mac-specific virtual overrides are available for apps to implement. The app object has special handling for these events and turns them into simple function calls that can be overridden in derived applications to provide an app-specific handling of them.

The first two methods that we overrode are called in response to creating a new file or opening existing files, such as when a file is dragged and dropped in the application icon in the dock. The MacOpenFiles method is new since wxPython 2.9.3 and should be used instead of the MacOpenFile method that was provided in previous versions.

The other method that most apps should implement in some form is the MacReopenApp method. This method is called when a user clicks on the application icon in the dock. In this implementation, we ensure that the app is brought back to the foreground in response to this action.

There's more...

If there are other OS X-specific actions you want your app to handle, it is also possible to add support for additional AppleEvents to a wxPython application. It is not a particularly easy task as it requires writing a native extension module to catch the event, block the event loop, and then restore the Python interpreter's state back to wx after handling the event. There is a pretty good example that can be used as a starting point on the wxPython Wiki page (refer to http://wiki.wxpython.org/Catching%20AppleEvents%20in%20wxMAC) if you find yourself needing to venture down this route.

2

Common User Controls

In this chapter, we will cover:

- ▸ Starting with the easy button
- ▸ Pushing all the buttons
- ▸ Offering options with CheckBoxes
- ▸ Using TextCtrl
- ▸ Processing key events
- ▸ Picking dates with DatePickerCtrl
- ▸ Exploring menus and shortcuts
- ▸ Displaying a context menu
- ▸ Working with ToolBars
- ▸ Managing UI states

Introduction

There are many common elements that can be found in nearly any software application that has a user interface. These elements include many well-known controls such as buttons, menus, and toolbars. In this chapter, we will take a look at how to start using and integrating these common user controls into your applications. We will do this by showing you how to create and add the controls to the user interface as well as how to make use of many of the common events. The events that are emitted by these controls are used to allow your application to interact and respond to actions initiated by the users of the interface.

Starting with the easy button

The button is probably one of the most commonly used UI controls in any application's user interface. The button control in wxPython has received some attention in recent versions and has had some useful new features added to it to make it an even more powerful control than it was in the past. In this recipe, we will explore some of the functionalities that the default button can provide, including the new features to support bitmaps that were added in wxPython 2.9.1.

How to do it...

Perform the following steps:

1. First, let's define a `Panel` class and start adding some buttons to it. It will act as the container to hold and organize the buttons we make. Using the following code:

    ```
    class MyPanel(wx.Panel):
        def __init__(self, parent):
            super(MyPanel, self).__init__(parent)

            # Sizer to control button layout
            sizer = wx.BoxSizer(wx.HORIZONTAL)
    ```

2. Next, we will create a simple stock button using a common ID with no label specified and add it with the following code:

    ```
    # Normal stock button
    button = wx.Button(self, wx.ID_OK)
    sizer.Add(button)
    ```

3. Now, let's make a button that has a custom bitmap and label applied to it (this is new since 2.9.1). This code will help us do this:

    ```
    # Button with a bitmap
    button = wx.Button(self, label="Play")
    bitmap = wx.Bitmap('monkeyTime.png')
    button.SetBitmap(bitmap)
    sizer.Add(button)
    ```

4. Then, last on the list, we will make a button and specify that it should show the authorization needed icon. (This is also new since 2.9.1). This is mostly a Windows-centric feature and may not have any effect on some platforms. The following code is all that is needed for this:

    ```
    # Button to show authorization is needed
    button = wx.Button(self, wx.ID_APPLY)
    button.SetAuthNeeded()
    sizer.Add(button)
    ```

5. Finally, to wrap it up, we will finish the layout and create an event handler for the buttons through the following code:

```
self.SetSizer(sizer)
self.Bind(wx.EVT_BUTTON, self.OnButton)

def OnButton(self, event):
    button = event.EventObject
    print("%s was pushed!" % button.Label)
    if button.GetAuthNeeded():
        print("Action requires authorization to proceed!")
    event.Skip()
```

How it works...

Adding this panel to an application and running it will show how what we did in these steps modifies the appearance of the buttons:

With the first button, the framework automatically applies the appropriate label to the button based on the stock ID that is set on the button. Many common buttons can be created this way, which allows the framework to apply some standard native behavior and labeling to them in some cases, depending on the underlying UI toolkit that is in use.

The second button displays a new feature that is added version 2.9.1 onward. The standard button now supports having bitmaps displayed with text. This feature has now made the need to use a BitmapButton control mostly non-existent. On some systems, there can be various bitmaps set for different pressed or hover states of the mouse; however, on OS X, the default bitmap is the only one that is displayed.

Finally, with the third button, we can take a look at how to add the authorization needed icon, which is mostly a Windows-specific feature in Windows Vista and later versions. When this is set, you can check in the event handler as we did and provide a confirmation dialog or request authorization to start another process with elevated permissions.

See also

▶ Refer to the *Using bitmaps* recipe in *Chapter 1, wxPython Starting Points*, for information on how bitmaps are handled.

▶ We made use of BoxSizer in this recipe. If you want more information on how sizer-based layouts work, take a look ahead at *Chapter 3, UI Layout and Organization*.

Pushing all the buttons

Even though the standard button can get the job done most of the time, there are other cases where you may want to provide a different look and feel for certain situations. So, in addition to the standard button, wxPython also has several other types of buttons that provide additional features to customize their look and feel.

How to do it...

You need to perform the following steps:

1. Let's start simply by stubbing out our panel that will hold the buttons in this example through this code:

```
import wx
import wx.lib.platebtn as platebtn

class MyPanel(wx.Panel):
    def __init__(self, parent):
        super(MyPanel, self).__init__(parent)

        # Layout sizers
        vsizer = wx.BoxSizer(wx.VERTICAL)
        sizer = wx.BoxSizer(wx.HORIZONTAL)
        vsizer.Add(sizer)
```

2. Now, let's create a couple of `ToggleButton` controls, as follows:

```
# Toggle Button
toggle = wx.ToggleButton(self, label="Toggle Me")
sizer.Add(toggle)
toggle = wx.ToggleButton(self, label="Me Too")
sizer.Add(toggle)
```

3. Next, let's add in a couple of custom `PlateButton` controls from `wx.lib` to the panel. To do so see the following code:

```
# PlateButton
plate = platebtn.PlateButton(self, label="PlateButton")
sizer.Add(plate)

plate = platebtn.PlateButton(self, label="WithMenu")
menu = wx.Menu("Action Menu")
menu.Append(wx.ID_OPEN, "Open it")
menu.Append(wx.ID_CLOSE, "Close it")
plate.SetMenu(menu)
sizer.Add(plate)
```

4. Finally, let's check out the new `CommandLinkButton` control that is added to the library version 2.9.2 onward and wrap up our layout as well as bind the needed event handlers. Use this code:

```
note = """Long detail message that informs user
more about what this action does."""
lbl = "CommandLink"
cmdLnk = wx.CommandLinkButton(self,
                               mainLabel=lbl,
                               note = note)
vsizer.Add(cmdLnk)

self.SetSizer(vsizer)
self.Bind(wx.EVT_TOGGLEBUTTON, self.OnToggle)
self.Bind(wx.EVT_BUTTON, self.OnButton)
```

5. Now that all the buttons are created, we can proceed to define our event handler methods using the following code:

```
def OnToggle(self, event):
    button = event.EventObject
    print("%s toggle button was pushed!" % button.Label)
    print("ToggleState: %s" % button.Value)

def OnButton(self, event):
    button = event.EventObject
    print("%s was pushed!" % button.Label)
    event.Skip()
```

How it works...

Each of these buttons provides a unique behavior and appearance; so, let's take a quick look at what each looks like in the following screenshot before we get into the details of each button type:

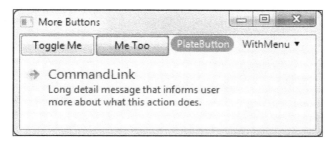

The `ToggleButton` control is much like the normal button except in that it exhibits two unique states. It can either be pressed or not pressed in order to toggle some action in the UI. This button emits its own special `EVT_TOGGLEBUTTON` event instead of the standard `EVT_BUTTON` event that is emitted by other button controls.

The `PlateButton` control is a custom, owner-drawn control provided by the `wx.lib.platebtn` module. By default, this control provides a flat transparent button that becomes highlighted when the mouse is hovered over it. In addition to this, it also supports adding a custom drop-down menu for various other options to control behavior and appearance.

Lastly, we looked at the `CommandLinkButton` control; this is a brand new control added since version 2.9.2. It is a native control on Windows 7 and later versions but implemented as a generic control on other platforms. It provides a flat clickable area that supports a header label and multiline description text to give more information about what clicking on it does.

There's more...

The `PlateButton` control has several optional style flags that can be set to change its appearance and behavior. Take a look at the following table:

Style flag	Description
PB_STYLE_NORMAL	This is the default style, as shown in the preceding example, with solid highlight color and rounded edges.
PB_STYLE_GRADIENT	When specified, this flag uses a gradient to draw the hover-over highlighting.
PB_STYLE_SQUARE	This makes a button be drawn as a rectangle with square edges.
PB_STYLE_NOBG	This is a Windows-only style flag. It turns off background redrawing and can set this flag to get better transparency behavior if the control's parent window is owner drawn.
PB_STYLE_DROPARROW	This draws the drop arrow on the button. This area generates a separate EVT_PLATEBTN_DROPARROW_PRESSED event when clicked on.
PB_STYLE_TOGGLE	This causes a button to operate like a ToggleButton control and generates EVT_TOGGLEBUTTON events instead of regular button events when clicked on.

Offering options with CheckBoxes

The CheckBox control in its usual configuration is similar to a type of binary input; it is either checked or not checked. So, as such, it is often used to offer selection options to "yes/no" questions in a user interface, such as an option to enable or disable a feature in an application's configuration screen. In this recipe, we will take a look at the ways of using a CheckBox control.

How to do it...

To offer options with checkboxes, you need to do the following:

1. First, we will start by making a panel that has three CheckBox controls on it through the following code:

```python
class MyPanel(wx.Panel):
    def __init__(self, parent):
        super(MyPanel, self).__init__(parent)

        # Layout sizers
        vsizer = wx.BoxSizer(wx.VERTICAL)

        # Toggle Button
        self.allCB = wx.CheckBox(self, label="All Selected",
                                 style=wx.CHK_3STATE)
        vsizer.Add(self.allCB)
        self.option1 = wx.CheckBox(self, label="Option 1")
        vsizer.Add(self.option1, flag=wx.LEFT, border=10)
        self.option2 = wx.CheckBox(self, label="Option 2")
        vsizer.Add(self.option2, flag=wx.LEFT, border=10)

        self.SetSizer(vsizer)
        self.Bind(wx.EVT_CHECKBOX, self.OnCheckBox)
```

2. Next, let's define the OnCheckBox method to handle the check events. We will use this handler to update the state of other controls. The first three-way checkbox will act as an indicator and a way to select or unselect all the suboptions:

```python
    def OnCheckBox(self, event):
        check = event.EventObject
        if check is self.allCB:
            self.option1.Value = check.Value
            self.option2.Value = check.Value
        else:
```

```
values = [self.option1.Value, self.option2.Value]
if all(values):
    self.allCB.Set3StateValue(wx.CHK_CHECKED)
elif any(values):
    self.allCB.Set3StateValue(wx.CHK_UNDETERMINED)
else:
    self.allCB.Set3StateValue(wx.CHK_UNCHECKED)
```

How it works...

In this recipe, we saw that a `CheckBox` control is not limited to only two states. The first `CheckBox` control created uses the `CHK_3STATE` style flag to enable the use of the third *undetermined* state. However, when clicked on by a user, this control still behaves like a normal checkbox, but it has a third visual state that can be used to show a partial selection.

The `OnCheckBox` event handler uses check events from each of the checkboxes to determine what state the other `CheckBox` controls should be set to. If the top `CheckBox` control is checked, it causes all the other checkboxes to be checked. If one of the two lower controls is checked and the other is unchecked, it causes the top `CheckBox` control to display the third state. Using a technique such as this, can give good visual feedback to indicate whether a full set of features is enabled or not and also give the user an easy way to select or unselect all options.

Using TextCtrl

The `TextCtrl` control is versatile; it allows the display and entry of textual data in an application. In its default form, `TextCtrl` is a single-line entry field that is often used on forms to allow users to input information such as names, places, and descriptions. From wxPython 2.9 onward, `TextCtrl` added some features to support auto-completion of input. This feature lets some input help be shown in a pop-up list that filters as the typing narrows down the available options. In this recipe, we will explore how to activate and use some of these features by making a custom the `TextCtrl` control that remembers previous entries that were made in it and offers them as input tips the next time data is typed into the field.

How to do it...

Perform the following steps:

1. First, let's create the class' definition and its constructor to set up the extensions and events that we need to handle in order to add the memory feature:

```
class MemoryTextCtrl(wx.TextCtrl):
    """TextCtrl that remembers previous entries"""
```

```
def __init__(self, parent):
    super(MemoryTextCtrl, self).__init__(parent)

    self._memories = set()

    self.Bind(wx.EVT_KILL_FOCUS,
              lambda event: self.Memorize())
    self.Bind(wx.EVT_SET_FOCUS,
              self.OnUpdateCompleteList)
```

2. Next, we will define the `OnUpdateCompleteList` event handler to take memories from previous entries in the control and set them to the AutoComplete list, as follows:

```
def OnUpdateCompleteList(self, event):
    # Set the autocomplete list with the
    # latest set of memories.
    self.AutoComplete(list(self._memories))
    event.Skip()
```

3. Lastly, we will define a couple of API functions to give us a little extra control over how the control behaves with this new feature:

```
def Memorize(self):
    """remember the current value"""
    if self.Value:
        self._memories.add(self.Value)

def Forget(self):
    """forget all remembered words"""
    self._memories.clear()
```

How it works...

The `MemoryTextCtrl` control has the added ability to memorize previous entries that were made in it and use them as input tips the next time values are added to the control. This is made possible by binding to two events: `EVT_KILL_FOCUS` and `EVT_SET_FOCUS`. When the user enters some text in the control and then presses *Tab* or clicks on another control, the kill focus event is generated. In this event handler, we can grab the current value of the control and store it in the control's memories. Then, the next time the control is tabbed or selected by the user, the set focus event will be generated; during this event, we will copy all memories into the control's `AutoComplete` choices array.

When values are present in the `AutoComplete` choices array, the control will check it during the processing of the keyboard input from a user. As characters are entered, if there are any partial matches, the control will pop up the list of possible matches to the user to allow a quick input of any of the matches.

To take a look at it in action, try out the sample code that accompanies this recipe. Enter a value in the first field, and then tab to the next field and repeat. If you start typing a word that starts with same letter as one of the previous ones, the auto-complete pop-up list will list the options from previous entries.

There's more...

The `TextCtrl` control also has a couple of other built-in `AutoComplete` methods that support auto-completing directory paths and filenames. These features are easily activated by just calling one of the following methods on `TextCtrl`:

Method	Description
AutoCompleteDirectories()	This displays a list of directories if the beginning of a directory path is typed into the control
AutoCompleteFileNames()	This works similarly to AutoCompleteDirectories, but it also includes files in the list of completion choices

See also

▶   Also take a look at the *Processing key events* recipe in this chapter for some additional examples on using `TextCtrl` and `AutoComplete`

Processing key events

The `KeyEvent` events are generated in any control that accepts keyboard input when a user presses keys on a keyboard. There are three distinct events that occur for a single key press. In this recipe, we will use `KeyEvents` to create a custom `TextCtrl` control that can generate a dynamic input suggestion list similar to the suggestions that Google shows when one types into the search box.

How to do it...

You need to do the following:

1.   Firstly, for this recipe, we need to include a couple of other modules from the Python standard library, as follows:

```
from urllib import urlopen
import re

from abc import ABCMeta, abstractmethod
import wx
```

2. To make the control's suggestion provider extensible, we will first define a simple interface class that will be responsible for providing suggestion options. This is defined as an abstract base class:

```
class CompleterDataSource:
    __metaclass__ = ABCMeta

    @abstractmethod
    def getSuggestions(self, phrase):
        """return list of strings"""
        pass
```

3. Now, we will define our `TextCtrl` subclass that uses an instance of the preceding data source interface. The constructor requires a valid instance of the data source; we will show how to invoke one with the following code:

```
class DataSourceTextCtrl(wx.TextCtrl):
    def __init__(self, parent, dataSource):
        super(DataSourceTextCtrl, self).__init__(parent)

        assert isinstance(dataSource, CompleterDataSource)
        self._dataSource = dataSource

        self.Bind(wx.EVT_KEY_DOWN, self.OnKeyDown)
        self.Bind(wx.EVT_CHAR, self.OnChar)
```

4. All that's left for this class now is to define the implementations of the two event handlers for the key down and character events. We will use EVT_KEY_DOWN to clear the previous suggestion list and EVT_CHAR to ask the data source for a new list of suggestions. Take a look at the following code:

```
    def OnKeyDown(self, event):
        self.AutoComplete([])
        event.Skip()

    def OnChar(self, event):
        char = unichr(event.KeyCode)
        if not char.isalnum():
            char = ""

        query = self.Value + char
        tips = self._dataSource.getSuggestions(query)
        if tips:
            self.AutoComplete(tips)
        event.Skip()
```

How it works...

The `DataSourceTextCtrl` control requires an instance of a `CompleterDataSource` object to provide it with suggestions to display in the `AutoComplete` list. As `CompleterDataSource` is an abstract base class (which means it uses `ABCMeta` from the `abc` module), it requires a specialized class, which is provided by the calling code. This data source is called on during key processing to provide tips based on the current input value.

The `EVT_KEY_DOWN` handler is called when `TextCtrl` has the focus and a key is pressed on the keyboard. This event is the first in the chain of three events that are generated for a key press. The next event that is generated is the `EVT_CHAR` event, which contains information about the character that is associated with the key that is pressed. Following this, there is also an `EVT_KEY_UP` event, which is generated when the key is no longer pressed down.

When the `OnChar` event handler is in use, the preceding control builds a query from the existing text and the new characters that are entered and uses it to ask the data source object to provide a list of suggestions. These suggestions are then put into the `AutoComplete` list for the control. Then, if the data source provides any tips, they are presented to the user.

There's more...

Check out the sample code that accompanies this recipe for an extended sample that uses this custom implementation of `CompleterDataSource` to fetch suggestion text from Google Search:

```python
class GoogleSuggestSource(CompleterDataSource):
    def getSuggestions(self, phrase):
        """Query google for suggestion list"""
        url = "http://google.com/complete/search?output=toolbar&q="
        if phrase:
            page = urlopen(url + phrase).read()
            suggestions = re.findall(r'data="([\w*\s*]+)"', page)
            return suggestions
```

This class requires a network connection, but it shows how powerful using a decoupled data source can be in making the functionality of the text control more extensible. The same pattern can be used to fetch data from any other sort of sources, such as a database or another web service.

This, and any other specialized data source, can be attached to the control to change how it provides tips, as follows:

```python
textCtrl = DataSourceTextCtrl(self, GoogleSuggestSource())
```

Once the control is created, it will defer all requests to display completion tips to the provided data source, which in this case will be retrieved from a Google web service, similar to when you start typing into the search box on Google's home page.

Picking dates with DatePickerCtrl

If your application requires getting date and/or time input from a user, this can be a difficult task due to the possible number of input formatting and validation issues. There is no need to fear, though; wxPython has several specialized controls to deal with date and time input. In this recipe, we will take a look at using `DatePickerCtrl` to select dates.

How to do it...

Here are the steps to perform for this recipe:

1. Firstly, let's start by making a little wrapper class around `DatePickerCtrl` to fix a layout issue that exists on some versions of Windows, with the native control being in use:

```
class DatePicker(wx.DatePickerCtrl):
    def __init__(self, parent, dt, style=wx.DP_DEFAULT):
        super(DatePicker, self).__init__(parent, dt=dt,
                                         style=style)

        self.SetInitialSize((120, -1))
```

2. Next, we will make a panel to contain the `DatePicker` control, as follows:

```
class MyPanel(wx.Panel):
    def __init__(self, parent):
        super(MyPanel, self).__init__(parent)

        # Layout sizers
        sizer = wx.BoxSizer(wx.VERTICAL)

        now = wx.DateTime.Now();
        self._dp = DatePicker(self, now,
                              wx.DP_DROPDOWN|wx.DP_SHOWCENTURY)
        sizer.Add(self._dp, 0, wx.ALL, 20)

        self.SetSizer(sizer)
```

3. For the final step, we will use the following code to create the frame to hold the panel as well as bind to the EVT_DATE_CHANGED event, which is emitted by DatePicker when selections are made:

```
class MyFrame(wx.Frame):
    def __init__(self, parent, title=""):
        super(MyFrame, self).__init__(parent, title=title)

        # Set the panel
        self.panel = MyPanel(self)

        self.Bind(wx.EVT_DATE_CHANGED, self.OnDateChange)

    def OnDateChange(self, evt):
        date = evt.GetDate()
        self.Title = date.Format()
```

How it works...

The DatePickerCtrl control is a space-efficient control to allow the selection of dates. The control uses a wx.DateTime object to hold and represent the data being presented by the control. The control can function in two primary styles. The style we chose in this recipe is DP_DROPDOWN. With this style set, the picker control is much similar to a ComboBox control, where when the drop arrow is selected, a pop-up window displaying a calendar control is shown:

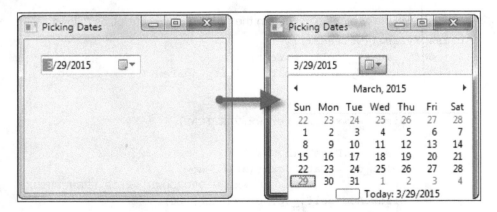

The other default style allows us to select a field in the text area and use either the up and down arrow keys or a button to increment or decrement the value.

When the selection is changed in the control, it generates an EVT_DATE_CHANGED event, which carries the new updated DateTime value that can be accessed by the event object's GetDate method. We used this value in the frame's OnDateChanged handler to update the title bar with the new value by calling Format on the DateTime object to convert it into a string.

 Note that we explicitly set the width of the control in this exercise to overcome an inconsistency in how the native version of the control gets sized on Windows. The control tends to not allocate enough minimal horizontal space, which causes part of the icon on the button to not be shown.

There's more...

There are also several other controls available to display and select date and time information in wxPython. Included in the following table is a quick reference guide to some additionally available options:

Control	Description
GenericDatePickerCtrl	This is a wx owner-drawn version of the DatePicker control, which is shown in this recipe.
CalendarCtrl	This control provides a full calendar display. It is located in the wx.calendar module, which needs to be imported in addition to the main wx module to get access to the control. There is both a native and generic version of this control available in the module. The generic one may be preferable in some cases if you require additional features and control over the appearance or want to include special markers on the calendar.
TimeCtrl	This control provides a functionality similar to DatePickerCtrl but for time values, instead. This control is available from the wx.lib.masked module as a custom Python control.

Exploring menus and shortcuts

Menus are a way to provide the user with a number of actions that can be performed by either clicking on them or using an associated keyboard shortcut. Menus allow us to categorize and organize any number of actions in lists and trees with submenus, all while keeping them out of sight until they are needed. This recipe will show you how to add menus to a frame and set up keyboard shortcuts to activate them by building up a little text editor application.

How to do it...

Here are the steps to be performed:

1. First, to make adding icons to the menus in this application easier, let's define a custom `Menu` wrapper class that will automatically get a bitmap from `ArtProvider` when one is available. This first little part just defines a way to map control IDs to ART IDs, as follows:

```
class EasyMenu(wx.Menu):
    _map = { wx.ID_CUT : wx.ART_CUT,
             wx.ID_COPY : wx.ART_COPY,
             wx.ID_PASTE : wx.ART_PASTE,
             wx.ID_OPEN : wx.ART_FILE_OPEN,
             wx.ID_SAVE : wx.ART_FILE_SAVE,
             wx.ID_EXIT : wx.ART_QUIT,
           }
```

2. Now, to finish up this class, we will add a helper method to attach items to a menu that uses the preceding art resource map through the following method:

```
def AddEasyItem(self, id, label=""):
    item = wx.MenuItem(self, id, label)
    art = EasyMenu._map.get(id, None)
    if art is not None:
        bmp = wx.ArtProvider.GetBitmap(art, wx.ART_MENU)
        if bmp.IsOk():
            item.SetBitmap(bmp)
    return self.AppendItem(item)
```

3. With our helper class out of the way, we can now define our `Editor` class, which is a frame that contains the menus and `TextCtrl` controls in it:

```
class Editor(wx.Frame):
    def __init__(self, parent, title=""):
        super(Editor, self).__init__(parent, title=title)
```

```
# Setup the menus
    menubar = wx.MenuBar()
    self.DoSetupMenus(menubar)
    self.SetMenuBar(menubar)

    # Set the main panel
    self.txt = wx.TextCtrl(self, style=wx.TE_MULTILINE)
```

4. As can be seen in the class declaration, we added a `DoSetupMenus` method to hold the logic in order to build up the application's menus. So now, it's time to add this method in to build up a simple **File** and **Edit** menu, as shown in the following code:

```
def DoSetupMenus(self, menubar):
    fileMenu = EasyMenu()
    self.RegisterMenuAction(fileMenu, wx.ID_OPEN, self.OnFile)
    self.RegisterMenuAction(fileMenu, wx.ID_SAVE, self.OnFile)
    fileMenu.AppendSeparator()
    self.RegisterMenuAction(fileMenu, wx.ID_EXIT, self.OnFile,
                            "Exit\tCtrl+Q")
    menubar.Append(fileMenu, "File")

    editMenu = EasyMenu()
    self.RegisterMenuAction(editMenu, wx.ID_CUT, self.OnEdit)
    self.RegisterMenuAction(editMenu, wx.ID_COPY, self.OnEdit)
    self.RegisterMenuAction(editMenu, wx.ID_PASTE,
                                self.OnEdit)
    menubar.Append(editMenu, "Edit")

def RegisterMenuAction(self, menu, id, handler, label=""):
    item = menu.AddEasyItem(id, label)
    self.Bind(wx.EVT_MENU, handler, item)
```

5. For the last steps, we will add the definitions of our `EVT_MENU` handlers. For the **File** menu, we will leave the **Open** and **Save** functionalities unimplemented in this recipe and come back to it in *Chapter 7, Requesting and Retrieving Information*, when we will take a closer look at the `FileDialog` class. Use the following code for this step:

```
def OnFile(self, event):
    if event.Id == wx.ID_OPEN:
        raise NotImplementedError("Open not implemented")
    elif event.Id == wx.ID_SAVE:
        raise NotImplementedError("Save not implemented")
```

```
        elif event.Id == wx.ID_EXIT:
            self.Close()
        else:
            event.Skip()
```

6. Finally, the definition for the handler of the **Edit** menu actions can be handled by using the following code:

```
def OnEdit(self, event):
    action = { wx.ID_CUT : self.txt.Cut,
               wx.ID_COPY : self.txt.Copy,
               wx.ID_PASTE : self.txt.Paste }
    if action.has_key(event.Id):
        action.get(event.Id)()
    else:
        event.Skip()
```

How it works...

Note that on some platforms, even if you have set a bitmap, it may be ignored due to system settings or to conform to the native platform's standards. For example, on Linux systems, the GTK+ environment has a global setting called `gtk-menu-images` that determines whether images are shown or not. (In Gnome 2.28 and higher versions, this is turned off by default.)

Now that you have taken a look at the code, let's go back and take a little more detailed look at it, starting with the EasyMenu class. We made this class to wrap up some of the details about adding MenuItem to a menu that has a bitmap on it. This class simply uses the defined control ID in the ART ID map to try and find out whether there is an appropriate bitmap available in the system's ArtProvider and then attaches it to MenuItem.

It's important to note that if you want to display Bitmap on MenuItem, Bitmap must be attached to MenuItem before MenuItem is attached to Menu!

Next, in our `Editor` class, we created a `MenuBar` object; `MenuBar` acts as the container for `Menu` objects and is attached to `Frame` through the frame's `SetMenuBar` method. In the `DoSetupMenu` method, we created all the `Menu` objects and their items as well as bound the event handlers to the menu events. This is done by first creating a `Menu` object, and then appending `MenuItem` objects to it using the `AddEasyItem` method, which we previously added to the `EasyMenu` class. An important point to note here is that `MenuBar` objects contain `Menu` objects, and `Menu` objects contain `MenuItem` objects.

In this recipe, all the `MenuItem` objects that we created use the stock IDs provided by wxPython for common actions. Using the stock IDs, most of our items automatically gained labels and shortcut keys, except for the `Exit` item, where we needed to specify our own shortcut. When a `MenuItem` object's label contains a `Tab` character in it, the label is automatically parsed for the text following the `Tab` to specify which keyboard shortcut is to be used.

To react to `MenuItem` clicks or the selection that is invoked when the shortcut is activated, we bound two common handlers to the `EVT_MENU` event for each `MenuItem` object. Here, the event's ID is used to map the selection to the appropriate action to be executed.

There's more...

When there is a large number of actions on a `Menu` object or a desire to categorize items with a menu, they can be grouped together by appending submenus. This can be done using the `Menu` object's `AppendMenu` method and passing it another `Menu` object to append, similar to how `MenuItem` is added.

Additional indicators and behaviors can be associated with menu items besides by just adding bitmaps. Using the `MenuItem` constructor or the kind parameter of the `Menu` class' `Append` method, a `MenuItem` object can have either a `CheckBox` (`ITEM_CHECK`) or a `RadioButton` (`ITEM_RADIO`) control.

See also

- ▸ Refer to the *Working with ToolBars* and *Managing UI states* recipes in this chapter, where we will add some extended functionality to the example code started in this recipe
- ▸ The *Selecting files with a FileDialog* recipe in *Chapter 7, Requesting and Retrieving Information*, will also revisit this recipe to add the **Open** and **Save** functionality

Displaying a context menu

Sometimes, an individual page or control on a page needs a way to give some additional options on which actions are available to be performed. The use of a context (or right-click) menu is often used to fill this role. In this recipe, we will look at how to create, show, and manage a context menu.

How to do it...

Here's how you can display a context menu:

1. In order to help manage the creation and destruction of a `Menu` object, we will make a small helper class that will be responsible for the `Menu` object, as follows:

```
class ContextMenuMgr(object):
    def __init__(self, parent):
        super(ContextMenuMgr, self).__init__()

        assert isinstance(parent, wx.Window)
        assert hasattr(parent, 'GetPopupMenu'), \
                "parent must implement GetPopupMenu"

        self.window = parent
        self.window.Bind(wx.EVT_CONTEXT_MENU,
                         self.OnContextMenu)
```

2. This helper class will have the following method, which is bound to the preceding owning `Window` object that is used as an event handler for the show context menu event:

```
    def OnContextMenu(self, event):
        menu = self.window.GetPopupMenu()
        if menu:
            self.window.PopupMenu(menu)
            menu.Destroy()
```

3. Now, to start the example code that will use the preceding class, we will simply define a couple of custom window IDs to use in the menu:

```
ID_BLUE = wx.NewId()
ID_RED = wx.NewId()
```

4. For the example usage class in this recipe, we will make a panel that has a `ContextMenuMgr` class through the following code:

```
class MyPanel(wx.Panel):
    def __init__(self, parent):
        super(MyPanel, self).__init__(parent)
```

```
self._menuMgr = ContextMenuMgr(self)

self.Bind(wx.EVT_MENU, self.OnMenu)
```

5. As part of the requirement for using `ContextMenuMgr`, this class must also give us a `GetPopupMenu` method to provide the `Menu` object to be displayed. We can do this using the following method:

```
def GetPopupMenu(self):
    menu = wx.Menu()
    menu.Append(ID_BLUE, "Blue")
    menu.Append(ID_RED, "Red")
    return menu
```

6. Lastly, we will add a menu event handler to the panel to handle events using context menu clicks, as follows:

```
def OnMenu(self, event):
    evtId = event.Id
    if evtId == ID_BLUE:
        self.BackgroundColour = wx.BLUE
        self.Refresh()
    elif evtId == ID_RED:
        self.BackgroundColour = wx.RED
        self.Refresh()
    else:
        event.Skip()
```

How it works...

The `ContextMenuMgr` class is used to help encapsulate the creation and destruction of a context menu. Unlike menus attached to the `MenuBar` object, the ones used as context menus require the caller to manage their lifetime. So, this class binds its `OnContextMenu` method to its parent window's `EVT_CONTEXT_MENU` event, which is emitted when the control is right-clicked on or the appropriate keyboard combination is pressed. Once this handler is called, it requests the menu object from the window and then shows it using the window's own `PopupMenu` method. The `PopupMenu` method returns once a menu selection is made or the menu is dismissed; at this point, the `Menu` object can be destroyed to free up the resources.

Then, in the example's usage, the `Panel` class simply creates a `ContextMenuMgr` class and registers to handle `EVT_MENU` events that may be emitted by the menu. If `ID_BLUE` or `ID_RED` is perceived by the handler, it would change its background color to match the selection.

See also

▶ Refer to the *Exploring menus and shortcuts* recipe in this chapter for more examples of using `Menu` objects

Working with ToolBars

A `ToolBar` object provides a quick visual way to display a series of icons that allow actions in the application to be performed by clicking on an icon associated with the desired task. A `ToolBar` object provides a functionality very similar to `Menu`, but it is most often displayed to the user and predominantly uses icons for identification instead of text. In this recipe, we will look at how to set up a `ToolBar` object on a `Frame` object by extending the `Editor` class from an earlier recipe in this chapter.

Getting ready

This recipe will use the code from the *Exploring menus and shortcuts* recipe as a base to build the additional use of a `ToolBar` upon.

How to do it...

You need to perform the following steps:

1. Much as we did in the *Exploring menus and shortcuts* recipe, we will start by making a simple wrapper class around the `ToolBar` object to automatically apply bitmaps when possible using the following code:

```
class EasyToolBar(wx.ToolBar):
    def AddEasyTool(self, id, label=""):
        art = ArtMap.get(id, None)
        if art is not None:
            bmp = wx.ArtProvider.GetBitmap(art, wx.ART_TOOLBAR)
            if bmp.IsOk():
                self.AddSimpleTool(id, bmp)
```

2. Now, just to make the new changes clearer, we will create a subclass of the `Editor` frame from the *Exploring menus and shortcuts* recipe and use it to add `ToolBar` to the base editor through the following class:

```
class EditorWithToolBar(Editor):
    def __init__(self, parent, title=""):
        super(EditorWithToolBar, self).__init__(parent, title)

        # Add in the toolbar
        toolbar = EasyToolBar(self)
        self.DoSetupToolBar(toolbar)
        toolbar.Realize()
        self.SetToolBar(toolbar)
```

3. As the last step, we will define the `DoSetupToolBar` method to add our set of tools to the toolbar, as follows:

```
def DoSetupToolBar(self, toolbar):
    toolbar.AddEasyTool(wx.ID_OPEN)
    toolbar.AddEasyTool(wx.ID_SAVE)
    toolbar.AddSeparator()
    toolbar.AddEasyTool(wx.ID_CUT)
    toolbar.AddEasyTool(wx.ID_COPY)
    toolbar.AddEasyTool(wx.ID_PASTE)
```

How it works...

A `ToolBar` object works much the same way as `Menu`. So, as a way to simplify and make its usage consistent with the `EasyMenu` class that was introduced earlier, we added the `EasyToolBar` class. This uses the same `ID` to `ART_ID` map that was refactored out of the `EasyMenu` class and into a shared global resource to simplify getting the appropriate bitmap resource to be displayed for a tool action.

The `ToolBar` object is added to `Frame` much the same way as a `MenuBar` object using the `Frame` object's `SetToolBar` method, which adds `ToolBar` to the `Frame` object's window area. An important thing to note about displaying a `ToolBar` object is that it is necessary to call the `ToolBar` object's `Realize` method in order to make it show the tool icons on screen. Failing to call this method will result in a blank and empty `ToolBar` object being displayed.

The last thing to note from this particular example is that we did not bind any special handlers to the events from `ToolBar`. This is because the `EVT_TOOL` event is the same as `EVT_MENU`, so all tool events will automatically be routed to the already existing menu handlers for the same actions.

There's more...

Newly since wxPython 2.9.1, the `ToolBar` object now supports adding a stretchable space between tools by calling the `AddStretchableSpace` method, which makes it possible to align tools away from the left side of the `ToolBar` object as the parent window changes its size.

A `ToolBars` object also supports adding several other types of tools in addition to the normal icon button-based ones. Take a look at the following table:

ToolBar methods	Description
`AddControl`	This is a generic method to add a simple control object to the `ToolBar` object, such as a button or `TextCtrl`
`AddCheckTool`	This adds a tool that can be toggled similar to a `CheckBox` or `ToggleButton` control
`AddRadioTool`	This adds a tool that behaves similar to a `RadioButton` control, where only one of the tools in the group can be selected at a time

The standard `AddTool` method also supports creating several special kinds of toolbar buttons by specifying different values to its kind parameter. The following table describes the different values that this parameter can be provided with:

Kind value	Description
`wx.ITEM_NORMAL`	This is the default value and creates a normal tool button.
`wx.ITEM_CHECK`	This creates a toolbar button that can be toggled from a pressed to nonpressed state.
`wx.ITEM_RADIO`	This creates a toolbar button that behaves similarly to `ITEM_CHECK` but groups other items of the same type together, only allowing one to be checked at a time.
`wx.ITEM_DROPDOWN`	This causes a menu drop-down button to be shown next to the normal tool button. It is necessary to call `SetDropdownMenu` on the toolbar afterwards to associate the menu. (This feature is only supported on Linux and Windows currently.)

See also

- ▶ The *Managing UI states* recipe in this chapter shows how to manage the enabled and disabled states of `ToolBar` items
- ▶ The *Selecting files with a FileDialog* recipe in *Chapter 7, Requesting and Retrieving Information*, will revisit this recipe to add the **Open** and **Save** functionalities

Managing UI states

In order to give good visual feedback to the users of an application, the user interface should let the user know when they can and cannot interact with an action that is provided by the interface. Managing the state of when a `ToolBar` or `MenuItem` object can be executed may quickly become a difficult and messy task if it is necessary to monitor and update an action in response to each and every action the user may take when using the UI. Fortunately, the `EVT_UPDATE_UI` event is provided to give the application an easy way to update the state of UI elements periodically during its idle time.

Getting ready

This recipe builds on the previous recipe in this chapter, *Working with ToolBars*, in order to show how to use `EVT_UPDATE_UI` to manage the state of toolbar icons.

How to do it...

You need to perform the following steps:

1. For this recipe, we will make a simple subclass of the `EditorWithToolBar` class from the previous recipe just to separate the new code from the old code and show the new handling of `EVT_UPDATE_UI`, as follows:

```
class EditorUpdateUI(EditorWithToolBar):
    def __init__(self, parent, title=""):
        super(EditorUpdateUI, self).__init__(parent, title)

        self.Bind(wx.EVT_UPDATE_UI, self.OnUpdateUI)
```

2. The second and last step is to simply define the `OnUpdateUI` event handler method that is bound to `EVT_UPDATE_UI` in the constructor. This will handle the updating of the state of UI elements through the following code:

```
def OnUpdateUI(self, event):
    evtId = event.Id
    if evtId in (wx.ID_COPY, wx.ID_CUT):
        event.Enable(self.txt.HasSelection())
    elif evtId == wx.ID_PASTE:
        event.Enable(self.txt.CanPaste())
    else:
        event.Skip()
```

How it works...

This was a fairly simple recipe, but let's now take a closer look at how it works. The wxPython application will emit `UpdateUIEvents` periodically during its idle time; these events are routed to each control in order to give it a chance to update its state as it relates to the current state of the application. In this example, the **Cut** and **Copy** actions are only allowed when the `TextCtrl` control has some text selected; otherwise, they are disabled. Likewise, the **Paste** operation is only allowed when there is text in the clipboard to paste into the `TextCtrl` control, which is checked using the `TextCtrl` control's `CanPaste` method. This event handler can be seen in action in the following screenshots:

As can be seen in the first image, the **Cut** and **Copy** actions are grayed out and disabled until a selection is made within `TextCtrl` in the second image. An important point to take away from using `EVT_UPDATE_UI` is that the state of the control being managed should be updated through the use of methods on the event and not by directly modifying the control itself. This is in order to allow the element for the same action to be updated regardless of the type of element being updated.

There's more...

In addition to enabling or disabling a control, `UpdateUIEvent` has some additional methods to update the states of UI elements in different ways, which are illustrated in the following table:

Method name	Description
`Check`	This is used to check or uncheck a control, such as `CheckBox` or a checkable menu item.
`SetText`	This is used to update the text shown in a control. This applies to controls with labels and other text displays.

In some cases, if an application has a very large number of elements, there could be a chance for some performance issues from the overhead of handling all `UpdateUIEvents`. To counter this, it is possible to adjust the interval period using the static `SetUpdateInterval` method on the `UpdateUIEvent` class. This method allows us to set the update interval in milliseconds, which can help adjust and reduce the number of `EVT_UPDATE_UI` events that are generated during runtime to reduce overheads when necessary.

3

UI Layout and Organization

In this chapter, we will cover:

- ► Laying out controls with Sizers
- ► Controlling layout behavior
- ► Grouping controls with a StaticBox control
- ► Creating an automatic wrapping layout
- ► Using the standard dialog button sizer
- ► Simplifying the panel layout
- ► Making dialog layout easy
- ► Building XML resource-based layouts
- ► Extending XRC for custom controls
- ► Advancing your UI with AuiManager

Introduction

Understanding how to use various controls and putting them to work in your application is just part of the equation in developing a user interface. The remaining part is being able to put the controls together in a functional layout on screen. The standard user interface on a computer is a two-dimensional plane of various rectangles being positioned and sized upon it.

A window can be organized using a static positioning of controls upon the two-dimensional plane, but what happens when the application is running on a different system where the screen resolution may be different or the native controls are shaped or sized slightly differently? Due to these potential issues and many others, avoiding the use of static layouts can be very advantageous. The solution, and the alternative, is to use the Sizer system in wxPython to create dynamic and flexible window layouts that can be adjusted according to changes. Sizers are a type of helper class that all container windows can use to help manage the sizing and positioning of their child controls based on proportions and relative positioning.

In this chapter, we will take a look at using Sizers to create window layouts as well as some other features and functionalities available through the wxPython library to create and lay out your user interfaces.

Laying out controls with Sizers

All container controls can have a Sizer class associated with them; this Sizer can be used to control the layout of the direct children of the control that the Sizer belongs to. There are several types of Sizer, each one providing slightly different capabilities and features to control the placement and sizing of the controls they manage; however, they all work on the same two-dimensional rectangle-based plane.

Among the available choices for Sizers, `BoxSizer` is the most basic, but it provides a simple and powerful way to control the layout of controls. This Sizer operates in one of two modes. It can lay out controls in either a single rectangular column or a row. Sizers can then be nested inside each other to create more complex layouts. In this recipe, we will explore some of the basics of using `BoxSizer` to layout controls on a panel.

How to do it...

For this recipe, you need to perform the following steps:

1. First, let's define the `__init__` method for the `Panel` class and its child controls, as follows:

```python
class MyPanel(wx.Panel):
    def __init__(self, parent):
        super(MyPanel, self).__init__(parent)

        # Define controls
        self.label = wx.StaticText(self, label="Label:")
        choices = ['a', 'b', 'c']
        self.choice = wx.Choice(self, choices=choices)
        self.info = wx.StaticText(self)
```

```
# Do Layout
self._doLayout()

self.Bind(wx.EVT_CHOICE, self.OnChoice,
          self.choice)
```

2. Next, let's start walking through the `_doLayout` method and create the main `BoxSizer` class for the panel:

```
def _doLayout(self):
    sizer = wx.BoxSizer(wx.VERTICAL)
    sizer.AddStretchSpacer()
```

3. Now, we will create another nested spacer to manage the first `StaticText` and `choice` controls through the following code:

```
row = wx.BoxSizer(wx.HORIZONTAL)
row.Add(self.label)
row.AddSpacer(10)
row.Add(self.choice)
```

4. With this horizontal row laid out, we can now add it to the main `sizer` with the following code:

```
sizer.Add(row, flag=wx.CENTER)
```

5. For the last part of the layout, we will add the final control to the main `sizer` and set `sizer` as the `sizer` for the panel using the following code:

```
sizer.Add(self.info, flag=wx.CENTER)
sizer.AddStretchSpacer()
self.SetSizer(sizer)
```

6. The last step in this recipe is defining the event handler for the `Choice` selection. The following code can be used for this:

```
def OnChoice(self, event):
    lbl = "'%s' was selected!" % event.String
    self.info.Label = lbl
    self.Layout()
```

How it works...

First, let's take a look at a graphical breakdown of the layout that was produced by the Sizers that we used in the `_doLayout` method:

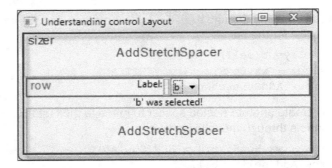

The preceding image tries to label the areas that are being managed by items added to the Sizer. Starting at the outer container, we can see the main `sizer` class, which is `BoxSizer` with the `VERTICAL` mode set. This means that the items added to it are added vertically from the top going downward. The first item is added by the `AddStretchSpacer` method, which adds empty space that will expand and contract as the outer window size changes.

Next, the second `row` Sizer is created with the `HORIZONTAL` mode set. This allows items to be added from left to right instead of top to bottom as with the `VERTICAL` mode. This is used to allow the label to be placed beside the `choice` control. The `row` Sizer is then added to `sizer` to let it become the next row in the layout of the main `sizer`. After this, the remaining control and spacer are added to the layout, as was done with the earlier items.

The last point to pay attention to in this recipe is the `OnChoice` event handler. Here, after assigning a new label to the `StaticText` control, there is a call to the `Layout` method. This method tells the window's Sizer to recalculate the layout and update the Sizers. This is necessary here to ensure that the control is properly repositioned by the main `sizer` after having its size changed by the new text.

See also

▶ Refer to the *Understanding the hierarchy of the UI* recipe in *Chapter 1, wxPython Starting Points*, for a review and explanation of the different types of UI components and their place in the hierarchy of the UI.

▶ Refer to the *Controlling layout behavior* recipe in this chapter for further explanation of how to make full use of the functionality Sizers provide.

Controlling layout behavior

In this recipe, we will take a deeper look at the optional parameters that can be applied to items that are added to a Sizer, which can control the proportional sizing and dynamic alignment of controls. Properly making use of these behavioral aspects of the layout can make the difference between the UI looking sloppy and great. They also allow the app to take advantage of various screen resolutions as well as allowing the components that make up the UI to properly adapt as the items around them change in size. So, in this recipe, we will take a look at using Sizer flags, borders, and proportions and how they affect the layout of controls.

Getting ready

Ensure that you have taken a look at the previous recipe in this chapter, *Laying out controls with Sizers*, to get an overview of the fundamentals of the Sizer API before proceeding with this recipe, which focuses on the behavioral aspects of Sizer-based layouts.

How to do it...

For this recipe, you need to perform the following steps:

1. First, let's make a custom `Panel` class and instantiate the five controls that will be used in the layout, as follows:

```
class RatingsPanel(wx.Panel):
    def __init__(self, parent):
        super(RatingsPanel, self).__init__(parent)

        # Define controls
        self._chLabel = wx.StaticText(self,
                                      label="Rating:")
        choices = ["Excellent", "Good", "Average", "Poor"]
        self._choice = wx.Choice(self, choices=choices)

        self._cmtLabel = wx.StaticText(self,
                                       label="Comment:")
        self._comment = wx.TextCtrl(self,
                                    style=wx.TE_MULTILINE)

        self._submit = wx.Button(self, label="Submit")

        # Do Layout
        self._doLayout()
```

2. Now, let's take a detailed walk through the _doLayout method, starting with setting up the layout of the top grouping of controls:

```
def _doLayout(self):
    main = wx.BoxSizer(wx.VERTICAL)

    topRow = wx.BoxSizer(wx.HORIZONTAL)
    topRow.Add(self._chLabel, 0,
               wx.RIGHT|wx.ALIGN_CENTER_VERTICAL, 10)
    topRow.Add(self._choice, 1,
               wx.EXPAND|wx.ALIGN_CENTER_VERTICAL)
    main.Add(topRow, 0, wx.EXPAND|wx.ALL, 5)
```

3. Next, let's add the comment entry field and its label using the following code:

```
commentRow = wx.BoxSizer(wx.HORIZONTAL)
commentRow.Add(self._cmtLabel,
               flag=wx.RIGHT,
               border=10)
commentRow.Add(self._comment, 1, wx.EXPAND)
main.Add(commentRow, 1, wx.EXPAND|wx.ALL, 5)
```

4. For the final step, we will add a button and attach the main `sizer` to the panel through this code:

```
main.Add(self._submit, 0, wx.ALL|wx.ALIGN_RIGHT, 5)
self.SetSizer(main)
```

How it works...

The Add method of the Sizer takes many optional parameters, which are used to influence how the controls are laid out on screen and how they react to changes in layout. Take a look at the following script:

```
Add(item, proportion, flags, border, userData)
```

Here's how this code can be broken down:

- ▶ **Item**: This is the object being added to the Sizer.
- ▶ **Proportion**: This is used to indicate whether the item can grow in proportion to its siblings and in the direction of the layout of the Sizer:
  - ❑ 0 means it's not changeable
  - ❑ > 0 allows a control to grow or shrink proportionally in relation to the value of the other children in the same Sizer
- ▶ **Flag**: This is the bit mask field that affects the behavior of the Sizer.

- ▸ **Border**: This is to add space padding around the item in pixels when a border flag is included in the `Flags` field.

- ▸ **userData**: This is a custom data object that can be attached to pass more complex sizing information, represented with the flags field. This is only really useful in making a custom `Sizer` subclass.

Now, armed with this information, let's take a look at the layout that is achieved in the preceding example code:

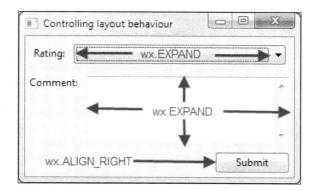

On the first row, compare the alignment of the label and `Choice` control to that of the previous recipe. Note how they are now lined up nice and square with each other and how the usage of the `EXPAND` flag and proportional value of 1 has caused the `Choice` control to stretch and fill the available horizontal space.

A similar approach is taken on the second row for the `Comment` field. The difference is that when the `HORIZONTAL` Sizer is added to the `VERTICAL` Sizer, it is also given the proportion of one and the `EXPAND` flag of the other. This allows the text control to expand and contract in both the horizontal and vertical directions as the available area changes.

Then, in the last row for the button, it is simply given a padded border and has the `ALIGN_RIGHT` flag applied to it to anchor it to the right of the available space.

There's more...

There are several flags that can be applied to achieve different behaviors. Take some time to experiment with the example code in this recipe to remove or add flags and take a look at how they affect the behavior of the layout. The following tables include some of the different flags that can be masked together when placing items in a Sizer:

Border flags

Flag	Description
wx.TOP	This applies border padding to the top of a control
wx.BOTTOM	This applies border padding to the bottom of a control
wx.LEFT	This applies border padding to the left of a control
wx.RIGHT	This applies border padding to the right of a control
wx.ALL	This applies border padding to all sides of a control

Behavior flags

Flag	Description
wx.EXPAND	This makes an item expand to fit the available space
wx.SHAPED	This makes an item expand while maintaining aspect ratio
wx.FIXED_MINSIZE	This keeps an item at its initial size
wx.RESERVE_SPACE_ EVEN_IF_HIDDEN	This reserves space for the control even if it is not currently visible

Alignment flags

Flag	Description
wx.ALIGN_CENTER	This aligns control toward the center of the available space
wx.ALIGN_LEFT	This aligns control to the left of the available space
wx.ALIGN_RIGHT	This aligns control to the right of the available space
wx.ALIGN_BOTTOM	This aligns control to the bottom of the available space
wx.ALIGN_CENTER_ VERTICAL	This center-aligns the control vertically in the available space
wx.ALIGN_CENTER_ HORIZONTAL	This center-aligns the control horizontally in the available space

Grouping controls with a StaticBox control

The StaticBox control is a type of static control that is used to group or organize controls that perform related actions together. It provides a label text and an outlining border around the grouped controls. In previous versions of wxPython, StaticBox had an irregular sibling relationship with the controls that it contained, which was, needless to say, outside the mold of the overall hierarchy of the framework. However, starting from version 2.9 onward, StaticBox can be treated similarly to a special panel that is the parent of the controls it contains. In this recipe, we will take a quick look at how to add controls to StaticBox.

How to do it...

Here are the steps for this recipe:

1. First, let's start off by making a little wrapper class around `StaticBox` to encapsulate `StaticBoxSizer` and add a couple of convenience methods, as follows:

```python
class GroupBox(wx.StaticBox):
    def __init__(self, parent, orient, label=""):
        super(GroupBox, self).__init__(parent, label=label)
        self._sizer = wx.StaticBoxSizer(self, orient)

def AddItem(self, item, proportion=0,
            flag=wx.ALL, border=5):
        self._sizer.Add(item, proportion, flag, border)

    @property
    def Sizer(self):
        return self._sizer
```

2. The next step is to put this class to use. We will use it to group a few buttons together through the following code:

```python
class MyPanel(wx.Panel):
    def __init__(self, parent):
        super(MyPanel, self).__init__(parent)

        # Layout sizers
        sizer = wx.BoxSizer(wx.VERTICAL)
        sbox = GroupBox(self, wx.HORIZONTAL,
                        "Button Group")
        for x in range(1, 4):
            button = wx.Button(self, label="Button %d" % x)
            sbox.AddItem(button)
```

3. Lastly, to finish off the layout in the __init__ method, we need to add GroupBox to the panel's layout. Take special note here that we will add GroupBoxes `StaticBoxSizer` to the layout and not `GroupBox` itself:

```python
        sizer.Add(sbox.Sizer, 0, wx.ALL, 20)
        self.SetSizer(sizer)
```

How it works...

The `StaticBox` control requires `StaticBoxSizer` in order to lay out itself and its controls. This specialized Sizer must be used to get the controls to lay out correctly in `StaticBox`. This Sizer shares a special relationship with the `StaticBox` control as it acts as a layout container for the box' child controls but also as a sort of container for the `StaticBox` control itself. As you can see in *Step 3*, we added `StaticBoxSizer` to the `Panel` layout instead of the control itself. This is slightly irregular from normal layout patterns as the Sizer controls the layout of `StaticBox` and its children but is not directly owned by `StaticBox`.

When displayed, `StaticBox`, as can be seen in the preceding screenshot, draws a border around the controls that are grouped within it as well as displaying an optional group label to give the user some context to what the purpose of the group of controls is.

There's more...

As can be noticed in the constructor of our `GroupBox` class, the orient argument is used to specify the direction of the box. The `StaticBoxSizer` class can be organized into either rows (`wx.VERTICAL`) or columns (`wx.HORIZONTAL`), as we did in this example. More complex layouts can also be achieved by the nesting of other Sizers and panels, as we will begin to look at in more detail in the next chapter.

Creating an automatic wrapping layout

Sizers allow the dynamic positioning and resizing of controls, though this layout is still typically on a fixed grid or in a single direction at a time, similar to `BoxSizer`. If you wish to allow controls to wrap and flow in both the horizontal and vertical directions as the space allows, you can use `WrapSizer`, which allows only this. It works much like `BoxSizer` in that it has a primary direction of layout, but as the space in the primary direction is used up, the sizer automatically adds new columns or rows in the secondary direction. In this recipe, we will have a quick introduction to using `WrapSizer`.

How to do it...

You need to perform these steps:

1. The usage is basically similar to `BoxSizer`; so, let's just set up a panel with 15 buttons on it to explore how this `sizer` works through the following code:

```
class WrappingPanel(wx.Panel):
    def __init__(self, parent):
        super(WrappingPanel, self).__init__(parent)

        sizer = wx.WrapSizer(wx.HORIZONTAL)

        # Add many buttons
        for x in range(15):
            button = wx.Button(self, label="Button %d" % x)
            sizer.Add(button, 0, wx.ALL, 5)

        self.SetSizer(sizer)
        self.SetInitialSize()
```

How it works...

The `WrapSizer` class is set up to use `HORIZONTAL` as its primary layout direction. Controls will be added to the layout from left to right, the same as `BoxSizer`. However, once the available horizontal space on the panel is used up by the buttons, additional rows will be added in the `VERTICAL` direction to contain the additional buttons. As the outer window changes size, such as when a user resizes the window, the available space is recalculated and the additional rows are added or removed as needed to best make use of the space.

Using the standard dialog button sizer

Each platform has varying conventions or standards for the way buttons are displayed on a dialog. For example, on Windows, the **OK** button is to the left of the **Cancel** button; however, on OS X, the **OK** button is to its right. wxPython provides a way to deal with these platform differences without the need for platform-specific code. In this recipe, we will explore how to use the `StdDialogButtonSizer` class to manage the layout of buttons on a dialog in a platform-independent way.

How to do it...

Here are the steps that you need to perform for this:

1. For this recipe, we will make a custom message dialog class that uses `StdDialogButtonSizer`. The first step is to define the class' special text Sizer for the message, which can be done through the following code:

```
class CustomMessageDialog(wx.Dialog):
    def __init__(self, parent, title, msg, flags):
        super(CustomMessageDialog, self).__init__(parent,
        title=title)

        sizer = wx.BoxSizer(wx.VERTICAL)

        msgSizer = self.CreateTextSizer(msg)
        sizer.Add(msgSizer, 0, wx.EXPAND|wx.ALL, 5)

        sizer.AddStretchSpacer()
```

2. The next and final step is to use the dialog's convenience function to create the button `sizer` using the flags passed on to the constructor. This can be achieved with the following code:

```
        bSizer = self.CreateStdDialogButtonSizer(flags)
        sizer.Add(bSizer, 0, wx.EXPAND|wx.BOTTOM, 5)

        self.SetSizer(sizer)
        self.SetInitialSize()
```

How it works...

The `CreateStdDialogButtonSizer` method will create standard stock buttons based on the `MessageBox` flags that are passed to the constructor.

As can be seen in the preceding screenshot, when the dialog is created using wx.OK|wx. CANCEL flags, an **OK** and **Cancel** button are also created. These buttons are put in the standard order, spaced, and positioned based on the platform's interface guidelines. In this example, on Windows, the buttons are grouped to the right with the **OK** button on the left-hand side. If this same exact code is run on OS X, the standard on the order will be reversed:

There's more...

The StdDialogButtonSizer class, as used in this example, is created by a helper method in the dialog class. This method can create and manage the layout of standard buttons using any of the standard button flag values. Take a look at the following table:

Flag	Description
wx.OK	This creates an **OK** button
wx.CANCEL	This creates a **Cancel** button
wx.YES	This creates a **Yes** button
wx.NO	This creates a **No** button
wx.APPLY	This creates an **Apply** button
wx.CLOSE	This creates a **Close** button
wx.HELP	This creates a **Help** button
wx.NO_DEFAULT	This creates a **No** button and sets it as the default action

This Sizer can also be used on its own in any other context by creating it and using its AddButton method to add a button to the layout. Note that it is necessary to use the AddButton method and not the base Add method to achieve the proper layout. The Sizer also only treats buttons with stock ID's for the preceding flags as well (that is, wx.ID_OK). Finally, the Sizer's Realize method must be called after the buttons are added to tell the Sizer to put them in the correct order based on the platform's standards.

Simplifying the panel layout

If you find yourself using the normal Sizer-based layouts to be somewhat tedious or cumbersome, there are some other options through the `sized_controls` library available in the `wx.lib` namespace. This library provides a number of specialized controls to help streamline and simplify the use of Sizers. These controls automatically create Sizers and add their child controls to them based on the layout mode of `SizedControl`. In this recipe, we will give an introduction to this library by making use of `SizedScrolledPanel` to lay out a number of controls.

How to do it...

Perform the following steps:

1. First, we will start by declaring a subclass of `SizedScrolledPanel` and setting the Sizer layout type to use through the following code:

```
class MyPanel(sized.SizedScrolledPanel):
    def __init__(self, parent):
        super(MyPanel, self).__init__(parent)

        self.SetSizerType("form")
```

2. Now, we can instantiate the controls to add them into the layout:

```
        label = wx.StaticText(self, label="Field 1:")
        text = wx.TextCtrl(self)
        text.SetSizerProp("expand", True)

        label2 = wx.StaticText(self, label="Field 2:")
        choice = wx.Choice(self, choices=['1', '2', '3'])
        choice.SetSizerProp("expand", True)
```

How it works...

When the `sized_controls` module is imported, it adds several extension methods into some Windows-based classes to use to manage the Sizer's properties. They are added because `SizedControls` classes, such as `SizedScrolledPanel`, automatically add their child controls to their internally managed Sizers as each control is instantiated. So, to modify the layout's behavior, it is necessary to call extension methods, such as `SetSizerProps`, to change the `sizer` flags for each item after they are already in a Sizer.

In this example, we used `SetSizerType` and passed it `form`. This generates a two-column grid layout; the controls are added to the layout from left to right and then top to bottom. This means that when using `SizedPanel`, the order in which the controls are instantiated is important as it determines where the controls are placed in the layout.

There's more...

The `SizedPanel` method supports several types of layouts through the use of the `SetSizerType` method. The available Sizer type options are as follows:

Sizer type argument	Description
`horizontal`	This is a horizontal `BoxSizer` option
`vertical`	This is a vertical `BoxSizer` option
`form`	This is a row-column grid layout
`table`	This is a configurable table layout; it requires option flags to be passed in to specify the number of rows and columns to use: ▶ **rows**: this specifies the number of rows to make ▶ **cols**: this specifies the number of columns to make
`Grid`	This works similarly to the table mode but also supports the following options flags: ▶ `hgap`: this specifies the pixel amount for the space between columns ▶ `vgap`: this specifies the pixel amount for the space between rows

The sizer properties for each item can be applied through the Windows object's `SetSizerProp` or `SetSizerProps` extension method with any of the following options:

Flag	Description
`proportion`	This is a number to set the control's proportional value
`hgrow`	This is used to set a proportion to allow a control to grow horizontally
`vgrow`	This used to set a proportion to allow a control to grow vertically
`halign`	This causes a control to align horizontally; the value can be `left`, `center`, or `right`
`valign`	This causes a control to align vertically; the value can be `top`, `center`, or `bottom`
`align`	This aligns the control and only accepts `center` as an option
`border`	This is used to set the border's direction; the value can be `left`, `right`, `top`, `bottom`, or `all`
`minsize`	When a `fixed` value is passed, this sets a fixed minimum size for an item
`expand`	This passes a value of `True` to set a control to expand and use the available space

See also

▶ Refer to the next recipe in this chapter, *Making dialog layout easy*, to learn more about using `SizedControls`

Making dialog layout easy

The `SizedControl` library, in addition to simplifying the layout of panels, also provides some integrated solutions for dialogs. Internally, `SizedDialog` uses `SizedPanel` to manage its controls as well as support the layout for `StdDialogButtonSizer`. This recipe will take a look at using `SizedDialog` to show how to quickly and easily build custom dialogs.

Getting ready

Ensure that you have taken a look at the previous recipe in this chapter, *Simplifying the panel layout*, before moving on to the rest of this recipe as this recipe heavily makes use of the content covered in the preceding one.

How to do it...

You need to perform the following steps:

1. In this recipe, we will mock up a dialog to configuring proxy settings. The first step is to derive a class from `SizedDialog`:

```
class ProxyConfigDlg(sized.SizedDialog):
    def __init__(self, parent, title):
        super(ProxyConfigDlg, self).__init__(parent, title=title)
```

2. Now, we need to set up the type of layout by getting a reference to `SizedPanel`:

```
pane = self.GetContentsPane()
pane.SetSizerType("grid", {"rows":3, "cols":2})
```

3. With the layout style set up, it's time to instantiate the controlscontrols, as is done in the following code:

```
proxyLbl = wx.StaticText(pane, label="Proxy URL:")
url = wx.TextCtrl(pane)
url.SetSizerProps(expand=True)

nameLbl = wx.StaticText(pane, label="Username:")
name = wx.TextCtrl(pane)
name.SetSizerProps(expand=True)
```

```
passLbl = wx.StaticText(pane, label="Password:")
name = wx.TextCtrl(pane, style=wx.TE_PASSWORD)
name.SetSizerProps(expand=True)
```

4. For the final step, we will create and add StdDialogButtonSizer, as follows:

```
bsz = self.CreateButtonSizer(wx.CANCEL|wx.OK))
self.SetButtonSizer(bsz)
self.SetInitialSize((300, 175))
self.Fit()
```

How it works...

The SizedDialog basically just wraps up SizedPanel in an easy-to-use package to build a dialog. The important point to note is that it is necessary to call GetContentPane to get a reference to this panel. This panel must be used as the parent for the controls in order to allow SizedPanel to manage the layout. In addition to this, the SetButtonSizer method should be used to add dialog buttons to the layout. This method ensures the correct placement of StdDialogButtonSizer in relation to SizedPanel.

Building XML resource-based layouts

wxPython also supports designer-like layout mechanisms using XML-based resource files, called XRC, that are supported by several wx-centric IDEs, such as XRCed, wxFormBuilder, and DialogBlocks. XRC uses hierarchical XML data to construct a window layout. This recipe will show you how to get started with XRC by building up a simple dialog.

How to do it...

1. We will start by going through an example XRC file that will be used to build a dialog. The first part will declare the dialog and a Sizer to lay out the contents of the dialog. Take a look at this code:

```
<?xml version="1.0" ?>
<resource>
  <object class="wxDialog" name="xrctestdlg">
    <title>Xrc Test Dialog</title>
    <style>wxDEFAULT_DIALOG_STYLE|wxRESIZE_BORDER</style>
    <object class="wxBoxSizer">
      <orient>wxVERTICAL</orient>
      <object class="spacer">
        <option>1</option>
        <flag>wxEXPAND</flag>
      </object>
```

2. Next, we will add a `CheckBox` control to the Sizer using the following code:

```
<object class="sizeritem">
  <object class="wxCheckBox" name="check_box">
    <label>CheckBox Label</label>
  </object>
  <flag>wxALL|wxALIGN_CENTRE_HORIZONTAL</flag>
  <border>5</border>
</object>
```

3. For the last part of the XRC file, we will add a button Sizer with some buttons, as follows:

```
<object class="sizeritem">
    <object class="wxStdDialogButtonSizer">
        <object class="button">
          <object class="wxButton" name="wxID_OK"/>
        </object>
        <object class="button">
          <object class="wxButton"
          name="wxID_CANCEL"/>
        </object>
      </object>
    <flag>wxEXPAND|wxALL</flag>
    <border>5</border>
  </object>
 </object>
  </object>
</resource>
```

4. Now, we will make a little example wrapper class to load the resource file into a dialog through the following class:

```
class ResourceDialog(object):
    def __init__(self, parent):
        super(ResourceDialog, self).__init__()

        resource = xrc.XmlResource("xrcdlg.xrc")
        self.dlg = resource.LoadDialog(parent,
                                      "xrctestdlg")

        checkId = resource.GetXRCID("check_box")
        self.dlg.Bind(wx.EVT_CHECKBOX, self.OnCheck,
                    id=checkId)
```

5. For the last step, we will finish up the class by defining the checkbox event handler and method to show the dialog object created from XRC:

```
def OnCheck(self, event):
    print("Checked: %s" % event.IsChecked())

def ShowModal(self):
    result = self.dlg.ShowModal()
    if result == wx.ID_OK:
        print("Ok Clicked!")
    else:
        print("Cancel Clicked!")
```

How it works...

The XRC format is a series of object nodes that defines the type of object and can contain other object nodes for objects that should be contained within the outer one. This builds up the structure of the UI, which in this recipe is a Dialog object that contains a Sizer. This in turn contains a CheckBox control and StdDialogButtonSizer.

To make use of the resource file, the wx.xrc module needs to be imported to get access to the XmlResource class, which is used to load the file. The resource object has several methods to load different types of objects. We used the LoadDialog method that passes the parent window and the name of the dialog resource from the xrctestdialog file. This loads a resource's definition and uses it to create the Dialog object.

The ResourceDialog class also showed a way to bind events to XRC-created controls. The XmlResource object can be used to look up the ID of any item by doing a name lookup in the resource with the GetXRCID method and using the resulting ID to bind to the EVT_CHECKBOX event handler.

There's more...

The `XmlResource` class also has methods to load several other types of resource objects from an XRC file. The following table is provided as a quick reference guide:

Method	Description
`LoadBitmap(name)`	This is used to load and return the named bitmap
`LoadDialog(parent, name)`	This is used to load and return the named dialog
`LoadFrame(parent, name)`	This is used to load and return the named frame
`LoadIcon(name)`	This is used to load and return the named icon
`LoadMenu(name)`	This is used to load and return the named menu
`LoadMenuBar(parent, name)`	This is used to load and return the named menu bar
`LoadObject(parent, name, className)`	This is used to load and return the named object of the `className` type
`LoadPanel(parent, name)`	This is used to load and return the named panel
`LoadToolBar(parent, name)`	This is used to load and return the named toolbar

Extending XRC for custom controls

If you have built up some of your own custom controls, there won't be a built-in handler for them in XRC. However, it's still possible to use XRC with your custom controls as XRC can be extended by defining custom XML handlers to instantiate your controls. In this recipe, we will show you how to create a custom XRC resource handler to load custom user-defined controls from an XRC file.

How to do it...

Here are the steps:

1. First, we will define the custom XRC handler to load a custom class called `PhoneButtonPanel`. The handler requires overriding two methods to check whether the handler can handle the XML tag and then create an instance of the object from the tag. The following code will help us do this:

```
class PhoneBtnPanelHandler(xrc.XmlResourceHandler):
    def CanHandle(self, node):
        return self.IsOfClass(node, "PhoneButtonPanel")

    def DoCreateResource(self):
        panel = PhoneButtonPanel(self.GetParentAsWindow())
        self.SetupWindow(panel)
        self.CreateChildren(panel)
        return panel
```

2. Next, we will define a simple custom `XmlResource` class to make use of this new handler through the following code:

```
class CustomXmlResource(xrc.XmlResource):
    def __init__(self, fileName):
        super(CustomXmlResource, self).__init__(fileName)

        # insert custom handler(s)
        self.InsertHandler(PhoneBtnPanelHandler())
```

3. For the final step, let's take a look at an XRC file that has a node for the custom `PhoneButtonPanel` in it, as follows:

```
<?xml version="1.0"?>
<resource>
  <object class="wxPanel" name="dialog_panel">
    <object class="wxBoxSizer">
      <orient>wxVERTICAL</orient>
      <object class="sizeritem">
        <object class="wxTextCtrl" name="display">
            <style>wxTE_READONLY|wxTE_RIGHT</style>
        </object>
        <flag>wxEXPAND</flag>
      </object>
      <object class="sizeritem">
        <object class="PhoneButtonPanel" name="buttons"/>
        <flag>wxALL|wxEXPAND</flag>
        <border>5</border>
      </object>
    </object>
  </object>
</resource>
```

How it works...

The `XmlResource` object is a SAX parser for the XML in an XRC file; it processes nodes in the file as they are seen and looks for a handler in its collection to find one that can handle the nodes as they are encountered. So, in order to handle custom control nodes, it is as simple as adding another handler to the chain of resource handlers.

The `XmlResourceHandler` has a number of methods to process the XML, but in most simple cases, it is only necessary to override `CanHandle` and `DoCreateResource`. The first method is called by the SAX processor to see whether the handler object can handle processing a specific node. The `DoCreateResource` method is used to create the resource object represented by the node.

With the `PhoneBtnPanelHandler` installed in the `CustomXmlResource` method's chain of handlers, it is now able to process the XRC file shown in *Step 3*, which contains an object node with `PhoneButtonPanel` in it.

There's more...

Check out the sample code that accompanies this chapter for an example application that creates a dialog using the resources from the XRC file in this recipe.

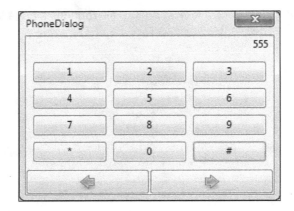

Advancing your UI with AuiManager

The `AuiManager` provides a docking panel layout framework for a frame. Panels can be added to the frame's layout through `AuiManager`. Users can be given options to rearrange the layout by undocking and redocking them where they like. The panes can also be pulled out into floating windows or closed and hidden altogether. wxPython currently has two versions of AUI libraries: there is the original C++ version in the `wx.aui` module as well as the new updated version in the `wx.lib.agw.aui` module. In this recipe, we will work with the newer `wx.lib` version, which has a more complete implementation and feature set available. So, let's get started with an introduction to using `AuiManager` to generate an advanced window layout.

How to do it...

You need to perform the following steps:

1. `AuiManager` works with a frame, so we will start by defining a frame that has some custom panels in it through the following code:

    ```
    import wx
    import wx.lib.mixins.listctrl as listmix
    import wx.lib.sized_controls as sized
    ```

```
import wx.lib.agw.aui as aui

class AuiFrame(wx.Frame):
    def __init__(self, *args, **kwargs):
        super(AuiFrame, self).__init__(*args, **kwargs)

        # Attributes
        self._mgr = aui.AuiManager(self)

        # Panels
        self._phone = PhoneDialerPanel(self)
        self._contacts = ContactList(self)
        self._callLog = wx.ListBox(self)

        # Layout
        self.SetupMgr()
        self.SetInitialSize((750, 350))
```

2. Next, let's step through the `SetupMgr` method, beginning by adding the central pane using the following method:

```
def SetupMgr(self):
    # Contacts Pane
    info = aui.AuiPaneInfo().Center().Name("Contacts")

    lbl = "Contact List"
    info = info.CloseButton(False).Caption(lbl)
    self._mgr.AddPane(self._contacts, info)
```

3. Now that the central pane is added, let's add the docked phone panel to its right:

```
    # Phone dialer pane
    self._phone.SetInitialSize()
    size = self._phone.BestSize
    info = aui.AuiPaneInfo().Right().Name("Phone")
    info = info.BottomDockable(False)
               .TopDockable(False)
    info = info.Layer(0).Caption("Phone")
    info = info.Fixed()
    self._mgr.AddPane(self._phone, info)
```

4. To wrap it up, we can just add the `ListBox` being used as a call log display right below the phone and tell the manager to update its layout. The following code will help:

```
    # Call Log
    info = aui.AuiPaneInfo().Right()
                            .Layer(0).Position(1)
```

```
info = info.Name("Log").Caption("Call Log")
info = info.BestSize(size).MinSize(size)
self._mgr.AddPane(self._callLog, info)

# Commit layout to manager
self._mgr.Update()
```

How it works...

The `AuiManager` manages a collection of `AuiPaneInfo` objects that are associated with different window objects. Each `AuiPaneInfo` object instructs the manager on how the pane is to be presented within the frame.

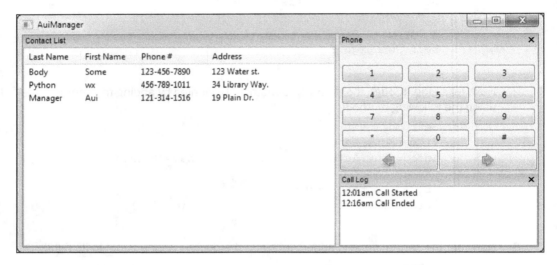

The three panes that we added in this recipe result in the preceding layout being created by the manager. Each pane gets its own title bar by default that can be used as a grab location to drag the panel out into its own floating window or to redock it in another location. The **Contact List** pane is set as the `Center` pane and cannot be undocked or relocated. To have panes stack on top of each other, like the `Phone` and `Call` Log panes, their pane information should indicate the same `Layer` value and then use `Position` to control their position within the layer. Directional properties, such as `Right`, `Left`, `Top`, or `Bottom`, are used to instruct which side of the `Center` pane to dock the pane on.

New items can be added and removed or the pane information can be modified on the items in the manager at any time. However, to reflect the changes in the display, it is necessary to call `Update` on the `AuiManager` object to instruct it to regenerate the layout.

There's more...

The `AuiManager` has a large number of features and possible ways to use it. Included in the following table are some additional pointers to explore.

Additional AuiPaneInfo options

The number of options available to configure pane behaviors is large, and we only covered a small number of options in this recipe. Included here is a list of some additional options that can be set to control which buttons are shown on the caption bar:

Property	Description
CloseButton(bool)	This is True by default but can be set to False to hide the close button on a pane.
MaximizeButton(bool)	This puts a maximize button on the caption bar. When clicked on, the pane will be expanded to take over all the space in the manager, making it the only visible pane.
MinimizeButton(bool)	This puts a minimize button on the caption bar. When clicked on, the pane will be minimized to an icon on a toolbar in the manager. This behavior can be further customized through the use of the `MinimizeMode` property. (This only works in the `wx.lib` version.)
PinButton(bool)	This sets whether a pin button should be shown on the caption bar. This allows a quick click to pop the pane out into a floating window.

Saving and restoring a window's state

Another great feature of `AuiManager` is that it allows for the layout to be serialized to a plain text format to allow the saving and restoring of specific window layouts and configurations to your app's user configuration or them to be used as prebaked layouts. Once all panes are loaded into the manager, its `SavePerspective` method captures the state of all the `AuiPaneInfo` objects in a string. Each pane is identified by its `Name` property when a perspective is loaded back into the manager using the `LoadPerspective` method.

So, if you wish to use `LoadPerspective` to reload a window's layout on the application's startup, you must first be sure to create all the panes and add them to the manager and then call `LoadPerspective` afterwards to restore the state of the pane info objects back to the previously saved state.

4
Containers and Advanced Controls

In this chapter, we will cover:

- ▸ Adding tabs with the Notebook control
- ▸ Enhancing ComboBox with bitmaps
- ▸ Configuring properties
- ▸ Taking control with FlatNotebook
- ▸ Styling text in StyledTextCtrl
- ▸ Annotating StyledTextCtrl
- ▸ Displaying hierarchical data with TreeCtrl
- ▸ Building a system tray application
- ▸ Surfing the Web in your app

Introduction

In earlier chapters, we looked at and learned a number of things about the fundamentals of building an application with wxPython. In this chapter, we will begin to take a look at some of the slightly more advanced controls that can be used to display more complex data to users of the application in useful and compelling ways. Throughout this chapter, we will build a number of small applications, each showing how to take advantage of some of the great user interface features that each control provides. Through these exercises, we will try to highlight some of the possibilities that you could put these controls to work for in your own applications.

Adding tabs with the Notebook control

The `Notebook` control is the basic means of creating a tabbed interface, which is a common way of allowing users to switch between pages or views in an application. The use of tabbed interfaces is one of the most prevalent ways to allow multidocument views in applications that show files or in any modern web browser. This recipe will show you how to set up `NotebookCtrl` and get started with creating tabbed interfaces.

How to do it...

Here are the steps you need to perform:

1. First, we will create a subclass of `wx.Notebook`, as follows:

```
class MyNotebook(wx.Notebook):
    def __init__(self, parent):
        super(MyNotebook, self).__init__(parent)

        # Setup an image list
        self.il = wx.ImageList(16, 16)
        print self.il.Add(wx.Bitmap("smile.png"))
        self.AssignImageList(self.il)

        self.Bind(wx.EVT_NOTEBOOK_PAGE_CHANGING,
                  self.OnChanging)
        self.Bind(wx.EVT_NOTEBOOK_PAGE_CHANGED,
                  self.OnChanged)
```

2. Next, we need to define the event handlers for the Notebook events that are bound to the constructor. Use the following methods:

```
    def OnChanging(self, event):
        result = wx.MessageBox("Allow Page Change?",
                               "Allow?", wx.YES_NO)
        if result == wx.NO:
            event.Veto()

    def OnChanged(self, event):
        print "Page Changed", event.Selection
```

3. To finish up this recipe, we will add in a quick example of using the preceding `Notebook` class. Take a look at this class:

```
class MyFrame(wx.Frame):
    def __init__(self, parent, title=""):
        super(MyFrame, self).__init__(parent, title=title)
```

```
# Set the panel
sizer = wx.BoxSizer()
self.nb = MyNotebook(self)
sizer.Add(self.nb, 1, wx.EXPAND)
self.SetSizer(sizer)

# Add some pages
page1 = wx.TextCtrl(self.nb, style=wx.TE_MULTILINE)
self.nb.AddPage(page1, "Page 1")
page1 = wx.TextCtrl(self.nb, style=wx.TE_MULTILINE)
self.nb.AddPage(page1, "Page 2", imageId=0)

self.SetInitialSize((400,250))
```

How it works...

The Notebook control supports displaying images as well as text on tabs for its pages. Images are provided to the control through an ImageList object, which can be loaded up with a collection of bitmaps that can then be assigned to pages through an index ID in ImageList.

There are two control-specific events that can be handled to control or react to page selection changes in the control. The EVT_NOTEBOOK_PAGE_CHANGING event is emitted when a new page is clicked on but before the change occurs. This event handler allows blocking and prevents the page from changing by calling Veto on the event object. This can be useful if the user needs to be notified and is asked to make a decision, such as applying some changes. The EVT_NOTEBOOK_PAGE_CHANGED event, on the other hand, is called after the newly selected page is activated.

Adding additional tabs to Notebook simply requires that the window objects being added are created as children of the Notebook control. The Add method takes a window object and page title to label the tab with. It also has an optional select value to specify whether the page should be selected when it's added as well as an optional index value to identify an item from an assigned ImageList to be displayed on the tab as well.

There's more...

The Notebook control's InsertPage method allows new pages to be inserted at a specific page index. The index starts from left to right, beginning at page 0, or from top to bottom in a Notebook control that uses either a NB_LEFT or NB_RIGHT style.

Pages can also be removed from the notebook in a few different ways. The RemovePage method removes the tab from Notebook but does not destroy the page. The DeletePage method, on the other hand, removes it from Notebook and also destroys it. To remove all pages from a Notebook control, the DeleteAllPages method can be called to handle the task.

See also

▶ Refer to the *Taking control with FlatNotebook* recipe later in this chapter for examples of an alternate Notebook control implementation

Enhancing ComboBox with bitmaps

The ComboBox control is similar to a Choice control, in that it allows us to make a single selection from a pop-up list of options. The list of options is configured as a list of strings, which in some cases may be slightly inconvenient for users to locate the choice they wish to select. This can be alleviated to some extent in certain circumstances by also displaying a related icon next to the choice to help make it more recognizable. In this recipe, we will make a ComboBox control to select a language option.

How to do it...

Here are the steps that you need to perform:

1. First, for this recipe we need to import a few submodules, which are as follows:

```
import wx
import wx.lib.langlistctrl as langlist
import wx.combo
```

2. Next, we will make a subclass of BitmapComboBox that enumerates all the possible language options in wxPython:

```
class LanguageComboBox(wx.combo.BitmapComboBox):
    def __init__(self, parent):
        super(LanguageComboBox, self).__init__(parent)

        for x in dir(wx):
            if x.startswith("LANGUAGE_"):
                langID = getattr(wx, x)
                flag = self.GetFlag(langID)
                name = wx.Locale.GetLanguageName(langID)

                self.Append(name, flag)
```

3. For the last step, we will add a method to pull bitmaps from the langlistctrl module and associate them with the items added in the previous step through the following code:

```
def GetFlag(self, langID):
    flag = langlist.GetLanguageFlag(langID)
    if flag.IsOk():
```

```
        if flag.Size != (16, 11):
            img = wx.ImageFromBitmap(flag)
            img.Rescale(16, 11)
            flag = img.ConvertToBitmap()
    return flag
```

How it works...

The `BitmapComboBox` control from the `wx.combo` module provides a ready built `ComboBox` control that can display images in its pop-up list. In the constructor of the `LanguageComboBox` control, we used introspection to enumerate all the language ID values defined in the in the `wx` module. The language IDs can be used to retrieve the associated bitmaps from the `langlistctrl` module, which contains a collection of bitmap resources. The `GetFlag` method is provided to ensure that all the flag images returned are of the same dimensions as the `BitmapComboBox` requires that all images are of the same size. Lastly, the name for each language can be retrieved through the `wx.Locale` object using the language ID, similar to how the bitmap is retrieved from the `langlistctrl` module.

There's more...

As hinted at in this recipe, there is another similar custom control provided by the `langlistctrl` module, which provides similar functionality in the form of `ListCtrl`. The `LanguageListCtrl` module also supports filtering based on the languages that are detected as available or by showing all possible languages, as was done in this recipe.

The `LanguageListCtrl` module's `SetUpFilter` method takes a filter flag of `LC_ONLY`, `LC_AVAILABLE`, or `LC_ALL`. The `LC_ONLY` filter applies to the optional list of language IDs that can be passed into the `SetupFilter` method. The `LC_AVAILABLE` filter looks at the `Locale` object to check whether there are catalogs available for the language. The `LC_ALL` filter, as the name suggests, enumerates all the language IDs on the system.

See also

▸ Take a look at the *Supporting internationalization* recipe in *Chapter 10, Getting Your Application Ready for Release*, for a recipe on how to make your app capable of being displayed in multiple languages

Configuring properties

The `PropertyGrid` control provides a highly customizable, specialized grid to edit name and value pairs. If you have ever used Visual Studio, it's very similar to the **Property Editor** window. Each named property can be set up with varying types of editor controls in the grid that suits the needs of the specific property's data. This control can be used to create a way to edit configuration values for any sort of data type as well as to view the property information of an item. In this recipe, we will make use of `PropertyGrid` to display and edit the attributes of a Python object.

How to do it...

Perform the following steps:

1. First, let's set up our module with the necessary imports and class constructor for the custom `PropertyGrid` control, with the following code:

```python
import inspect
import wx
import wx.propgrid as propgrid

class ObjectInspector(propgrid.PropertyGrid):
    def __init__(self, parent):
        super(ObjectInspector, self).__init__(parent)
        self.Bind(propgrid.EVT_PG_CHANGED, self.OnChange)
```

2. Next is the event handler for the change event that was bound to the preceding code. This will attempt to set a new value to the object for the changed property, as follows:

```python
def OnChange(self, event):
    prop = event.GetProperty()
    name = prop.GetName()
    val = prop.GetValue()
    try:
        setattr(self.obj, name, val)
    except Exception, err:
        print(err)
```

3. The next method is used to set the object that has its properties displayed. We will break it in two parts here, beginning with the first part that filters the methods and appends all the attribute fields. Take a look at the following code:

```python
def SetObject(self, obj):
    self.Clear()
    self.obj = obj
    methods = list()
    if obj is not None:
```

```
prop = propgrid.PropertyCategory("Attributes")
self.Append(prop)
for name, val in inspect.getmembers(obj):
    if callable(val):
        methods.append((name, val))
    else:
        self.AddAttribute(name, val)
```

4. For the second half, we will do the same with all the methods and put them in their own category section, as follows:

```
# Add Method category
self.Append(propgrid.PropertyCategory("Methods"))
for name, val in methods:
    self.AddMethod(name, val)


self.GetGrid().FitColumns()
```

5. The next method is a helper method used to map a Python type to a `PropertyGrid` field type:

```
def GetProperty(self, attr, val):
    pmap = { bool : propgrid.BoolProperty,
             int : propgrid.IntProperty,
             str : propgrid.StringProperty,
             unicode : propgrid.StringProperty,
             wx.Colour : propgrid.ColourProperty,
             wx.Font : propgrid.FontProperty
           }
    prop = pmap.get(type(val))
    if prop is None:
        sval = str(val)
        prop = propgrid.StringProperty(attr, value=sval)
        prop.Enable(False)
        return prop
    return prop(attr, value=val)
```

6. This next method is used to add individual attributes to the grid, as follows:

```
def AddAttribute(self, name, val):
    prop = self.Append(self.GetProperty(name, val))
    if val is None:
        prop.Enable(False)
    elif isinstance(val, bool):
        prop.SetAttribute("UseCheckbox", True)
```

7. The last method in this recipe is used to populate the method section. It attempts to get the docstring for each method and display it as the value for the method in the grid:

```python
def AddMethod(self, name, m):
    doc = inspect.getdoc(m)
    if doc is None:
        doc = "No Description"
    prop = propgrid.StringProperty(name, value=doc)
    prop.Enable(False)
    self.Append(prop)
```

How it works...

The `PropertyGrid` control uses `PGProperty` objects to control the display and control of each individual row in the grid. Various `Property` objects, such as `BoolProperty` and `IntProperty` in this recipe, are specialized subclasses that are used to handle specific types of data. As can be seen in the following screenshot, the `BoolProperty` object for the `AutoLayout` property shows a checkbox and the `ColourProperty` object for the `BackgroundColour` property shows a color-select dialog when clicked on:

This recipe made use of the `inspect` module from the Python standard library to inspect the object passed in the control's `SetObject` method. Then, some basic introspection is used to interrogate the types of each member in the object to attempt to map them to the best suited property type.

When a value changes in the right-hand side column of the `PropertyGrid` object, the `EVT_PG_CHANGED` event is emitted. The `event` object has a reference to the `Property` object that was modified and generates the event. Our `OnChange` event handler for this method retrieves the name and value from the property grid and uses them to try and set the new value back to the object.

There's more...

The `wx.propgrid` module provides a fair number of `Property` field types for the most common types. However, if you need to support some unsupported or custom type, it is also possible to make a custom property object to handle it. The `PyProperty` class provides a virtual interface that can be overridden to describe the handling needed for the property type. At a minimum, the custom property class needs to override the `ValueToString` and `StringToValue` methods to convert the property's value type back and forth. Refer to the sample code that accompanies this chapter for a simple example of the use of a property class to handle a `wx.Size` object.

Taking control with FlatNotebook

The `FlatNotebook` control is a custom notebook control provided by the `wx.lib` module. It offers many additional basic and advanced features over the simple `wx.Notebook` class that is offered by the main library. For example, tabs are able to have close buttons on them along with several different visual display styles, and tabs can be dragged and reordered. As `FlatNotebook` is an owner-drawn control, it provides a lot more options for taking control of the behavior of your application. In this recipe, we will take a look at some of the useful features that `FlatNotebook` has to offer.

How to do it...

Perform the following steps:

1. First, we will define the constructor for a subclass of `FlatNotebook`, as follows:

```
import wx
import wx.lib.agw.flatnotebook as fnb

class EditorBook(fnb.FlatNotebook):
    def __init__(self, parent):
        mystyle = fnb.FNB_DROPDOWN_TABS_LIST|\
                fnb.FNB_FF2|\
                fnb.FNB_SMART_TABS|\
                fnb.FNB_X_ON_TAB
        super(EditorBook, self).__init__(parent,
                                        agwStyle=mystyle)

        self.Bind(fnb.EVT_FLATNOTEBOOK_PAGE_CLOSING,
                self.OnClosing)
```

2. Next, we will define the event handler for the page-closing event through the following code:

```
def OnClosing(self, event):
    pgNum = event.GetSelection()
    page = self.GetPage(pgNum)
    if page.IsModified():
        msg = "Document is modified continue closing?"
        resp = wx.MessageBox(msg, "Close Page?",
                             wx.YES_NO|wx.CENTER| \
                             wx.ICON_QUESTION)
        if resp == wx.NO:
            event.Veto()
            return
    event.Skip()
```

How it works...

The `FlatNotebook` control provides a very similar feature set to that of the regular notebook that we looked at earlier in this chapter. In this little example, though, we can see a number of differences that can be activated using the special style flags that are supplied to the `agwStyle` keyword of the `FlatNotebook` object's constructor. Take note that this additional style keyword was added in wxPython 2.8 onward to handle AGW-specific styles that can be applied to widgets in the `wx.lib.agw` modules. The list of style flags used in this recipe enables a number of features that are not available on the basic Notebook control. The first style flag, `FNB_DROPDOWN_TABS_LIST`, adds a drop-down menu to the tab area to list all the tabs and allow selection. The `FNB_FF2` flag is simply a style flag that draws the flags with a look and feel similar to the tabs in the Firefox 2 web browser. The `FNB_SMART_TABS` flag enables switching tabs via a keyboard shortcut: *Alt + Tab*. The last flag used is `FNB_X_ON_TAB`, which enables a close button on each tab.

Unlike the basic notebook, it is also possible to allow users to directly close tabs in the control. In this recipe, we used the `EVT_FLATNOTEBOOK_PAGE_CLOSING` event to get notified when a page is being closed.

There's more...

The appearance and behavior of `FlatNotebook` can be customized greatly depending on the `agwStyle` flags that are passed in to the constructor. Included here is a quick reference to the styles and what they do:

Tab style flag	Description
FNB_DEFAULT	These are the default `FlatNotebook` style tabs
FNB_FANCY_TABS	These are square tabs with gradient filling

Tab style flag	Description
FNB_FF2	These are Firefox 2-style tabs
FNB_RIBBON_TABS	These are Ribbon bar-style tabs
FNB_VC71	These are Visual Studio 2003-style tabs
FNB_VC8	These are Visual Studio 2005-style tabs

Appearance flags	Description
FNB_TABS_BORDER_SIMPLE	This uses a thin border around the page
FNB_BOTTOM	This places tabs at the bottom of a window instead of at the top
FNB_BACKGROUND_GRADIENT	This paints the tab background with a gradient
FNB_COLOURFUL_TABS	This is for us to use colorful tabs (VC8 tab style only)

Behavior flags	Description
FNB_NO_X_BUTTON	This doesn't display the close button on the right-hand side of the tab area
FNB_NO_NAV_BUTTONS	This doesn't display the tab navigation buttons on the right-hand side of the tab area
FNB_MOUSE_MIDDLE_CLOSES_TABS	Through this flag, the middle mouse button can be used to let the user close tabs
FNB_NODRAG	This doesn't allow tabs to be reordered by dragging and dropping
FNB_X_ON_TAB	This puts a close button on each tab
FNB_DCLICK_CLOSES_TABS	Through this, tabs can be closed by double-clicking on them
FNB_SMART_TABS	Through this, a selected tab can be changed by the *Alt* + *Tab* keyboard shortcut
FNB_DROPDOWN_TABS_LIST	This makes a button show a pop-up menu for changing a selected tab
FNB_ALLOW_FOREIGN_DND	This allows tab dragging and dropping operations between different FlatNotebook controls
FNB_HIDE_ON_SINGLE_TAB	This hides the tab area when only one tab is in the notebook
FNB_NO_TAB_FOCUS	This doesn't allow tabs to get focus
FNB_HIDE_TABS	This doesn't show the tab area
FNB_NAV_BUTTONS_WHEN_NEEDED	This hides the navigation buttons when all the tabs fit in the available space

▶ Refer to the *Adding tabs with the Notebook control* recipe earlier in this chapter for examples of some basic notebook features which can also be used in the `FlatNotebook`

Styling text in StyledTextCtrl

The `StyledTextCtrl` class is an advanced text-editing component provided by the `wx.stc` module. This class is a `wx` wrapper around the Scintilla code editor control. This control is primarily geared toward editing source code files. It provides a large set of features for enhanced code-editing support. In this recipe, we will look at how to set up syntax highlighting for Python source code files using `StyledTextCtrl`.

How to do it...

Perform the following steps:

1. This recipe will be split into two classes. Starting here with a base class to set up some programming language-independent settings on `StyledTextCtrl`. Take a look at the following code:

```
import wx
import wx.stc as stc
import keyword

class CodeEditorBase(stc.StyledTextCtrl):
    def __init__(self, parent):
        super(CodeEditorBase, self).__init__(parent)

        # Attributes
        font = wx.Font(10, wx.FONTFAMILY_MODERN,
                           wx.FONTSTYLE_NORMAL,
                           wx.FONTWEIGHT_NORMAL)
        self.face = font.GetFaceName()
        self.size = font.GetPointSize()

        # Setup
        self.SetupBaseStyles()
```

2. Next, we will add a helper function to toggle showing and hiding the line number margin:

```
    def EnableLineNumbers(self, enable=True):
        if enable:
```

```
                    self.SetMarginType(1, stc.STC_MARGIN_NUMBER)
                    self.SetMarginMask(1, 0)
                    self.SetMarginWidth(1, 25)
                else:
                    self.SetMarginWidth(1, 0)
```

3. Now, we will just add some methods to set up the base text styling and help with styling in the subclasses through the following code:

```
        def GetFaces(self):
            return dict(font=self.face, size=self.size)

        def SetupBaseStyles(self):
            faces = self.GetFaces()
            default = "face:%(font)s,size:%(size)d" % faces
            self.StyleSetSpec(stc.STC_STYLE_DEFAULT, default)
            line = "back:#C0C0C0," + default
            self.StyleSetSpec(stc.STC_STYLE_LINENUMBER, line)
            self.StyleSetSpec(stc.STC_STYLE_CONTROLCHAR,
                              "face:%(font)s" % faces)
```

4. With the base class defined, let's turn our attention to creating a specialized editor for Python source files. Define the following subclass:

```
class PythonCodeEditor(CodeEditorBase):
    def __init__(self, parent):
        super(PythonCodeEditor, self).__init__(parent)

        # Setup
        self.SetLexer(wx.stc.STC_LEX_PYTHON)
        self.SetupKeywords()
        self.SetupStyles()
        self.EnableLineNumbers(True)
```

5. The STC_LEX_PYTHON lexer supports keyword highlighting; so now, let's tell it what the keywords for the language are by getting them from the keyword module, as follows:

```
        def SetupKeywords(self):
            kwlist = " ".join(keyword.kwlist)
            self.SetKeyWords(0, kwlist)
```

6. For the last two steps, we need to set the styles for each lexer token type. In this first part, we will define some style description template strings and set up the styles on some of the basic syntax items in a Python code file through the following code:

```
        def SetupStyles(self):
            # Python styles
            faces = self.GetFaces()
```

```
fonts = "face:%(font)s,size:%(size)d" % faces
tmpl = "fore:%s," + fonts
default = "fore:#000000," + fonts

# Default
self.StyleSetSpec(stc.STC_P_DEFAULT, default)
# Comments
self.StyleSetSpec(stc.STC_P_COMMENTLINE, tmpl % "#007F00")
# Number
self.StyleSetSpec(stc.STC_P_NUMBER, tmpl % "#007F7F")
# String
self.StyleSetSpec(stc.STC_P_STRING, tmpl % "#7F007F")
# Single quoted string
self.StyleSetSpec(stc.STC_P_CHARACTER, tmpl % "#7F007F")
# Keyword
self.StyleSetSpec(stc.STC_P_WORD, tmpl % "#00007F,bold")
```

7. Now, just to finish it up for the remaining lexer syntax items, we will add the following code:

```
# Triple quotes
self.StyleSetSpec(stc.STC_P_TRIPLE, tmpl % "#7F0000")
# Triple double quotes
self.StyleSetSpec(stc.STC_P_TRIPLEDOUBLE,
                  tmpl % "#7F0000")
# Class name definition
self.StyleSetSpec(stc.STC_P_CLASSNAME,
                  tmpl % "#0000FF,bold")
# Function or method name definition
self.StyleSetSpec(stc.STC_P_DEFNAME,
                  tmpl % "#007F7F,bold")
# Operators
self.StyleSetSpec(stc.STC_P_OPERATOR, "bold," + fonts)
# Identifiers
self.StyleSetSpec(stc.STC_P_IDENTIFIER, default)
# Comment-blocks
self.StyleSetSpec(stc.STC_P_COMMENTBLOCK,
                  tmpl % "#7F7F7F")
# End of line where string is not closed
eol_style = "fore:#000000,back:#E0C0E0,eol," + fonts
self.StyleSetSpec(stc.STC_P_STRINGEOL, eol_style)
```

How it works...

The `StyledTextCtrl` class supports building syntax highlighting for many different programming languages. To activate this, the lexer needs to be selected using the `SetLexer` method and by passing it a corresponding lexer ID. All lexer IDs are defined in the `wx.stc` module and begin with `STC_LEX_`. Each lexer has a corresponding set of syntax IDs that are used by the lexer to style sections of text. In this recipe, we made use of the Python lexer to apply the styles defined in the `SetStyles` method to set the text styling properties in the display.

The `StyleSetSpec` method takes a string to define the styling for the text associated with the style ID. The style spec string is formatted as follows:

```
ATTRIBUTE:VALUE,ATTRIBUTE,VALUE,MODIFIER
```

Take a look at the following table:

Attribute	Description
fore	This is the foreground color; this can either be a color name or a hex color code
back	This is the background color; this can either be a color name or a hex color code
face	This is the name of the font to be used
size	This is a point size for the font to use

The modifiers that can optionally follow a value are as follows:

Modifier	Description
bold	This makes the text bold
italic	This italicizes the text
eol	This extends the specified background style to the end of the current line
underline	This underlines the text

Some lexers, such as the Python lexer, have one or more keyword styles; in this case, the keyword style is `STC_P_WORD`, the `SetKeywords` method tells the text control what the keywords are by passing a list of strings, and the first number argument is the keyword index. This will usually be zero unless the lexer supports multiple different keyword sets.

There's more...

The `StyledTextCtrl` class has built-in lexers and syntax highlighting for over 100 different types of programming languages and other plain text format files. So, it can be leveraged to provide syntax highlighting and other advanced features for probably every programming language you may have ever heard of and more. There are too many to list here, but you can easily find the list of available lexers by looking at all the lexer IDs that are prefixed with `STC_LEX_` in the `wx.stc` module.

See also

▸ Refer to *Annotating StyledTextCtrl* for another recipe that explores some of the features available in this control

▸ Take a look at *Chapter 9, Creating and Customizing Components,* for a recipe about making your own text-styling lexer using `StyledTextCtrl`

Annotating StyledTextCtrl

The new version of the `StyledTextCtrl` class in wxPython 3.0 uses an updated version of Scintilla, which has added a new feature to add annotations to the text being shown in the buffer. Annotations can be used to display read-only text underneath each line of editable text. The annotations can be used to display inline diagnostic messages to the user. In this recipe, we will use them to extend `PythonCodeEditor` from the previous recipe to show `pep8` warning messages in the editor.

Getting started

This recipe uses an external module called `pep8`, which should be installed prior to trying this recipe. The `pep8` module can be installed using `pip` or by downloading it from `pypi` (`https://pypi.python.org/pypi/pep8`).

How to do it...

1. First, we need to import some extra modules from `stdlib` as well as the `pep8` module to help us out this time as well as bringing in the sample module from the previous recipe. Take a look at the following code:

```python
import sys
import pep8
import StringIO
import wx
import wx.stc as stc
# Recipe 5 module
import codeEditor

# Constants
ANNOTATION_ERROR = 20
ANNOTATION_WARN = 21
```

2. Now, we will subclass `PythonCodeEditor`, enable the use of annotations in it, and define two styles that can be used in the annotations through the following code:

```
class Pep8Editor(codeEditor.PythonCodeEditor):
    def __init__(self, parent):
        super(Pep8Editor, self).__init__(parent)

        # Setup annotation settings
        self.AnnotationSetVisible(stc.STC_ANNOTATION_BOXED)
        errStyle = "fore:#8B0000,bold,back:#FF967A"
        self.StyleSetSpec(ANNOTATION_ERROR, errStyle)
        warnStyle = "fore:#DD6A00,bold,back:#F5DEB3"
        self.StyleSetSpec(ANNOTATION_WARN, warnStyle)
```

3. To perform the `pep8` check, we will override the `SaveFile` method of the control and use this as the signal to run the check. See this code:

```
def SaveFile(self, fileName="",
             fileType=wx.TEXT_TYPE_ANY):
    super(Pep8Editor, self).SaveFile(fileName, fileType)

    # perform pep8 analysis after save
    self.AnnotationClearAll()
    self.DoPep8Check(fileName)
```

4. The `DoPep8Check` method will redirect the output of the checker and use the output to generate annotations, as follows:

```
    def DoPep8Check(self, fileName):
        checker = pep8.Checker(fileName)

        stdio = sys.stdout
        sys.stdout = results = StringIO.StringIO()
        try:
            checker.check_all()
        finally:
            sys.stdout = stdio

        results.seek(0)
        findings = results.readlines()
        if findings:
            processed = self.ProcessFindings(findings)
            self.AddFindings(processed)
```

5. The text captured from `stdout` is processed into a series of line number and message pairs by the following `ProcessFindings` method::

```python
def ProcessFindings(self, findings):
    processed = dict()
    for finding in findings:
        finding = finding.strip()
        parts = finding.split(':')
        line = int(parts[1]) - 1
        msg = parts[-1].strip()
        if processed.has_key(line):
            processed[line] += "\n" + msg
        else:
            processed[line] = msg
    return [ (l, m) for l, m in processed.iteritems() ]
```

6. The last step takes the processed findings and creates annotations in the control to display directly below the line that the `pep8` finding is associated with. Here's the code to be executed for this:

```python
def AddFindings(self, findings):
    for line, msg in findings:
        self.AnnotationSetText(line, msg)
        if msg.startswith("E"):
            self.AnnotationSetStyle(line, ANNOTATION_ERROR)
        else:
            self.AnnotationSetStyle(line, ANNOTATION_WARN)
```

How it works...

In the class constructor, we set up some basic settings for using annotations. The `AnnotationSetVisible` method sets whether the annotations are visible and how they are displayed. There are three possible options to pass to this method:

- ▶ `STC_ANNOTATION_HIDDEN`: The annotations are hidden
- ▶ `STC_ANNOTATION_BOXED`: The annotations are displayed within a box
- ▶ `STC_ANNOTATION_STANDARD`: The annotations are displayed as inline text

Adding an annotation to a line of text just requires calling the `AnnotationSetText` method, which takes the message's text and attaches it as an annotation to the given line. Annotations can be made multiline by including `\n` to separate each line in the annotation. In the following screenshot, you can take a look at how annotations are added to the text buffer. When this recipe runs a `pep8` check on itself, there were two findings for line **61**, which are accumulated together by the `ProcessFindings` method:

```
50    def ProcessFindings(self, findings):
51        processed = dict()
52        for finding in findings:
53            finding = finding.strip()
54            parts = finding.split(':')
55            line = int(parts[1]) - 1
56            msg = parts[-1].strip()
57            if processed.has_key(line):
          W601 .has_key() is deprecated, use 'in'
58                processed[line] += "\n" + msg
59            else:
60                processed[line] = msg
61        return [ (l, m) for l, m in processed.iteritems() ]
          E201 whitespace after '['
          E202 whitespace before ']'
```

The `AnnotationSetStyle` method is used to set how the text is styled in the annotation. This method takes a line that the annotation is on, and a style ID of any style that the text buffer is set up to use currently can be applied to style the text in the annotation. In this recipe, we defined two new style IDs using some arbitrary numbers that are outside the style ID range used by the Python lexer. The two styles are an error and a warning style to differentiate the two types of messages from the pep8 checker. All error messages start with an E followed by an error ID.

There's more...

Within an annotation, individual lines and even individual characters can be styled in more than one style. The `AnnotationSetStyle` method works similarly to `AnnotationSetStyle`, but takes a byte array to describe the style of each individual character instead. The API for this method is quite cumbersome to use and very lightly documented, but hopefully, with the following additional pointers, you will find a way through.

The second parameter for `AnnotationSetStyle` should be a string containing an octal byte, which in turn contains the style ID for each character in the annotation, including whitespace characters. So, for our preceding example, the \024 octal would set the error style for the corresponding character, and \025 would set the warning style. So, consider the following annotation string:

```
"hello world"
```

Here, the following style string would set `hello` to be displayed using the error style and `world` to be displayed in the warning style:

```
"\024\024\024\024\24\24\025\025\025\025\025"
```

Displaying hierarchical data with TreeCtrl

`TreeCtrl` provides a way to create and display data in a hierarchy. The control contains a series of nodes that can have child nodes, which in turn can have their own child nodes. This nested data display allows users to expand and collapse the nodes to see more or less as need be. In this recipe, we will use `TreeCtrl` to create an outline view of an XML file.

How to do it...

Perform the following steps:

1. For this recipe, in addition to the `wx` module, we will use the `ElementTree` module from the Python standard library. Take a look at the following script:

```
import xml.etree.ElementTree as ET
import wx
```

2. Next, let's start on a custom subclass of `wx.TreeCtrl` to specialize it to display XML data using the following code:

```
class XMLOutliner(wx.TreeCtrl):
    def __init__(self, parent, xmlText):
        super(XMLOutliner, self).__init__(parent)

        rootElement = ET.fromstring(xmlText)
        root = rootElement.tag
        self._root = self.AddRoot(root)
        self.SetPyData(self._root, rootElement)
        self._populateTree(self._root, rootElement)

        self.Bind(wx.EVT_TREE_ITEM_GETTOOLTIP, self.OnToolTip)
```

3. The `_populateTree` method is a simple recursive method for walking through XML data and creating `TreeCtrlItems` for each XML node, as seen in the following code:

```
def _populateTree(self, parentNode, element):
    for child in element:
        node = self.AppendItem(parentNode, child.tag)
        self.SetPyData(node, element)
        self._populateTree(node, child)
```

4. The next two methods are used to handle the get tooltip event that was bound to in the constructor. When the user lets the mouse hover over an item in the tree node, we will display the XML text as a tooltip through the following code:

```
def _getDetails(self, element):
    xmlText = ET.tostring(element)
    items = xmlText.split('\n')
```

```
                    return items[0]

        def OnToolTip(self, event):
            node = event.GetItem()
            data = self.GetPyData(node)
            tip = self._getDetails(data)
            event.SetToolTip(tip)
```

How it works...

A `TreeCtrl` control is a series of connected nodes very similar to how an XML file is a structured collection of nodes. To simplify converting raw XML text to display in the `TreeCtrl` object, the `ElementTree` module from the Python standard library is used to parse text into `Element` objects. The `TreeCtrl` control requires a root node to attach other child nodes to, so in the constructor, we used the tag name of the XML file's root node as the root node of `TreeCtrl`.

Once the root node is created in `TreeCtrl`, we can begin appending the child nodes beginning at the root. The `_populateTree` method recursively loops over each child node and its child nodes until all the leaf nodes are attached. Each time a node is attached, the `SetPyData` method is used to attach the related `Element` object as client data to `TreeItem`. Attaching this data to the item will allow us to easily retrieve it later when an action with the given node is performed.

The `TreeCtrl` control's `EVT_TREE_ITEM_GETTOOLTIP` event is fired when the mouse cursor hovers over `TreeItem` for a few moments. This event handler allows the application to provide a `ToolTip` string to display as hover-over information in `TreeCtrl`. For this recipe, we used the raw XML string from the `Element` object that we saved in each `TreeItem` after creating them to show the full details of the node as it was in the text file.

There's more...

The `TreeCtrl` control is fairly versatile, with a large feature set. There are a large number of style flags and events that can be used to modify its appearance and behavior to suit the application's needs. Let's take a quick look at the available style flags and some of the events that can be used to further enhance the use of `TreeCtrl`:

Style flag	Description
TR_EDIT_LABELS	This allows the user to edit the labels of `TreeItems`. When used, the user can cause a `TextCtrl` control to show up when clicking on the node.
TR_NO_BUTTONS	This doesn't show any buttons next to the `TreeItems`. This hides the normal buttons for expanding and contracting the nodes.
TR_HAS_BUTTONS	This shows the buttons next to the `TreeItems`.

Style flag	Description
TR_NO_LINES	This doesn't show the vertical lines that connect the nodes.
TR_FULL_ROW_ HIGHLIGHT	This extends the selected background color across the whole row of TreeItems.
TR_LINES_AT_ROOT	This is used to only show connecting lines between root nodes, and it only applies if TR_HIDE_ROOT is applied and TR_NO_ LINES is not applied.
TR_HIDE_ROOT	This doesn't display the root node.
TR_MULTIPLE	This allows multiple items to be selected at a time.
TR_SINGLE	This only allows a single selection at a time.

As mentioned, TreeCtrl also has many events that can be bound to. Listed here is just a partial collection of some of the more commonly useful ones:

Event	Description
EVT_TREE_BEGIN_LABEL_ EDIT	This event is raised if the TreeCtrl control uses the TR_ EDIT_LABELS style, and the user has attempted to initiate an edit session. The application can call Veto() on the event object to prevent TextCtrl from being shown.
EVT_TREE_ITEM_ACTIVATED	This is raised when the user activates a TreeItem, either by selecting it and pressing the *Enter* key or by double-clicking on it.
EVT_TREE_ITEM_EXPANDING	This is raised when a node is about to be expanded. It can be used to either prevent the node from expanding by calling Veto() on the event object or to allow delaying actually appending the nodes until they need to be displayed.
EVT_TREE_ITEM_MENU	This is similar to EVT_TREE_ITEM_GETTOOLTIP, but is instead called when the context menu for an item is requested. We can handle this event to provide a custom context menu for TreeItems.

Building a system tray application

If you want to build a simple menu-based application that does not require a full GUI, the TaskBarIcon class provides a way to build a TaskBar application that integrates with the operating system's window manager, such as TaskBar (Windows/Linux), Dock, or status area on OS X. This recipe will show you how to build a simple weather checker application using the TaskBarIcon class in wxPython.

Getting started

This recipe uses the `OpenWeatherMap` API to get weather information. From October 2015, they require that you have an API key to use this service. Obtaining a key is free and simply requires signing up on their site. So, before starting this recipe, visit `http://openweathermap.org/appid#get` to learn how to get an API key.

How to do it...

Perform the following steps:

1. Firstly for this recipe, we will need a couple of extra imports from the Python standard library to help us out and define some menu IDs for later use. We can use the following code for this:

```
import urllib
import json
import wx

URL = "http://api.openweathermap.org/data/2.5/weather?q=%s"
ID_GET_CITY = wx.NewId()
ID_ENTER_KEY = wx.NewId()
```

2. Define the constructor for our custom `TaskBarIcon` class using the following:

```
class WeatherTray(wx.TaskBarIcon):
    def __init__(self, frame):
        super(WeatherTray, self).__init__()
        self.apiKey = ""
        self.frame = frame
        self.data = { 'desc' : "Unknown", 'temp' : "??" }
        self.UpdateData("London,UK")
        self.Bind(wx.EVT_MENU, self.OnMenu)
```

3. This next method is used to as a helper method to build up the URL to query the `OpenWeatherMap` website with:

```
    def GetRequestURL(self, city):
        formatted = city.replace(' ', "%20")
        query = URL % formatted

        # Add User API Key
        apiKey = "&APPID=%s"
        query += (apiKey % self.apiKey)
        return query
```

4. The `UpdateData` method fetches JSON that contains the weather data for the currently specified city from the `OpenWeatherMap` API service. Take a look at this method:

```python
def UpdateData(self, city):
    try:
        # Query the OpenWeatherMap site
        query = self.GetRequestURL(city)
        url = urllib.urlopen(query)
        j = json.load(url)

        weather = j['weather'][0]
        temp = j['main']['temp']
        self.data = dict()
        self.data['desc'] = weather['main']
        self.data['icon'] = weather['icon']
        c = float(temp) - 273.15
        self.data['temp'] = c
    except Exception, err:
        print "Error getting data: %s" % err

    self.city = city
    self.UpdateIcon()
```

5. Next, the `UpdateIcon` function tries and retrieves the icon for the current weather from the same web service to use as its display icon in the tray, as follows:

```python
def UpdateIcon(self):
    img = None
    try:
        loc = "http://openweathermap.org/img/w/%s.png"
        url = urllib.urlopen(loc % self.data['icon'])
        img = wx.ImageFromStream(url, wx.BITMAP_TYPE_PNG)
        img = wx.BitmapFromImage(img)
    except:
        img = wx.Bitmap('errIcon.png')
    icon = wx.IconFromBitmap(img)
    self.SetIcon(icon)
```

6. When `TaskBarIcon` is right-clicked on, the framework calls the `CreatePopupMenu` method on the object. So here, we will override this method in order to make the pop-up menu that will be used by this application. For this, use the following code:

```python
def CreatePopupMenu(self):
    menu = wx.Menu()

    data = (self.city,
```

```
                    "Weather: %s" % self.data['desc'],
                    "Temp: %s C" % self.data['temp'])
        for d in data:
            item = menu.Append(wx.ID_ANY, d)
            item.Enable(False)

        menu.AppendSeparator()
        menu.Append(ID_GET_CITY, "Enter city name...")
        menu.Append(ID_ENTER_KEY, "Enter API Key...")
        menu.AppendSeparator()
        menu.Append(wx.ID_CLOSE)
        return menu
```

7. The pop-up menu contains four items, but only two of them are clickable; one is to close the application, and another allows the city to be changed. So here, we will define the `menu` event handler to perform these actions:

```
def OnMenu(self, event):
    if event.Id == wx.ID_CLOSE:
        self.Destroy()
    elif event.Id == ID_GET_CITY:
        msg = "Enter City Name (City,Country):"
        t = wx.GetTextFromUser(msg,
                               default_value=self.city)
        if t:
            self.UpdateData(t)
    elif event.Id == ID_ENTER_KEY:
        t = wx.GetTextFromUser("Enter OpenWeatherMap Key:",
                               default_value=self.apiKey)
        if t:
            self.apiKey = t
            self.UpdateData(self.city)
    else:
        event.Skip()
```

8. The final step is to create the `App` object and `TaskBarIcon` instance, as follows:

```
class WeatherTrayApp(wx.App):
    def OnInit(self):
        # Make a hidden frame as some platforms require
        # a top level window to keep the app loop running.
        frame = wx.Frame(None)
        self._trayIcon = WeatherTray(frame)
        return True
```

How it works...

When started, `WeatherTrayApp` creates an instance of `WeatherTray`. The use of `TaskBarIcon` requires that its `SetIcon` method is called to set the image used as the UI component of the control. Once this is set, it appears as an icon in the system tray, as shown by the little cloud in the following screenshot. To get started using this example app, right-click on the icon and enter your API key:

When right-clicked on, the framework will call TaskBarIcon's `CreatePopupMenu` method, which is overridden by our subclass. In this method, we created and returned the menu object to present it to the user. The top three items of this menu are read-only to the user, showing detailed information about the weather that was retrieved from the weather service during `UpdateData`. Two additional options are available to allow the city to be changed as well as to exit the application.

When the city is changed, the new value is used to requery the `openweathermap` service to get the new data for the requested city. This data is then used to update the icon as well as the data that would be shown on the next menu click.

There's more...

New on the OS X platform, in wxPython 3.0, the TaskBar icon can be set up to be showed in either the Dock or the main system status bar area by specifying an optional argument to the object constructor. Take a look at the following table:

Icon type ID	Description
`wx.TBI_CUSTOM_STATUSITEM`	This creates the icon in the system status area (which is the common menu bar area on top of the screen).
`wx.TBI_DEFAULT_TYPE`	This is the default parameter as of wxPython 3.0; it is the same as `TBI_DOCK`.
`wx.TBI_DOCK`	This creates the application as an icon in the Dock. This is the default behavior that was available in earlier versions of the library.

Surfing the Web in your app

Another great feature available in wxPython 3.0 is the new full-featured web browser control available in the `wx.html2` module. This control provides a full rendering engine for the display of HTML with CSS and JavaScript. It uses a Webkit backend on GTK/OSX and an IE backend on MSW. This control provides a great way to display the documentation or HTML-based help files. It also lets us be leveraged to make a hard client for web-based applications that you may want to provide direct access for within your app. In this recipe, we will show how to get started with the `WebView` class by implementing a very simple web browser application using it.

How to do it...

You need to perform the following steps:

1. First, let's take a look at the modules that need to be imported for this application, as follows:

```
import wx
import wx.html2 as html2
```

2. Next, this application will consist of two main components: a navigation bar and a browser window. First, we will start by defining the navigation bar class, as follows:

```
class NaviBar(wx.Panel):
    def __init__(self, parent, browser):
        super(NaviBar, self).__init__(parent)

        self._url = wx.TextCtrl(self,
                                style=wx.TE_PROCESS_ENTER)
        self._url.SetHint("Enter URL here and press enter...")

        back = wx.Button(self, style=wx.BU_EXACTFIT)
        back.Bitmap = wx.ArtProvider.GetBitmap(wx.ART_GO_BACK,
                                               wx.ART_TOOLBAR)
        fw = wx.Button(self, style=wx.BU_EXACTFIT)
        fw.Bitmap = wx.ArtProvider.GetBitmap(wx.ART_GO_FORWARD,
                                             wx.ART_TOOLBAR)
```

3. With all the controls for the navigation bar defined, the layout is next, as shown in the following code:

```
        sizer = wx.BoxSizer(wx.HORIZONTAL)
        sizer.Add(back, 0, wx.ALL, 5)
        sizer.Add(fw, 0, wx.ALL, 5)
        sizer.Add(self._url, 1, wx.EXPAND)
        self.SetSizer(sizer)
```

4. To finish up the navigation bar, all we have left to do is bind the events, as is done here:

```
b = browser
self.Bind(wx.EVT_TEXT_ENTER,
        lambda event: b.LoadURL(self._url.Value))
self.Bind(wx.EVT_BUTTON, lambda event: b.GoBack(), back)
self.Bind(wx.EVT_BUTTON, lambda event: b.GoForward(), fw)
self.Bind(wx.EVT_UPDATE_UI,
        lambda event: event.Enable(b.CanGoBack()),
        back)
self.Bind(wx.EVT_UPDATE_UI,
        lambda event: event.Enable(b.CanGoForward()),
        fw)
```

5. With `NaviBar` out of the way, the next is to define the web browser frame, we will use the following class for this:

```
class WebFrame(wx.Frame):
    def __init__(self, parent, title):
        super(WebFrame, self).__init__(parent, title=title)

        self._browser = html2.WebView_New(self)
        self._bar = NaviBar(self, self._browser)

        sizer = wx.BoxSizer(wx.VERTICAL)
        sizer.Add(self._bar, 0, wx.EXPAND)
        sizer.Add(self._browser, 1, wx.EXPAND)
        self.SetSizer(sizer)

        self.Bind(html2.EVT_WEBVIEW_TITLE_CHANGED,
                self.OnTitle)

    def OnTitle(self, event):
        self.Title = event.GetString()
```

How it works...

Wow, look at that! With less than 70 lines of code, we built a very simple yet functional cross platform web browser application that supports browsing to a specified URL as well as basic forward and backward history navigation.

The NaviBar class provides a means of interaction with the user by providing back and forward buttons as well as TextControl to accept URL entry. The TextControl control uses the TE_ PROCESS_ENTER style to allow event handling when the *Enter* key is pressed. I used this event handler to get the text from TextControl and pass it as a URL to WebView's LoadURL method. This method handles everything related to opening the HTML file, which can be local or at an internet address as shown in the following screenshot. The buttons are also linked to execute the methods available in the WebView control to check whether there is any browser history to enable or disable the buttons and to instruct WebView to navigate in the requested direction.

The WebView control does many of its actions asynchronously, such as the loading or reloading of pages. There are a handful of events that can be handled to get callbacks during parts of the loading process. In this example, we handled EVT_WEBVIEW_TITLE_CHANGED in order to get notifications when a new title is found in a loaded URL. When this event occurs, our application uses it to update the frame's title to match that of the website.

There's more...

As mentioned, there are several other events that can be handled on the `WebView` control. Included here is a quick reference for the additionally available events that can be bound to:

Event	Description
EVT_WEBVIEW_NAVIGATING	This is called before the control tries to get a resource. It can be used to allow or disallow navigation to the resource.
EVT_WEBVIEW_NAVIGATED	This is called after it is confirmed that the resource would be requested.
EVT_WEBVIEW_LOADED	This is called after a resource is fully loaded and displayed.
EVT_WEBVIEW_ERROR	This is called if a navigation error occurs.
EVT_WEBVIEW_NEWWINDOW	This is called if the browser requests a new window to be created to load content into.

5

Data Displays and Grids

In this chapter, we will cover:

- ► Displaying lists of data
- ► Editing data lists
- ► Implementing a data source
- ► Getting started with the data grid
- ► Displaying dynamic data
- ► Modeling your data
- ► Displaying your data model

Introduction

The primary purpose of many computer applications is to display and analyze data. Many types of data can be represented in a tabular format, and wxPython has several different controls to help in displaying this type of data. In this chapter, we will take a tour of some of the main ways to display data in a wxPython application. This includes recipes on how to use ListCtrls, Grids, and DataViewCtrls components to display and interact with data in various ways within an application.

Displaying lists of data

If your application needs to generally display small amount of tabular data, the standard `ListCtrl` component can be a quick and easy way to present this data to users. `ListCtrl` can operate in a number of visual modes that present data in a different way to the user. The report mode is the mode that we are going to take a look at in this recipe as it allows us to build a multicolumn table to display the data in.

How to do it...

Here are the steps that you need to perform:

1. First, let's make a custom `ListCtrl` base class to add some useful helper functions to, as follows:

```
class BaseList(wx.ListCtrl):
    def __init__(self, parent):
        super(BaseList, self).__init__(parent,
                                      style=wx.LC_REPORT)

        self.Bind(wx.EVT_LIST_ITEM_RIGHT_CLICK, self.OnRClick)
        self.Bind(wx.EVT_MENU, self.OnMenu, id=wx.ID_COPY)
        self.Bind(wx.EVT_MENU, self.OnMenu, id=wx.ID_SELECTALL)
```

2. Next, let's define the event handlers that were specified in the constructor using this code:

```
def OnRClick(self, event):
    menu = wx.Menu()
    menu.Append(wx.ID_COPY)
    menu.Append(wx.ID_SELECTALL)
    self.PopupMenu(menu)
    menu.Destroy()


def OnMenu(self, event):
    if event.Id == wx.ID_COPY:
        self.Copy()
    elif event.Id == wx.ID_SELECTALL:
        self.SelectAll()
    else:
        event.Skip()
```

3. To support the event handlers, let's add some methods to get data out of `ListCtrl` through the following:

```
def Copy(self):
    """Copy selected data to clipboard"""
    text = self.GetSelectedText()
    data_o = wx.TextDataObject()
    data_o.SetText(text)
    if wx.TheClipboard.IsOpened() or wx.TheClipboard.Open():
        wx.TheClipboard.SetData(data_o)
        wx.TheClipboard.Flush()
        wx.TheClipboard.Close()
```

4. This next method retrieves all the selected text from the control:

```
def GetSelectedText(self):
    items = list()
    nColumns = self.ColumnCount
    for item in range(self.ItemCount):
        if self.IsSelected(item):
            items.append(self.GetRowText(item))
    text = "\n".join(items)
    return text
```

5. This method is used to get the text from a specific row in `ListCtrl`:

```
def GetRowText(self, idx):
    txt = list()
    for col in range(self.ColumnCount):
        txt.append(self.GetItemText(idx, col))
    return "\t".join(txt)
```

6. To wrap up this base class, this last method provides a `Select all items` function in the control:

```
def SelectAll(self):
    """Select all items"""
    for item in range(self.ItemCount):
        self.Select(item, 1)
```

7. Now, with the base class defined, let's make a specific instance of it to display a list of employees as an example, with the following code:

```
class PersonnelList(BaseList):
    def __init__(self, parent):
        super(PersonnelList, self).__init__(parent)

        # Add column headers
        self.InsertColumn(0, "ID")
        self.InsertColumn(1, "Name")
        self.InsertColumn(2, "Email")
        self.InsertColumn(3, "Phone#")

    def AddEmployee(self, id, name, email, phone):
        item = self.Append((id, name, email, phone))
```

How it works...

The `BaseList` class is defined to provide some common useful functions that are not available in the `ListCtrl` class. This base class specifies the `LC_REPORT` style, which means that the list can be built with one or more columns with a header:

The `OnRClick` event handler displays a context menu, and the `OnMenu` event handler provides the handling of the events from the context menu. When an item in the list is right-clicked on, the context menu is shown and the `OnMenu` handler performs the *Copy* or *SelectAll* action, depending on what is selected.

The `Copy` method is added to copy the text of the selected items to the clipboard. Getting at the text in each cell of the control can be a little inconvenient with the base API, so two additional helper methods are also created to support the *Copy* action. The `GetSelectedText` method iterates over each item in the control to find selected rows. Then, for each selected row, it iterates over each of the columns in the row to get text from each cell. This is necessary as the text for each cell is stored in `ListItem`, which represents each cell in the control. The strings retrieved from each cell are then joined together in a single formatted string before being placed on the clipboard.

The `PersonnelList` class is added as an example of how to set up the columns in `ListCtrl`. The `InsertColumn` method takes an index and label value to create the column and its header. The label value is used as the header text for the column. To add items to a multicolumn `ListCtrl` component, the values are passed in as a tuple of strings—one tuple per row and one item in the tuple per column—as can be seen in the `AddEmployee` convenience method.

There's more...

The `ListCtrl` component can operate in a number of visual modes that produce different layouts for data. Take a look at the following table:

Style flag	Description
`LC_LIST`	The control will have a single column and operate similar to a `ListBox` component

Style flag	Description
LC_ICON	This displays a grid of large icons, similar to the icon view in Windows Explorer
LC_SMALL_ICON	This displays a grid of small icons
LC_REPORT	This creates a single or multicolumn report view with an optional header

The LC_REPORT mode used in this recipe also has some additional style flags that can be applied to modify the behavior of the control and how it is displayed. Take a look at the following table:

Style flag	Description
LC_VIRTUAL	The application stores and provides data to the control on demand. This mode is useful to improve performance when there is a larger amount of data to be displayed. When using this style, the control should override the OnGetItemText, OnGetItemImage, and OnGetItemAttr methods to provide the requested data on demand.
LC_NO_HEADER	This hides the header row of the list.
LC_HRULES	This adds horizontal divider lines between rows.
LC_VRULES	This adds vertical divider lines between columns.

See also

  ▸   Refer to the next recipe in this chapter, *Editing data lists*, to use some of the ListCtrl component's additional features

Editing data lists

ListCtrl provides a nice way to display tabular data to users, though in its normal form, it only offers a read-only display of data. If you also wish to allow users to interact with and edit data, there are some additional steps that need to be taken. The LC_EDIT style flag can be used to allow the editing of data, but this only works for the first column of ListCtrl. Luckily, to overcome this limitation and enable the editing of any cell in LC_REPORT mode, the wx.lib.mixins.listctrl module has a mixin class to help provide this functionality. So, let's take a look at how to make a ListCtrl editable.

Getting ready

We will use the example code from the previous recipe in this chapter, *Displaying lists of data*, as a base for showing the extended functionality of editing ListCtrl in this recipe. So, ensure that you check over the contents of the preceding recipe before continuing with this one.

How to do it...

Here are the steps to perform in this recipe:

1. First, we need a few extra modules to help us with this recipe, which are as follows:

```python
import re
import wx
import wx.lib.mixins.listctrl as listmix
# Module from recipe 1
import baseList

RE_NAME = "[A-Z][a-z]*"
RE_EMAIL = ".+@email\.com"
RE_PHONE = "[0-9]{3}\-[0-9]{4}"
```

2. Next, we will define a subclass of `PersonnelList` from the previous recipe, which uses `TextEditMixin`, using the following code:

```python
class PersonnelEditList(baseList.PersonnelList,
                        listmix.TextEditMixin):
    def __init__(self, parent):
        super(PersonnelEditList, self).__init__(parent)
        listmix.TextEditMixin.__init__(self)

        self.Bind(wx.EVT_LIST_BEGIN_LABEL_EDIT, self.OnEdit)
        self.Bind(wx.EVT_LIST_END_LABEL_EDIT, self.OnValidate)
```

3. Now, let's define the `OnEdit` event handler, which we will use to allow or disallow editing on some columns:

```python
def OnEdit(self, event):
    if event.Item.Column == 0:
        # Don't allow edit of ID column values
        event.Veto()
    else:
        event.Skip()
```

4. All that's left now is to define the `OnValidate` event handler to check user data and prevent bad input:

```python
def OnValidate(self, event):
    """Check input values and reject if bad data is present"""
    item = event.Item
    validator = { 1 : RE_NAME,
                  2 : RE_EMAIL,
                  3 : RE_PHONE }.get(item.Column)
    ok = re.match(validator, item.Text)
```

```
if not ok:
    event.Veto()
else:
    event.Skip()
```

How it works...

The TextEditMixin component adds a pop-up TextCtrl, which is shown over a cell in the ListCtrl when a selected cell is clicked on a second time or when using the *Tab* key to traverse from one editor cell to the next. The TextEditMixin component raises the EVT_LIST_BEGIN_LABEL_EDIT event prior to showing TextCtrl. As was done in this recipe, this event can be used to prevent TextCtrl from being shown by calling Veto on the event for columns that should not allow editing. When the TextCtrl loses focus or the *Enter* key is pressed, the TextEditMixin raises the EVT_LIST_END_LABEL_EDIT event. In this recipe, we used this event to check whether the data that was entered was valid for the given column. If the text that was entered did not match the given pattern, Veto would be called on the event to prevent the cell from being updated to the user's input.

There's more...

The wx.lib.mixins.listctrl module also has a number of other mixin classes that can be used to further extend and enhance a ListCtrl with additional features and capabilities. Take a look at the following table:

Mixin class	Description
CheckListCtrlMixin	This adds checkboxes to the first column of ListCtrl
ColumnSorterMixin	This adds some helper methods to support sorting ListCtrl when a column header is clicked on
ListCtrlAutoWidthMixin	This automatically resizes the set column to take up any remaining width that is available
ListRowHighlighter	This automatically changes the background color of alternating rows in ListCtrl

Implementing a data source

For most usages of the grid control, your application must define a custom data source to provide the data on demand when the grid requests to display it. The use of a data source allows virtualizing data storage to prevent duplicating the storage of data in both the control and the backing data field. In this recipe, we will take a look at how to create a custom PyGridTableBase to use as a data source for grid.

How to do it...

Perform the following steps:

1. First, in this recipe, we will retrieve backing data from the GitHub API, so we need to import a few extra modules from the Python standard library. We will do this as follows:

```
import urllib
import json
import wx
import wx.grid as gridlib
```

2. Let's start by defining the custom `PyGridTableBase` class to provide data to the grid:

```
class MyDataSource(gridlib.PyGridTableBase):
    def __init__(self):
        super(MyDataSource, self).__init__()

        # Github change history for wxPython
        self._RetrieveData()

    def _RetrieveData(self):
        url = "https://api.github.com/repos/RobinD42/wxPython/"
        query = "commits?path=%s&per_page=100"
        changes = query % "CHANGES.txt"
        fp = urllib.urlopen(url+changes)
        headers = dict(fp.info())
        self._data = json.load(fp)
```

3. Now, there are a handful of methods that must be overridden; these first two tell the grid the number of rows and columns available from the data source. Define the following methods:

```
    def GetNumberRows(self):
        """Override to tell grid how many columns to show"""
        return len(self._data)

    def GetNumberCols(self):
        """Override to tell grid how many rows
        of data there are"""
        return 3
```

4. This next override is called by the grid every time it needs a value to display for a given cell:

```
    def GetValue(self, row, col):
        """Get the value for a specific cell from data source"""
```

```
        data = self._data[row]['commit']
        keys = { 0 : ('author', 'date'),
                 1 : ('author', 'name'),
                 2 : ('message',) }
        value = ""
        temp = data
        for key in keys[col]:
            value = temp[key]
            temp = value
        return value
```

5. These last two overrides are optional and are used to customize the labels on the row and column headers:

```
def GetColLabelValue(self, col):
    """Get the label for the column"""
    cols = ["Date", "Name", "Comment"]
    return cols[col]

def GetRowLabelValue(self, row):
    """Get label for the given row"""
    return str(row + 1)
```

6. For the last step, we will create a simple grid and assign it to use an instance of the preceding data source with the following code:

```
class MyFrame(wx.Frame):
    def __init__(self, parent, title):
        super(MyFrame, self).__init__(parent, title=title)

        sizer = wx.BoxSizer()
        self._grid = gridlib.Grid(self)
        self._data = MyDataSource()
        self._grid.SetTable(self._data)
        self._grid.EnableEditing(False)
        self._grid.AutoSizeColumns()

        sizer.Add(self._grid, 1, wx.EXPAND)
        self.SetSizer(sizer)
        self.SetInitialSize()
```

How it works...

The `PyGridTableBase` object's job is to take raw data from whichever source it may come and to provide the grid with the data through a common well-defined interface. The example in this recipe shows the basic methods that must be implemented and overridden by a subclass of `PyGridTableBase` in order for it to fulfill its role of the `Grid` object that is responsible for displaying the data.

The data source in this recipe uses a fixed query to get a set of JSON result values about the first 100 revisions of the wxPython changelog from GitHub. The JSON data is downloaded when the data source is first created and then provided to the grid on demand by the `GetValue` method, which is used to return data for a specific cell in the grid. Through the `GetValue` method, the data source projects only three columns from the returned JSON data, the commit timestamp, the author's name, and the check-in comment.

The other overrides are called by `Grid` in a similar way to help set up the scroll bar's virtual space by asking the `GetNumberRows` method to find out how many rows of data there are. Likewise, it gets the number of columns in the horizontal direction by asking the `GetNumberCols` method. The values returned by these two simple methods set up the overall dimensions of the grid and are used by the grid to determine how many cells there are and what values can be passed into `GetValue` to get the actual string to display.

There's more...

In this recipe, the custom data source is implemented as a read-only view of data. However, it's also possible to allow data to be modified by implementing some additional overrides available on the `PyGridTableBase` class, which are as follows:

Overridable method	Description
`SetValue(row, col, value)`	This is similar to `GetValue` but is called to update a value in the data source if a user edits a cell in the UI
`DeleteRows(pos, num)`	This deletes a number of records from the data source, starting at `pos`
`InsertRows(pos, num)`	This inserts some new empty rows at the given index position
`AppendRows(num)`	This adds a number of empty rows at end of the data table

See also

> ▶ Refer to the next recipe in this chapter, *Getting started with the data grid*, for some additional examples on using a grid table data source and formatting data in the display

Getting started with the data grid

The `Grid` control provides a spreadsheet-like display of data using a separate data source that provides the data to the `Grid` control. The `Grid` control in wxPython is a generic widget used to display tabular data. In this recipe, we will explore some of the basic capabilities of the grid control by creating a grid that can be used to edit CSV-formatted files.

Getting ready

This recipe will assume some basic familiarity with the `PyGridTableBase` class that was discussed in the previous recipe, *Implementing a data source*; so, ensure that you take a quick review of the preceding recipe before getting into this one.

How to do it...

Here are the steps that you need to perform in this recipe:

1. First, we will use a couple of extra imports from the standard library to help out in this recipe, so let's add them in, as follows:

```
import csv
from StringIO import StringIO
import wx
import wx.grid as gridlib
```

2. Next, let's start on the data source for the grid by defining the following class:

```
class CSVDataSource(gridlib.PyGridTableBase):
    def __init__(self):
        super(CSVDataSource, self).__init__()
        self._data = None
        self._header = None
        self._readOnly = list()

        self._roAttr = gridlib.GridCellAttr()
        self._roAttr.SetReadOnly()
        c = wx.SystemSettings.GetColour(wx.SYS_COLOUR_GRAYTEXT)
        self._roAttr.TextColour = c
```

3. This next method is to help support importing CSV data into the grid:

```
    def LoadFile(self, fileName):
        reader = csv.reader(file(fileName, 'r'))
        self._data = [row for row in reader]
        self._header = self._data.pop(0)
        self._readOnly = list()
```

4. Now, we also need a method to get the data back out of the data source in the CSV format. We can do this with the following:

```python
def GetData(self):
    if not self._data:
        return ""

    buff = StringIO()
    writer = csv.writer(buff)
    writer.writerow(self._header)
    writer.writerows(self._data)
    return buff.getvalue()
```

5. The following two methods are to make it easy to disable editing on a single column. The `GetAttr` method is called by grid when it needs to get information on how to display the cell:

```python
def SetColReadOnly(self, col):
    self._readOnly.append(col)

def GetAttr(self, row, col, kind):
    if col in self._readOnly:
        self._roAttr.IncRef()
        return self._roAttr
    return None
```

6. The following helper function is to support data sorting:

```python
def Sort(self, col, ascending):
    self._data.sort(None,
                    lambda data: data[col],
                    not ascending)
```

7. The next group of methods are basic overrides of the base table object needed to represent data in grid:

```python
def GetNumberRows(self):
    return len(self._data) if self._data else 0

def GetNumberCols(self):
    return len(self._header) if self._header else 0

def GetValue(self, row, col):
    if not self._data:
        return ""
    else:
        return self._data[row][col]

def SetValue(self, row, col, value):
```

```
        if self._data:
            self._data[row][col] = value

    def GetColLabelValue(self, col):
        return self._header[col] if self._header else None
```

8. With the data source now out of the way, let's work on a custom `Grid` class to use this data source:

```
class CSVEditorGrid(gridlib.Grid):
    def __init__(self, parent):
        super(CSVEditorGrid, self).__init__(parent)

        self._data = CSVDataSource()
        self.SetTable(self._data)

        self.Bind(gridlib.EVT_GRID_COL_SORT, self.OnSort)
```

9. This event handler is called when a column header is clicked on to sort the data based on the given column:

```
    def OnSort(self, event):
        self._data.Sort(event.Col,
                        self.IsSortOrderAscending())
```

10. To support the easy loading and exporting of data from grid, the following two methods are added:

```
    def LoadFile(self, fileName):
        self._data.LoadFile(fileName)
        self.SetTable(self._data)
        self.AutoSizeColumns()

    def SaveFile(self, fileName):
        with file(fileName, 'w') as fileObj:
            fileObj.write(self._data.GetData())
```

11. Finally, to finish it up, a simple accessor method to set a grid column as read-only can be defined as follows:

```
    def SetColReadOnly(self, col):
        self._data.SetColReadOnly(col)
```

How it works...

With a relatively less amount of code, we created a control that can be used as an editing component for pretty much any type of CSV files. Grid gets most of its capabilities from what is provided by its data source. The `LoadFile` method of the data source processes the CSV file and loads it into memory. Here, the first row of the data is treated as column header labels. The `GetData` method, on the other hand, takes the latest version of the data and converts it back into a CSV string.

The grid queries the data source for information about cells with the `GetAttr` method. The `GridCellAttribute` class returned by this method can be used to modify the appearance or behavior of an individual cell in the grid. In this recipe, we used this capability to add a quick way to disable editing in individual columns of data by returning a `GridCellAttribute` class. This will display grayed-out text and has a read-only attribute set, as can be seen in the following example application:

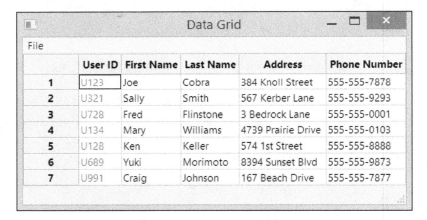

Now, in the actual `Grid` window class, there isn't much to do as most of the heavy lifting had already been taken care of by the data source, though we did add a few features to help support user interaction. The `EVT_GRID_COL_SORT` event is used to get a notification when a column header is clicked on, and this is then used to resort the data in the data source, which in turn causes the grid display to be resorted.

The `LoadFile` method on the `Grid` class is used to tell the data source to load a new data file into memory, and then `SetTable` is called to reset the grid's data source. We are reusing the same data source instance, but calling `SetTable` is necessary as it is the easiest way to get grid to refresh the display when the underlying table changes.

There's more...

The following two sections include some additional details on customizing and managing `GridCellAttributes`.

Custom Editors

The `GridCellAttribute` class provides a large number of options to customize the appearance and even the type of editor control used when a cell needs to be edited. The data source's default editor is `TextCtrl`, but this can be customized to a number of other controls by overriding `GetAttr` and returning `GridCellAttribute`, which uses `SetEditor` to set a specialized editor type.

Managing Attributes

If you use more than just a couple of `GridCellAttribute` classes, using `GridCellAttrProvider` can help simplify the management and application of the attributes. This class provides a way to set a common attribute per row or column, quite similar to how we manually managed disabling columns in this recipe. An instance of `GridCellAttrProvider` can be created, and then we can use the `SetAttr`, `SetRowAttr`, or `SetColAttr` methods to load it up with `GridCellAttributes` for specific cells, rows, or columns. The provider can then be assigned to the `GridTableBase` object using its `SetAttrProvider` method.

The `GridTableBase` object's overridden `GetAttr` method can be used to further customize grid attributes on the fly. In this overridden method, we can simply get the attribute from the provider and apply any overriding modifications to the attribute prior to returning it to the grid.

See also

- ▸ Refer to the *Displaying dynamic data* recipe in this chapter for another example of using the grid to display dynamic data
- ▸ Refer to the *Customizing grid labels* recipe in *Chapter 8, User Interface Primitives*, for a recipe on how to use custom grid renderers

Displaying dynamic data

In the previous two recipes in this chapter, we looked at how to work with `GridTableBase` to make a data source and considered some additional information about grid itself. In these previous examples, we worked with static data that was preloaded into the data table; however, in this recipe, we will work with a dynamic data source that can update grid dynamically when the data in the data source changes.

How to do it...

Perform the following steps for this recipe:

1. First, let's import all the libraries we will need for this recipe, which are as follows:

```
import os
import stat
import time
import wx
import wx.grid as gridlib
```

2. Next, let's start by making a little data class to help put information about a file in a human readable format:

```
class FileInfo:
    def __init__(self, path):
        self.path = path
        fstat = os.stat(path)
        ltime = time.localtime(fstat[stat.ST_MTIME])
        self.modified = time.asctime(ltime)
        self.type = "Directory" if os.path.isdir(path) else "File"
        self.size = self.DisplaySize(fstat[stat.ST_SIZE])

    def DisplaySize(self, bits):
        for unit in ['B','KB','MB','GB']:
            if abs(bits) < 1024.0:
                return "%3.1f%s" % (bits, unit)
            bits /= 1024.0
        return "%.1f%s" % (bits, 'TB')
```

3. Now, we are ready to start on the data source. This data source will monitor a directory for new, deleted, or renamed files. The following class will handle this:

```
class DirDataSource(gridlib.PyGridTableBase):
    def __init__(self, directory):
        super(DirDataSource, self).__init__()

        self._dir = directory
        self._snapshot = os.listdir(self._dir)
        self._timer = wx.Timer()
        self._timer.Start(1000)

        self._timer.Bind(wx.EVT_TIMER, self.OnRefresh)
```

4. The next methods provide the interface to supply data to the grid:

```python
def GetNumberRows(self):
    return len(self._snapshot)

def GetNumberCols(self):
    return 4 # file, modified, type, size

def GetValue(self, row, col):
    fname = self._snapshot[row]
    path = os.path.join(self._dir, fname)
    info = FileInfo(path)
    val = [fname, info.modified, info.type, info.size]
    return val[col]

def GetColLabelValue(self, col):
    cols = ("File", "Modified", "Type", "Size")
    return cols[col]
```

5. Now, here is the part that is used to check for changes in the monitored directory. This event handler is invoked by the `Timer` object once a second:

```python
def OnRefresh(self, event):
    currentData = os.listdir(self._dir)
    if currentData == self._snapshot:
        return # no change

    curNumRows = len(self._snapshot)
    newNumRows = len(currentData)
    self._snapshot = currentData

    if curNumRows != newNumRows:
        self.ProcessUpdates(curNumRows, newNumRows)

    msgId = gridlib.GRIDTABLE_REQUEST_VIEW_GET_VALUES
    msg = gridlib.GridTableMessage(self, msgId)
    self.View.ProcessTableMessage(msg)
```

6. The last is another helper method to inform grid that the number of rows in the table has changed. Take a look at the following code:

```python
def ProcessUpdates(self, curNumRows, newNumRows):
    self.View.BeginBatch()
    if newNumRows < curNumRows:
        msg = gridlib.GridTableMessage(self,
                gridlib.GRIDTABLE_NOTIFY_ROWS_DELETED,
                curNumRows - newNumRows,
```

```
                              curNumRows - newNumRows)
            self.View.ProcessTableMessage(msg)

    if newNumRows > curNumRows:
        msg = gridlib.GridTableMessage(self,
                    gridlib.GRIDTABLE_NOTIFY_ROWS_APPENDED,
                    newNumRows - curNumRows)
        self.View.ProcessTableMessage(msg)
    self.View.EndBatch()
```

How it works...

This recipe uses simple time-based polling to check for changes in a directory, specifically to find out whether files were added, removed, or renamed. When a change is detected in the directory, `GridTable` uses its reference to the grid window to invoke `ProcessTableMessage`. Depending on the message that is sent for processing, the grid begins to redo its layout by rerequesting information from `GridTable`.

The `GRIDTABLE_NOTIFY_ROWS_DELETED` message takes two parameters: the first is the index of the first row that is deleted, and the second is the number of rows that are deleted. The first parameter does not really matter in this case as we follow this message with `GRIDTABLE_REQUEST_VIEW_GETVALUES`, which tells grid to refresh the values in the visible cells. The `GRIDTABLE_NOTIFY_ROWS_APPENDED` message takes one parameter, which is the number of rows that are added to the end of the grid. Again, as the get value's message follows, the important part about sending this message is to tell the grid that the number of items has changed, so it can adjust the scrolling.

There's more...

The methods to manage dynamic data presented in this recipe can be readily applied to more practical applications, where your data source may be a database or another network location. For example, if you set a watch on a database table for anything inserted or deleted from a background thread, you can use the trigger notification and requery to get the data and then update the view, as we did in this recipe.

See also

▸   Refer to *Chapter 8, User Interface Primitives*, for a recipe about providing custom renders in Grid to see how the display of the grid can be customized

Modeling your data

The `DataViewCtrl` control allows a flexible way to display rich data. The `DataViewCtrl` control can use different data model classes to represent and provide data to the view that can then present the data, such as `ListCtrl` or `TreeCtrl`. In this recipe, we will take a look at getting started with `DataViewCtrl` by creating a custom `DataViewModel` class to provide data to the control.

How to do it...

Perform the following steps:

1. First, we need to import an extra module as `DataViewCtrl` and related classes are in a submodule of the wx namespace:

```
import inspect
import wx
import wx.dataview as dv
```

2. Next, let's define a Python object that will be our data model. This class will be used to represent the structure of class inheritance for a Python object, as follows:

```
class HierarchyInfo:
    def __init__(self, item, parent):
        self.item = item
        self.parent = parent

        self.name = item.__name__
        self.docs = item.__doc__
        if self.docs:
            self.docs = self.docs.replace("\n", "")
        self.subs = list()

        self._searchSubs()

    def _searchSubs(self):
        if hasattr(self.item, '__subclasses__'):
            for t in self.item.__subclasses__():
                self.subs.append(HierarchyInfo(t, self))
```

3. Now, let's start by creating a custom `PydataViewModel` to serve data to `DataViewCtrl`, as follows:

```
class ClassDataModel(dv.PyDataViewModel):
    def __init__(self, data):
        super(ClassDataModel, self).__init__()
        self.data = data
        self.objmapper.UseWeakRefs(True)
```

4. This and the subsequent methods are overrides used to adapt data to the view. This first method is used by the control to build a structure of `DataViewItems` to be used by the view:

```
def GetChildren(self, parent, children):
    # check root node
    if not parent:
        for item in self.data:
            children.append(self.ObjectToItem(item))
        return len(self.data)

    node = self.ItemToObject(parent)
    for item in node.subs:
        children.append(self.ObjectToItem(item))
    return len(node.subs)
```

5. This override tells the container how many columns the data model has:

```
def GetColumnCount(self):
    return 3
```

6. This next override is overridden to always return `true` as we want to display all columns' data for the parent nodes:

```
def HasContainerColumns(self, item):
    return True
```

7. This method is called to check whether a given `DataViewItem` has child items or not. Returning `True` results in the node being expandable in the view, as follows:

```
def IsContainer(self, item):
    if not item:
        return True

    obj = self.ItemToObject(item)
    return len(obj.subs) > 0
```

8. The next override is called when the view needs to find the parent item when expanding nodes:

```
def GetParent(self, item):
    if not item:
        return dv.NullDataViewItem

    obj = self.ItemToObject(item)
    if obj.parent is None:
        return dv.NullDataViewItem
    else:
        return self.ObjectToItem(obj.parent)
```

9. The `GetValue` method must be overridden to return the value for the requested column of the given item. So, we will simply map the correct property of the object to the requested column:

```
def GetValue(self, item, col):
    obj = self.ItemToObject(item)
    vMap = { 0 : obj.name,
             1 : str(len(obj.subs)),
             2 : obj.docs
           }
    return vMap[col]
```

10. We will not allow the editing of data in this model, so we will just provide an empty implementation for `SetValue` using the following code:

```
def SetValue(self, value, item, col):
    pass
```

11. Now, to wrap up this class, we will add one more optional override to control the appearance of the subclass count column and display its values in bold text, as follows:

```
def GetAttr(self, item, col, attr):
    if col == 1:
        attr.Bold = True
        return True
    return False
```

12. For the last step, let's put the data model to use through the following code:

```
class ClassViewer(wx.Frame):
    def __init__(self, parent, title):
        super(ClassViewer, self).__init__(parent, title=title)

        # Look at all classes in wx namespace
        data = list()
        for x in dir(wx):
            item = getattr(wx, x)
            if inspect.isclass(item):
                data.append(HierarchyInfo(item, None))

        dvc = dv.DataViewCtrl(self, style=dv.DV_VERT_RULES)
        model = ClassDataModel(data)
        dvc.AssociateModel(model)

        autosize = wx.COL_WIDTH_AUTOSIZE
        dvc.AppendTextColumn("Class", 0, width=autosize)
        dvc.AppendTextColumn("Subclasses", 1, width=autosize,
```

```
                                    align=wx.ALIGN_CENTER)
        dvc.AppendTextColumn("Docstring", 2, width=autosize)

        sizer = wx.BoxSizer()
        sizer.Add(dvc, 1, wx.EXPAND)
        self.SetSizer(sizer)
        self.SetInitialSize((500,400))
```

How it works...

We did quite a few things in this recipe, but before we get to the details, let's take a quick look at what we built:

Starting with the `HierarchyInfo` class, we built a data structure to represent the class hierarchy of a class object that was passed in. The _searchSubs method looks at all the known subclasses and attaches additional `HierarchyInfo` classes all the way down the class tree until it hits a leaf class that has no more additional subclasses. A collection of this data is used by the `ClassDataModel` class, which is used by `DataViewCtrl` to translate raw data into a format that the view can display.

Making a custom data model class, as we did in this recipe, requires overriding several virtual methods, which each allow the view to acquire some information about the data that it needs to display as well as how to display it. The `GetChildren` method is called to build up and describe the data structure of each item to the view. The parent parameter is the node that is queried about, and the child parameter is an output list that all the children of the given node should be added to. It's during this function that the objects are converted to `DataViewItem` for the view to manage.

The important point to note when working on implementing these methods is the mapping of the data object back from and forth to (`HierarchyInfo`) `DataViewItem`. This is accomplished using the `ItemToObject` and `ObjectToItem` methods. Internally, in your model, you would want to work with the object, but when handing it back to the view, it needs to be passed as `DataViewItem`.

There's more...

In this recipe, we built a custom data model using the basic model type. There are, however, some other built-in model types that can be used to help model the basic list or tree structured data. Take a look at the following table:

Data model class	Description
`DataViewIndexListModel`	This provides a simple model API to address an item by an index in a list or collection.
`DataViewVirtualListModel`	This is similar to `IndexListModel`, but the view does not store the items. The data model keeps the data and the view asks for only the data it needs to display at the time. This allows an optimized display of a large amount of data.
`DataViewListStore`	This provides a ListCtrl-like API to build up a model to display a list or tabular data. The class stores the data and can be used directly without the need to derive a subclass.
`DataViewTreeStore`	This provides a TreeCtrl-like API to build up a model for hierarchical data. This model can be used directly without subclassing.

See also

 ▸ Refer to the next recipe in this chapter, *Displaying your data model*, for some more information on working with `DataViewCtrl` to manage the display of data

Displaying your data model

The `DataViewCtrl` control has several different ways to display the data that is provided by its data model object. The view and the model objects both influence each other; the view contains settings for the columns of data that are shown, and it sets what type of data they should display. The model is responsible for providing data to the view in the appropriate format when the view requests it. The model also has some control over how the data is displayed by way of providing `DataViewItemAttr` objects to control the styling of text. In this recipe, we will explore the use of `DataViewCtrl` a little further by looking at some of its custom column types and how to access data from its event handlers.

Getting ready

In this recipe, we will extend and reuse the data model class from the previous recipe, so ensure that you take a look over the preceding topic prior to continuing with this one.

How to do it...

Perform the following steps:

1. First, we need to import some modules to help with this recipe, including a module with some of the code from the previous recipe. For this, we will use the following code:

```
import inspect
import wx
import wx.dataview as dv

# Recipe 6 module
import dataModel as dm
```

2. Now, we will make a few small extensions to the base model class to support some additional display options that we will enable in the view later on using the following code:

```
class ExtendedModel(dm.ClassDataModel):
    def GetValue(self, item, col):
        obj = self.ItemToObject(item)
        bmp = wx.ArtProvider.GetIcon(wx.ART_FOLDER_OPEN,
                            wx.ART_MENU, (16,16))
        sf = dv.DataViewIconText(self.GetSourceFile(obj), bmp)
        vMap = { 0 : obj.name,
                 1 : str(len(obj.subs)),
                 2 : self.IsBase(obj),
                 3 : sf
               }
        return vMap[col]
```

3. The next two methods are some helper methods used by the preceding overridden `GetValue` method:

```
    def IsBase(self, obj):
        bases = obj.item.__bases__
        lcount = len(bases)
        return lcount == 0 or (lcount == 1 and object in bases)

    def GetSourceFile(self, obj):
        try:
            return inspect.getsourcefile(obj.item)
        except:
            return "Unknown"
```

4. Now, let's make a subclass of `DataViewCtrl` to encapsulate our custom settings using the following code:

```
class ClassDataView(dv.DataViewCtrl):
    def __init__(self, parent, data):
        style = dv.DV_ROW_LINES | dv.DV_HORIZ_RULES
        super(ClassDataView, self).__init__(parent, style=style)

        self.model = ExtendedModel(data)
        self.AssociateModel(self.model)

        flags = dv.DATAVIEW_COL_SORTABLE|\
                dv.DATAVIEW_COL_RESIZABLE
        autosize = wx.COL_WIDTH_AUTOSIZE
        self.AppendTextColumn("Class", 0, width=autosize,
                              flags=flags)
        self.AppendTextColumn("Subclasses", 1, width=autosize,
                              align=wx.ALIGN_CENTER)
        self.AppendToggleColumn("IsBase", 2, width=autosize)
        self.AppendIconTextColumn("Source File", 3,
                                  width=autosize, flags=flags)

        self.Bind(dv.EVT_DATAVIEW_ITEM_CONTEXT_MENU,
                  self.OnContext)
```

5. For the last step to wrap it up, we will define the `OnContext` event handler to take a look at how we can access data in the model from `DataViewEvent` through the following:

```
    def OnContext(self, event):
        menu = wx.Menu()
        iconTxt = self.model.GetValue(event.GetItem(), 3)
        fname = iconTxt.GetText()
        menu.Append(wx.ID_OPEN, "Open Module '%s'" % fname)

        obj = self.model.ItemToObject(event.GetItem())
        docLbl = obj.docs or "No info Available"
        item = menu.Append(wx.ID_ANY, docLbl)
        item.Enable(False)

        self.PopupMenu(menu)
        menu.Destroy()
```

How it works...

Let's take a look at the changes we made to how data is displayed compared to how it was displayed in the previous recipe:

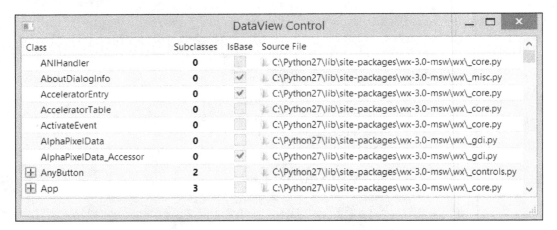

As can be seen in the preceding screenshot, we used two additional types of columns in the view. The first is added by `AddToggleColumn`, which uses a checkbox to display a Boolean value. To support the use of this column, the `GetValue` method in the model must return a Boolean value. The last column is changed to an icon text column, and instead of displaying the docstring, it now shows the file that the class is located in. For columns appended using the `AppendIcontTextColumn` method, the data model must return a `DataViewIconText` object that contains the label and text to display in the cell.

In the `ClassDataView` class, we bound to the context menu event for `DataViewCtrl`. This event handler is called when an item is right-clicked on. The event handler is passed a `DataViewEvent` object that contains information about what is clicked on to raise the event. This event object has several properties and methods to access data related to the item in the control. However, they currently return references to typed items from the underlying C++ code, which provides limited help in our Python application.

To help work around these current limitations, we kept a reference to the `PyDataViewModel` object directly in the class in order to maintain access to its `ItemToObject` method to convert the `DataViewItem` to Python objects. The `DataViewCtrl` class has a `Model` property already, but this property returns a `DataViewModel` that does not have the object mapper methods exposed. This is why we need to keep an extra reference to the custom `ExtendedModel` instance that we are using. So, between this and the access to `DataViewItem` that the event's `GetItem` method returns, we can gain access to Python data objects and use the data in event handlers, as was done to make the pop-up menu in this recipe.

There's more...

In addition to the built-in column types that use their own renderers to render nonstring data, you can also create your own custom renders to display or style the data in any way you want. A custom render allows you to define how the cell is drawn by overriding some methods and using a provided `DeviceContext` (refer to *Chapter 8, User Interface Primitives*, for using `DeviceContext`).

To use a custom renderer, it is necessary to create a subclass of `PyDataViewCustomRenderer` and override the necessary virtual methods to define the custom behavior of how the cell is rendered. Then, to add a column to the view that uses the custom renderer, a `DataViewColumn` object should be created that is assigned an instance of the renderer, and the column object should be added to the view with the view's `AppendColumn` method.

6
Ways to Notify and Alert

In this chapter, we will cover the following recipes:

- ► Showing MessageBox
- ► Using InfoBar
- ► Providing extra tips on usage
- ► Displaying transient notifications
- ► Making a splash at startup
- ► Giving busy feedback
- ► Showing information about your app

Introduction

Nearly all software applications that have a user interface need, at some point in time, to alert or notify their users about events that occur in the application or to simply display information. There are many ways to display information and notify that may be more appropriate than others, depending on the circumstances. Some notifications may require acknowledgement from the user while others may not. In this chapter, we will take a look at several different ways to display information and provide feedback and notifications to the user.

Showing MessageBox

`MessageBox` is one of the most common and recognizable UI components of nearly any application on any platform. It provides a very simple way to present information to the user and requires their acknowledgement of the information that is presented. It can also be used as a way to request and get responses to questions and decisions that the program may need to ask the user about. In this recipe, we will take a look at some of the different ways to show `MessageBox`.

How to do it...

Perform the following steps:

1. Let's make a simple `Frame` class that will show `MessageBox` when a button is clicked on. The first step is to define the class and do a simple layout, as follows:

```python
class MyFrame(wx.Frame):
    def __init__(self, parent, title):
        super(MyFrame, self).__init__(parent, title=title)

        panel = wx.Panel(self)
        button = wx.Button(panel, label="Show MessageBox")
        hsizer = wx.BoxSizer()
        hsizer.AddStretchSpacer()
        hsizer.Add(button, 0, wx.ALIGN_CENTER_VERTICAL)
        hsizer.AddStretchSpacer()
        vsizer = wx.BoxSizer(wx.VERTICAL)
        vsizer.Add(hsizer, 1, wx.ALIGN_CENTER_HORIZONTAL)
        panel.SetSizer(vsizer)

        sizer = wx.BoxSizer(wx.VERTICAL)
        sizer.Add(panel, 1, wx.EXPAND)
        self.SetSizer(sizer)

        self.Bind(wx.EVT_BUTTON, self.OnButton, button)
```

2. Now, for the second and last step, let's define the event handler method and show `MessageBox`, with the following code:

```python
def OnButton(self, event):
    style = wx.YES_NO|wx.CENTER|wx.ICON_INFORMATION
    result = wx.MessageBox("Heres the message text!",
                           "Here is the Title",
                           style)
    if result == wx.NO:
```

```
        print("Answer was no!")
    else:
        print("Answer was yes!")
```

How it works...

The first thing to take note of is that `wx.MessageBox` is a function and not a class. This function takes some input parameters that describe what kind of `MessageDialog` and message to display. It then displays a modal `MessageDialog`, and then when the dialog is dismissed, it returns a return code to indicate how the dialog is dismissed.

In this instance, as shown in the preceding image, we decided to show **Yes** and **No** buttons, which are specified with the `wx.YES_NO` style flag as well as an icon that indicates that the message box contains an informational message. So, when this dialog is closed, the `MessageBox` function will return either `wx.YES` or `wx.NO` for a return value, which can be used to determine the decision that the user has made.

There's more...

The `wx.MessageBox` function supports showing several variations of a `MessageDialog`, depending on the style parameter flags passed in. Included here is a quick reference for the available styles that can be used.

Button flags

The flags in the following table can be used to determine the kinds of buttons are placed in the dialog:

Style flag	Description
`wx.OK`	This shows an **Ok** button
`wx.CANCEL`	This shows a **Cancel** button
`wx.YES_NO`	This shows **Yes** and **No** buttons
`wx.HELP`	This shows a **Help** button
`wx.NO_DEFAULT`	This makes the **No** button the default one
`wx.CANCEL_DEFAULT`	This makes the **Cancel** button the default one
`wx.OK_DEFAULT`	This makes the **Ok** button the default one

Icon flags

One of these flags can be combined with the preceding flags to set the icon type of the dialog. Note that the requested icon may be ignored or not shown in some cases, depending on the interface guidelines for the platform. Take a look at the following table:

Style flag	Description
wx.ICON_NONE	This doesn't show an icon if the platform allows it
wx.ICON_WARNING	This shows a warning icon
wx.ICON_ERROR	This shows an error icon
wx.ICON_QUESTION	This shows a question mark icon
wx.ICON_INFORMATION	This shows an information symbol icon

Using InfoBar

The `InfoBar` control is a new control that was added in wxPython 3.0. This control acts similarly to the small informational bar that pops into view at the top of some web browsers. It can be used to present simple messages or get responses to questions, just as a `MessageBox` function can, but it is presented in a less obtrusive way, which does not require acknowledgement from the user or prevents them from continuing to use the program. In this recipe, we will look at how to integrate an `InfoBar` control into your application's frames.

How to do it...

You would need to perform the following steps:

1. First, let's start by making a subclass of `InfoBar` that we will add an *Auto Dismiss* feature to through the following code:

```python
class AutoDismissInfo(wx.InfoBar):
    def __init__(self, parent, hideAfter=-1):
        super(AutoDismissInfo, self).__init__(parent)

        self._timer = wx.Timer(self)
        self._limit = hideAfter

        self.Bind(wx.EVT_TIMER, lambda event: self.Dismiss(),
                  self._timer)
```

2. Next, we will override the `ShowMessage` method to start the timer that is used to automatically dismiss `InfoBar` using this method:

```
def ShowMessage(self, msg, flags):
    if self._timer.IsRunning():
        self._timer.Stop()

    super(AutoDismissInfo, self).ShowMessage(msg, flags)

    if self._limit > 0:
        self._timer.Start(self._limit, True)
```

3. Now, let's put the `InfoBar` control to use in a simple `Frame` class, as follows:

```
class MyFrame(wx.Frame):
    def __init__(self, parent, title):
        super(MyFrame, self).__init__(parent, title=title)

        # Hide messages after 3 seconds
        self.info = AutoDismissInfo(self, 3000)
        self.CreateStatusBar()
        self.SetStatusText("Move the mouse over the window!")
        panel = wx.Panel(self)

        sizer = wx.BoxSizer(wx.VERTICAL)
        sizer.Add(self.info, 0, wx.EXPAND)
        sizer.Add(panel, 1, wx.EXPAND)
        self.SetSizer(sizer)

        panel.Bind(wx.EVT_ENTER_WINDOW, self.OnEnter)
        panel.Bind(wx.EVT_LEAVE_WINDOW, self.OnLeave)
```

4. The last step is to define the event handler functions that we will use to display the `InfoBar` control. Whenever the mouse cursor enters or leaves the window, we will update a new informational message:

```
def OnEnter(self, event):
    self.info.ShowMessage("Mouse has entered the window!",
                          wx.ICON_INFORMATION)

def OnLeave(self, event):
    self.info.ShowMessage("Mouse has left the window!",
                          wx.ICON_WARNING)
```

How it works...

As you just saw, the usage of `InfoBar` is quite simple as in its basic usage, it only requires to be created and added as either the first or last item in its parent window's Sizer. The `InfoBar` control can only be displayed at the top or bottom of the window; this is important in how it is placed in the layout.

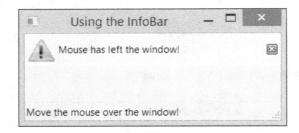

Other than this, the bar can be shown or updated by calling its `ShowMessage` method, which pops the bar into view if it's not currently shown, and we can update the display text with the latest that's passed in. In this recipe, we used an event where the mouse cursor enters or leaves the panel as the trigger for when to show and update the message.

There's more...

The `InfoBar` control can also support some message-box-like functionality by adding buttons to the bar. The `InfoBar` control's `AddButton` method can be used to add buttons to the bar. When a button is clicked on, the bar will be closed. Take note, though, that the `InfoBar` object will consume the button event, and it will not be propagated to the parent window. So, in order to handle the button event, it is necessary to use `Bind` with the `EVT_BUTTON` event handler directly to the `InfoBar` object. In the event handler, also make sure to call skip on the event to let the base handler receive the event and dismiss the window.

See also

▸ Also, check out the *Displaying transient notifications* recipe later in this chapter for another way to display transient or noncritical messages in an application

Providing extra tips on usage

ToolTips are small, transient pop-up windows that are automatically displayed when the mouse cursor is hovered over a window. These popups can be used to provide context-sensitive help messages about what changing the state of a control might do or what a field in a dialog is for. Nearly every control type can have a ToolTip associated with it. This recipe shows how to add ToolTip text to windows in your application.

How to do it...

1. First, let's define a `Panel` subclass with some controls on it through the following code:

```
class MyPanel(wx.Panel):
    def __init__(self, parent):
        super(MyPanel, self).__init__(parent)

        self._timer = wx.Timer(self)
        self._countDown = 10

        self._msg = wx.StaticText(self, label="")
        self._go = wx.Button(self, label="Go")
        tip = "Start a countdown to exit the application."
        self._go.ToolTipString = tip
        self._stop = wx.Button(self, label="Stop")
        self._stop.Enable(False)
        tip = "Cancel the application exit."
        self._stop.ToolTipString = tip

        self._doLayout()

        self.Bind(wx.EVT_BUTTON, self.OnButton)
        self.Bind(wx.EVT_TIMER, self.OnTimer)
```

2. Next, let's do the layout of the controls, as follows:

```
def _doLayout(self):
    sizer = wx.BoxSizer(wx.VERTICAL)

    sizer.Add(self._msg, 0,
              wx.ALIGN_CENTER_HORIZONTAL|wx.ALL, 10)
    bsizer = wx.BoxSizer(wx.HORIZONTAL)
    bsizer.Add(self._go, 0, wx.ALL, 5)
    bsizer.Add(self._stop, 0, wx.ALL, 5)
    sizer.Add(bsizer, 0,
```

```
                        wx.ALIGN_CENTER_HORIZONTAL|wx.BOTTOM, 10)

        self.Sizer = sizer
```

3. Now, let's define the button event handler using this method:

```
def OnButton(self, event):
    if event.EventObject is self._go:
        self._timer.Start(1000)
        self._go.Enable(False)
        self._stop.Enable(True)
    else:
        self._timer.Stop()
        self._go.Enable(True)
        self._stop.Enable(False)
```

4. The final step is to define the onTimer event handler, with this code:

```
def OnTimer(self, event):
    if self._countDown > 0:
        self._countDown -= 1
        msg = "Exiting in %d seconds..." % self._countDown
        self._msg.Label = msg
        self.Layout()
    else:
        wx.GetApp().Exit()
```

How it works...

This recipe is quite simple as the framework takes care of most the work. In the `Panel` constructor, we just used each of the buttons' `ToolTipString` properties to set the ToolTip message to be shown. The ToolTip messages are added to give more context to the action that each button performs. When the mouse cursor hovers over the enabled button and pauses for a moment, the ToolTip message will be shown, and then as the mouse moves again, the tip will be automatically dismissed.

Using the `ToolTipString` property of a window is the easiest way to add a tool tip. However, if you need a little more control over how long the delay should be before it's shown or its maximum width, you can also create a ToolTip object, set up its behavior, and assign it directly to a window's ToolTip property instead.

Displaying transient notifications

If your application needs to occasionally get the user's attention and present some information that may not be critical or require acknowledgement, the `ToasterBox` window can be a nice and unobtrusive way to show simple messages to the user. In this recipe, we will make a small `TrayIcon` application that acts as a timer, which pops up a notification every time a set amount of time has elapsed.

How to do it...

Here are the steps that you need to perform:

1. First, we need an additional import from `wx.lib` to access `ToasterBox`. For this, we will uses the following code:

    ```
    import wx
    import wx.lib.agw.toasterbox as tb

    ID_GET_DUR = wx.NewId()
    ID_START = wx.NewId()
    ```

2. Next, let's make a custom `TaskBarIcon` object to manage our alarm notifications, as follows:

    ```
    class AlarmIcon(wx.TaskBarIcon):
        def __init__(self, topWindow):
            super(AlarmIcon, self).__init__()

            self._topWindow = topWindow
            self._timer = wx.Timer(self)
            self._duration = 10

            bmp = wx.Bitmap("clock.png")
            icon = wx.IconFromBitmap(bmp)
            self.SetIcon(icon, "Alarm Clock")
            self.ResetAlarm()

            self.Bind(wx.EVT_MENU, self.OnMenu)
            self.Bind(wx.EVT_TIMER, self.OnAlarm)
    ```

3. Now, let's add a pop-up menu to the icon to give some options and control over the application to the user through the following code:

    ```
    def CreatePopupMenu(self):
        menu = wx.Menu()
        menu.Append(ID_GET_DUR, "Set Duration")
        menu.AppendSeparator()
    ```

```
            item = menu.Append(ID_START, "Start")
            item.Enable(not self._timer.IsRunning())
            item = menu.Append(wx.ID_STOP)
            item.Enable(self._timer.IsRunning())
            menu.AppendSeparator()
            menu.Append(wx.ID_EXIT)
            return menu
```

4. Next, we need to define the menu's event handler. This is defined by the following method:

```
        def OnMenu(self, event):
            if event.Id == ID_GET_DUR:
                msg = "Enter the alarm timer duration."
                num = wx.GetNumberFromUser(msg, "Duration (sec):",
                                            "Timer Setting",
                                            self._duration, 0, 360)
                self._duration = num
                self.ResetAlarm()
            elif event.Id == ID_START:
                self.ResetAlarm()
            elif event.Id == wx.ID_STOP:
                self._timer.Stop()
            elif event.Id == wx.ID_EXIT:
                self._topWindow.Destroy()
                self.Destroy()
            else:
                event.Skip()
```

5. Next, let's define the `Timer` event handler and the helper function, as follows:

```
        def OnAlarm(self, event):
            notify = tb.ToasterBox(None,
                                    closingstyle=tb.TB_ONCLICK)
            notify.SetPopupPauseTime(self._duration * 1000)
            msg = "Its time! Its time!\nClick to dismiss!"
            notify.SetPopupText(msg)
            notify.SetPopupPositionByInt(3) # bottom right
            notify.Play()

        def ResetAlarm(self):
            if self._timer.IsRunning():
                self._timer.Stop()
            self._timer.Start(self._duration * 1000)
```

6. For the final step, we just need to wrap the icon up in an app object:

```
class AlarmClock(wx.App):
    def OnInit(self):
        frame = wx.Frame(None)
            self.icon = AlarmIcon(frame)
            return True
```

How it works...

In the preceding recipe, we built a small tray icon application that runs a timer and displays a `ToasterBox` window as a notification every time the timer reaches its set interval. We also created a hidden `Frame` object so that the application has a top-level window. This is done as some platforms require a top-level window to keep the main loop running.

A `ToasterBox` object is created in the `Timer` event and set up to display notifications to the user. The `ToasterBox` object is displayed when its `Play` method is called; this begins the animation to show the message on screen. The `ToasterBox` object can be configured in several ways to set how it should be shown. In our application, we set the display period to be until the next notification period by calling its `SetPopupPauseTime` method. The `TB_ONCLICK` option passed to the `ToasterBox` constructor allows the user to dismiss the notification sooner by clicking on it. Lastly, the `SetPopupPositionByInt` method takes a 0-3 value to specify a screen-based location to display the notification at. The value 3 used by this application specifies the lower right-hand side of the screen. An important note to take away from using this control is to not keep references or attempt to reuse instances. Each instance will auto-destroy itself after it is dismissed, and attempting to reuse the object will result in undefined behavior.

There's more...

By default, `ToasterBox` provides a simple window that slides into view, displays some text, and then disappears after a moment. However, being a generic control in `wx.lib`, it can also be customized to the application's needs. By making use of the `TB_COMPLEX` style flag, which can be provided to ToasterBox's `tbstyle` constructor parameter, it is possible to customize the display window and even add any other additional controls to the display that you wish. This can be accomplished by calling ToasterBox's `GetToasterBoxWindow` method, which will return a panel that can have controls added to it similar to any panel.

See also

▶ See the *Using InfoBar* recipe earlier in this chapter for another way to display transient informational notifications

Making a splash at startup

Splash windows can be used to show information during the launching of a program and are most commonly used for applications that require some time to initialize. They provide a means to give quick feedback to the user to show that the application is in the process of starting up and that it is not hung or nonresponsive. In this recipe, we will show how to create an advanced splash screen control that is capable of displaying progress messages during the startup of an application.

How to do it...

1. First, let's start by defining the custom `SplashScreen` class, with the following code:

```python
class ProgressSplash(wx.SplashScreen):
    def __init__(self, bmp, splashStyle, timeout, parent):
        super(ProgressSplash, self).__init__(bmp, splashStyle,
                                             timeout, parent)

        self._msg = wx.StaticText(self)

        # Create status display area
        self.CreateStatusBar()
        sbarHeight = self.StatusBar.Size.height
        self.SetSize((self.Size.width,
                     sbarHeight + bmp.Height))
```

2. We will also override the `PushStatusText` method of the splash screen to ensure that `StatusBar` is refreshed after each text update through the following code:

```python
def PushStatusText(self, text, number=0):
    super(ProgressSplash, self).PushStatusText(text, number)
    # Force ui update
    self.StatusBar.Refresh()
    self.StatusBar.Update()
```

3. Now, let's start on making a sample application that shows how to use the customized splash screen:

```python
class SlowStartingApp(wx.App):
    def OnInit(self):
        self.mainw = wx.Frame(None, title="MyApp")

        bmp = wx.Bitmap('splash_img.png')
        splashStyle = wx.SPLASH_CENTRE_ON_SCREEN|\
                      wx.SPLASH_NO_TIMEOUT
        self.splash = ProgressSplash(bmp, splashStyle,
                                     -1, self.mainw)
        self.splash.Show()
```

```
# Begin the application setup tasks
# on next iteration of event loop
wx.CallAfter(self.Initialize)
return True
```

4. Now, let's take a look at how updates can be pushed to the splash window during the application's initialization method:

```
def Initialize(self):
    self.LoadConfig()
    self.ConnectToServer()
    self.InitializeUI(mainw)

def LoadConfig(self):
    # simulate long configuration load
    self.splash.PushStatusText("Loading config...")
    wx.Sleep(1)

def ConnectToServer(self):
    # simulate setting up connections
    self.splash.PushStatusText("Connecting...")
    wx.Sleep(2)
    self.splash.PushStatusText("Connection Ok...")
    wx.Sleep(1)

def InitializeUI(self, window):
    # simulate setup of UI
    self.splash.PushStatusText("Initializing UI...")
    wx.Sleep(1)
    window.Show()
```

How it works...

A splash window is really just a specialized `Frame` class that is set up to display an image; however, in this recipe, we extended it by adding `StatusBar` to display the status messages that the main application can push to it during startup. The example application creates and shows an instance of the `ProgressSplash` class. Then, it begins its initialization procedures. As this code could block the main loop, we used `CallAfter` to defer the execution of the method until the next iteration of the main loop. This should ensure that the messages showing the progress dialog are processed before the startup procedures begin. Then, in several places during startup, which might take some time to complete, an update message is pushed to the window to give feedback to the user about the progress of what is happening. We overrode the `PushStatusText` method to force a synchronous redrawing of `StatusBar` each time a message is pushed to ensure that it is visible before another task starts, which might block the event being processed on the main loop. Finally, once all the startup steps are completed, the `ProgressSplash` window is dismissed by calling its `Destroy` method, and the application's main window is shown.

There's more...

There is another splash window implementation in the `wx.lib.agw.advancedsplash` module. This extended splash window implementation has some features to display a shaped window by specifying the `AS_SHADOW_BITMAP` style and a `shadowcolour` mask value to be used to mask out the portions of the bitmap that should be displayed as transparent on the screen. So, go ahead and check out this alternate implementation if you want to display a non-rectangular-shaped splash screen.

See also

- ▶ Continue to the next recipe in this chapter, *Giving busy feedback*, for another way to give progress feedback to users during long-running tasks

Giving busy feedback

Sometimes, applications require some time to process a command, and while doing so, the user has to be given some feedback so that he/she doesn't think that the application is frozen. This can be accomplished in several ways, but one common way is to provide animated feedback in the form of a progress bar or gauge. In this recipe, you will see how to animate a gauge to give feedback while a long-running task is completed on a background thread.

How to do it...

Here are the steps to be performed:

1. First, we need to import some extra modules for this recipe, so let's take a quick look at the needed imports:

```
import threading
import wx
```

2. Next, we will use a background thread to do the calculations. For this, see the following:

```
class FibonacciCalc(threading.Thread):
    def __init__(self, n, completeFunc):
        super(FibonacciCalc, self).__init__()
        assert callable(completeFunc)
        self.n = n
        self.complete = completeFunc

    def run(self):
        def fib(n):
            a,b = 1,1
```

```
            for i in xrange(n - 1):
                a,b = b,a+b
            return a

        val = fib(self.n)
        self.complete(val)
```

3. Now, let's start building up the UI that the user can use to invoke the calculation. Here's the class that will define this:

```
class ResultDisplay(wx.Frame):
    def __init__(self, parent, title):
        super(ResultDisplay, self).__init__(parent,
                                            title=title)

        sizer = wx.BoxSizer(wx.VERTICAL)
        panel = self._BuildPanel()
        sizer.Add(panel, 1, wx.EXPAND)
        self.SetSizer(sizer)

        self.SetInitialSize()
```

4. Next, we will build up the controls for the display as follows:

```
    def _BuildPanel(self):
        panel = wx.Panel(self)
        msg = "Enter the nth Fibonacci # to calculate:"
        self.msg = wx.StaticText(panel, label=msg)
        self.ntxt = wx.TextCtrl(panel, value="500000")
        style = wx.TE_READONLY|wx.TE_RICH2
        self.result = wx.TextCtrl(panel, style=style)
        self.calc = wx.Button(panel, label="Calculate")
        self.calc.Bind(wx.EVT_BUTTON, self.OnCalculate)
        self.gauge = wx.Gauge(panel)
        self.timer = wx.Timer(self)
        self.Bind(wx.EVT_TIMER,
                  lambda e: self.gauge.Pulse(),
                  self.timer)
        return self._LayoutPanel(panel)
```

5. Next, let's finish up the layout of the panel:

```
    def _LayoutPanel(self, panel):
        sizer = wx.BoxSizer(wx.VERTICAL)
        hsizer = wx.BoxSizer(wx.HORIZONTAL)
        hsizer.Add(self.msg, 0, wx.ALL, 5)
        hsizer.Add(self.ntxt, 0, wx.RIGHT, 5)
```

```
sizer.Add(hsizer, 0, wx.ALIGN_CENTER_HORIZONTAL)

flags = wx.EXPAND|wx.ALIGN_CENTER_HORIZONTAL
sizer.Add(self.result, 1, flags)
sizer.Add(self.gauge, 0, flags, 5)
self.gauge.Show(False)

sizer.Add(self.calc, 0, wx.ALIGN_CENTER_HORIZONTAL)
panel.SetSizer(sizer)
return panel
```

6. Now, when a calculation is requested, we will show the progress bar and start its feedback while the calculation is started on a background thread, as follows:

```
def OnCalculate(self, event):
    self.ShowFeedBack(True)
    self.calc.Enable(False)

    num = int(self.ntxt.Value)
    t = FibonacciCalc(num, self.OnComplete)
    t.start()
```

7. The next step is to handle the result when it is reported from the other thread. Use the following code:

```
def OnComplete(self, value):
    def SafeUpdate(value):
        self.ShowFeedBack(False)
        self.result.Value = str(value)
        self.calc.Enable(True)

    wx.CallAfter(SafeUpdate, value)
```

8. The last part is the helper method to show and hide the progress bar:

```
def ShowFeedBack(self, show):
    self.gauge.Show(show)
    self.result.Show(not show)
    if show:
        self.timer.Start(250)
    else:
        self.timer.Stop()
    self.Layout()
```

How it works...

The example application in this recipe performs a calculation that may take a noticeable time to complete. Prior to starting the calculation, a gauge is shown to notify the user that the application is busy. While the background thread is working, a timer is used to pulse the gauge and update its current position to give continuous feedback to the user:

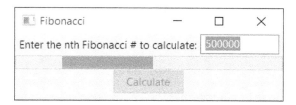

Once the calculation is completed on the background thread, it uses the provided callback function to signal that the calculation is done and updates the UI with the result. As OnComplete is called from a background thread, which is not the same thread that the UI is running in, it is necessary to use CallAfter. The CallAfter method can be used to pass the execution of a function back to the main thread, where it is safe to make updates to the state of the UI.

Showing information about your app

If you are planning on distributing your application to others, it may be a good idea to add AboutBox as a place to show some general information about your application. This information commonly includes the application's version number, author or company name, and any copyright information. In this recipe, we will make a simple application and show how to incorporate AboutBox in it.

How to do it...

Here are the steps that you need to perform:

1. First, let's create a Frame that has a Menu option to show AboutBox, as follows:

```
class AboutRecipeFrame(wx.Frame):
    def __init__(self, parent, title):
        super(AboutRecipeFrame, self).__init__(parent,
                                               title=title)

        # Attributes
        self.panel = wx.Panel(self)

        # Setup Menus
```

```
menubar = wx.MenuBar()
helpmenu = wx.Menu()
helpmenu.Append(wx.ID_ABOUT, "About")
menubar.Append(helpmenu, "Help")
self.SetMenuBar(menubar)

# Setup StatusBar
self.CreateStatusBar()
self.PushStatusText("See About in the Menu")

# Event Handlers
self.Bind(wx.EVT_MENU, self.OnAbout, id=wx.ID_ABOUT)
```

2. All that's left now is to put together the information we want to show and then use it to create an `AboutBox`. Here's how:

```
def OnAbout(self, event):
    """Show the about dialog"""
    info = wx.AboutDialogInfo()

    # Make a template for the description
    desc = ["\nwxPython Cookbook Chapter 6\n",
            "Platform Info: (%s,%s)",
            "License: Public Domain"]
    desc = "\n".join(desc)

    # Get the platform information
    py_version = [sys.platform,
                  ", Python ",
                  sys.version.split()[0]]
    platform = list(wx.PlatformInfo[1:])
    platform[0] += (" " + wx.VERSION_STRING)
    wx_info = ", ".join(platform)

    # Populate with information
    info.SetName("AboutBox Recipe")
    info.SetVersion("1.0")
    info.SetCopyright("Copyright (C) Joe Programmer")
    info.SetDescription(desc % (py_version, wx_info))

    # Create and show the dialog
    wx.AboutBox(info)
```

How it works...

The first part of this recipe is the creation of the **About** menu item. This item is a standard item on each platform. On Windows and GTK, it appears in the **Help** menu, and on OS X, it appears in the **Application** menu. As the standard `ID_ABOUT ID` is used, wxPython will automatically move the **About** menu item to the appropriate location when run on OS X.

Next is the `AboutDialogInfo` class, which is used to contain the data to show in `AboutBox`. This object is populated by using its various set functions to put in the information to display. In this recipe, we just used a small number of them to ensure that we ended up with a native dialog. There are many additional fields that can be filled out to include the application's licensing information as well as lists of contributors, but using the additional fields may result in a generic dialog being used on some platforms. Once the `AboutDialogInfo` object is populated with all the information that you want to display, you can use the `AboutBox` function to create and show a dialog that presents all the information as a modal dialog:

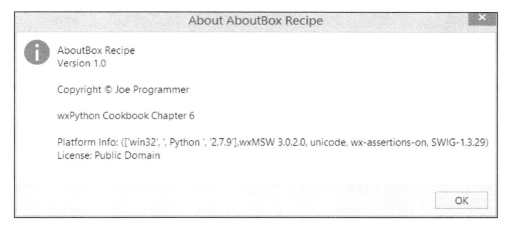

There's more...

As mentioned, the `AboutDialogInfo` class supports a number of additional parameters that can be used to add additional information to `AboutBox`. Only the GTK platform supports most of these additional fields natively, so using them will result in the framework falling back to the generic version of the dialog on Windows and OS X. Take a look at the following table:

Additional fields	Description
`SetArtists`	This sets a list of names to give credits to graphic artists
`SetDevelopers`	This sets a list of names to give credits to developers
`SetDocWriters`	This sets a list of names to give credits to documentation writers
`SetIcon`	This sets a custom display icon on the dialog

Additional fields	Description
`SetLicense`	This sets a full license text to be displayed
`SetTranslators`	This sets a list of names to give credits to translators
`SetWebsite`	This sets a URL to create a hyperlink from

See also

▶ The *Exploring menus and shortcuts* recipe in *Chapter 2, Common User Controls,* for more examples on using menus and stock IDs

7

Requesting and Retrieving Information

In this chapter, we will cover:

- ▸ Selecting files with FileDialog
- ▸ Searching text with FindReplaceDialog
- ▸ Filtering through choices
- ▸ Retrieving multiple selections
- ▸ Using Print dialogs
- ▸ Guiding selections with Wizard

Introduction

Being able to retrieve input from users in an application is a critical task that nearly any application needs to perform. There are many common types of input information that applications use to perform a wide array of common tasks. This includes operations such as opening and saving files, choosing documents to print, getting search queries to use to perform searches on data, and many others. In this chapter, we will take a look at several commonly provided controls and dialogs in the wxPython library to discuss how to perform many of these common everyday tasks as well as discuss a few of the less-known controls to consider the kinds of tasks that they can help you solve.

Selecting files with FileDialog

Many applications operate on files as their input and output; `FileDialog` is the standard way to allow users to either choose files to open or input a file path to save the current document on. In this recipe, we will take a look at how to use `FileDialog` to open and save text files.

Getting ready

This recipe will add the `Open` and `Save` functionalities to the text editor application that we started back in *Chapter 2, Common User Controls*. It only covers the functionality of `FileDialog`, but you may want to jump back to the *Exploring menus and shortcuts* and *Working with ToolBars* recipes from *Chapter 2, Common User Controls*, for a refresher on how the base code in this recipe is started.

How to do it...

Perform the following steps:

1. First, let's start by importing the needed modules and overriding the base class' constructor, as follows:

    ```
    import wx

    # Code from Chapter 2 Working with Toolbars
    import chapter2Editor as c2e

    class FileEditor(c2e.EditorWithToolBar):
        def __init__(self, parent, title):
            super(FileEditor, self).__init__(parent, title)

            types = ["Python (*.py)|*.py",
                     "Text Files (*.txt)|*.txt"]
            self.wildcard = "|".join(types)
            self._file = None
    ```

2. Now, let's add a property to keep track of the path of the file that we are editing:

    ```
    @property
    def file(self):
        return self._file

    @file.setter
    def file(self, value):
    ```

```
self._file = value
if self._file:
    self.Title = self._file
```

3. Next, we need to override the event handler for the menu and toolbar events to add in handlers for the `Save` and `Open` actions:

```
def OnFile(self, event):
    """Override base event handler"""
    if event.Id == wx.ID_OPEN:
        self.OpenFile()
    elif event.Id == wx.ID_SAVE:
        self.SaveFile()
    else:
        super(FileEditor, self).OnFile(event)
```

4. Now that everything is set up, it's time to first use `FileDialog` in `Open` mode to open files. We can do this using the following code:

```
def OpenFile(self):
    dlg = wx.FileDialog(self, "Open File",
                        wildcard=self.wildcard,
                        style=wx.FD_OPEN)
    if dlg.ShowModal() == wx.ID_OK:
        path = dlg.GetPath()
        with open(path, "rb") as handle:
            text = handle.read()
            self.txt.SetValue(text)
            self.file = path
    dlg.Destroy()
```

5. The last step is to add support to save the changes back in a file on the disk:

```
def SaveFile(self):
    if self.txt.IsModified():
        if self.file is None:
            # Save As
            style = wx.FD_SAVE|wx.OVERWRITE_PROMPT
            dlg = wx.FileDialog(self, "Save As",
                                wildcard=self.wildcard,
                                style=style)
            if dlg.ShowModal() == wx.ID_OK:
                self.file = dlg.GetPath()
        self.WriteToDisk(self.file)

def WriteToDisk(self, fileName):
```

```
with open(fileName, "wb") as handle:
    handle.write(self.txt.Value)
self.file = fileName
```

How it works...

Starting in the constructor, we defined a wildcard string. This is a specially formatted string used by `FileDialog` to set up filters of the file types that users are allowed to open. This string is formatted as a series of pipes (|) or delimited tokens. The first part is a free description string, and the second token is a list of wildcard patterns to match the file type. Multiple patterns can be specified for a given file type by separating each wildcard with a semicolon (;).

`FileDialog` operates primarily in two different modes: `Open` or `Save`. The only real difference between the two is in the appearance and text on the affirmative button of the dialog. In each case, users have the ability to either select or enter a filename at a given path on the system. Once the dialog is dismissed, the full entered path can be retrieved from the dialog with its `GetPath` method.

In the save dialog case, we first checked whether we already have a path, and if so, we could simply use this to save the text from the control to the file. If not, we could show `FileDialog` to get the path for the new file from the user to write the data to.

See also

- ▶ Take a look at the *Exploring menus and shortcuts* recipe in *Chapter 2, Common User Controls*, to note where the example application in this recipe was started

Searching text with FindReplaceDialog

In many applications that display textual data, it can be useful to provide a way to search this data for keywords or sequences of text. `FindReplaceDialog` can be used for this task. The dialog allows us several options to control how a search is to be carried out as well as to specify the string that is being looked for in the data. However, it is the application's responsibility to take this data and perform the actual search. In this recipe, we will take a look at how to retrieve data from the dialog and use it to perform a basic search.

Getting ready

This recipe will use the class created in the previous recipe of this chapter, *Selecting files with FileDialog*, as a base to show how to use `FindReplaceDialog`, so you may want to take a quick look back at the preceding recipe before proceeding with this one.

How to do it...

Here are the steps that you need to perform:

1. First, we need to import the code from the previous recipe and extend the art map, as follows:

```
import wx
import fileEditor as FE # previous recipe module

# extend the art map
FE.ArtMap[wx.ID_FIND] = wx.ART_FIND
FE.ArtMap[wx.ID_REPLACE] = wx.ART_FIND_AND_REPLACE
```

2. Next, we need to subclass `FileEditor` and add some attributes to manage `FindDialog`:

```
class TextEditorWithFind(FE.FileEditor):
    def __init__(self, parent, title):
        super(TextEditorWithFind, self).__init__(parent, title)

        self.finddlg = None
        self.finddata = wx.FindReplaceData()
        self._SetupFindActions()
```

3. This next function adds the menu, toolbar, and event handlers for the search feature that we will add:

```
def _SetupFindActions(self):
    menub = self.MenuBar
    editMenu = menub.GetMenu(1)
    editMenu.AppendSeparator()
    self.RegisterMenuAction(editMenu, wx.ID_FIND,
                            self.OnEdit)
    self.RegisterMenuAction(editMenu, wx.ID_REPLACE,
                            self.OnEdit)

    toolb = self.ToolBar
    toolb.AddSeparator()
    toolb.AddEasyTool(wx.ID_FIND)
    toolb.AddEasyTool(wx.ID_REPLACE)
    toolb.Realize()

    # Find Dialog actions
    self.Bind(wx.EVT_FIND, self.OnFind)
    self.Bind(wx.EVT_FIND_NEXT, self.OnFind)
    self.Bind(wx.EVT_FIND_REPLACE, self.OnReplace)
    self.Bind(wx.EVT_FIND_REPLACE_ALL, self.OnReplaceAll)
    self.Bind(wx.EVT_FIND_CLOSE, self.OnFindClose)
```

4. The next method is used to create `FindReplaceDialog` in the mode, depending on whether a find or replace action is requested:

```
def _InitFindDialog(self, mode):
    if self.finddlg:
        self.finddlg.Destroy()
    style = (wx.FR_NOUPDOWN|wx.FR_NOMATCHCASE
             |wx.FR_NOWHOLEWORD)
    if mode == wx.ID_REPLACE:
        style |= wx.FR_REPLACEDIALOG
        title = "Find/Replace"
    else:
        title = "Find"
    dlg = wx.FindReplaceDialog(self, self.finddata,
                                title, style)
    self.finddlg = dlg
```

5. Now, we will override the event handler to show the dialog. Execute the following for this:

```
def OnEdit(self, event):
    if event.Id in (wx.ID_FIND, wx.ID_REPLACE):
        self._InitFindDialog(event.Id)
        self.finddlg.Show()
    else:
        super(TextEditorWithFind, self).OnEdit(event)
```

6. Now that we have everything in place to show `FindReplaceDialog`, we will start adding event handlers for the buttons on the dialog through the following code:

```
def OnFind(self, event):
    findstr = self.finddata.GetFindString()
    if not self.FindString(findstr):
        wx.Bell() # beep at the user for no match
```

7. These next two methods handle the **Replace** buttons on the dialog:

```
def OnReplace(self, event):
    rstring = self.finddata.GetReplaceString()
    fstring = self.finddata.GetFindString()
    cpos = self.GetInsertionPoint()
    start, end = cpos, cpos
    if fstring:
        if self.FindString(fstring):
            start, end = self.txtctrl.GetSelection()
    self.txtctrl.Replace(start, end, rstring)
```

```
def OnReplaceAll(self, event):
    rstring = self.finddata.GetReplaceString()
    fstring = self.finddata.GetFindString()
    text = self.txt.GetValue()
    newtext = text.replace(fstring, rstring)
    self.txt.SetValue(newtext
```

8. When the dialog is closed, it sends an event; we will use an event handler for this event to destroy the dialog, as follows:

```
def OnFindClose(self, event):
    if self.finddlg:
        self.finddlg.Destroy()
```

9. The last step is a helper function that finds and highlights matches in the text control:

```
def FindString(self, findstr):
    text = self.txt.GetValue()
    csel = self.txt.GetSelection()
    if csel[0] != csel[1]:
        cpos = max(csel)
    else:
        cpos = self.txt.GetInsertionPoint()

    if cpos == self.txt.GetLastPosition():
        cpos = 0

    # Simple case insensitive search
    text = text.upper()
    findstr = findstr.upper()
    found = text.find(findstr, cpos)
    if found != -1:
        end = found + len(findstr)
        self.txt.SetSelection(end, found)
        self.txt.SetFocus()
        return True
    return False
```

How it works...

The `FindReplaceDialog` dialog's appearance is controlled by the flags set in `FindReplaceData`, which is passed to the dialog's constructor. We kept a reference to this data because the dialog also uses this data object as a way to pass information about the kind of search to perform back on the parent window:

The data entered in the **Find what** or **Replace with** field is copied into the `FindReplaceData` object when one of the action buttons is clicked on in the dialog. For example, in the `OnFind` event handler that is executed when the **Find Next** button is clicked on, we retrieved the search string that is entered in the dialog by calling the `GetFindString` method of `FindReplaceData`. Then, in `FindString`, we used the current cursor position as a starting point to begin the search; if a match is found, the method will set the selection in the control to highlight the match and make it visible to the user.

There's more...

In this recipe, we disabled some of the search options in the dialog that allow the user to specify whether the search is for **Match whole word only** and/or **Match case**. When these options are available, it is also necessary to factor them in to how the search is performed. In order to check whether the user has selected either of these options, the `FindReplaceData` object's `GetFlags` method can be used to retrieve a bitmask that can be checked to see which options were selected if any. Take a look at the following table:

Find option flags	Description
`wx.FR_DOWN`	The down option is selected, and the search should be done going toward the end of the document
`wx.FR_MATCHCASE`	The **Match case** check box is selected, and the search should be performed as case sensitive
`wx.FR_WHOLEWORD`	The **Match whole word only** check box is selected, and the search should be performed to match the entire word

Filtering through choices

Sometimes, there is a need to present users with the number of times they need to choose some or all of the items. There are several ways to perform this task, one of which is using the `ItemsPicker` control. This control allows presenting a list of choices in the `ListBox` control and filtering them into another `ListBox` control of selections. In this recipe, we will see how to make use of `ItemsPicker` to select from a group of choices.

How to do it...

Perform the following steps:

1. First, let's make a window to hold the `ItemsPicker` control, as follows:

```
class ListMaker(wx.Frame):
    def __init__(self, parent, choices, title):
        super(ListMaker, self).__init__(parent, title=title)
        style = IP.IP_REMOVE_FROM_CHOICES
        self.picker = IP.ItemsPicker(self, choices=choices,
                                     ipStyle=style)
        style = wx.TE_RICH2|wx.TE_MULTILINE
        self.txt = wx.TextCtrl(self, style=style)
        self._DoLayout()
        self.picker.Bind(IP.EVT_IP_SELECTION_CHANGED,
                         self.OnChange)
```

2. Next, let's do the layout of `ItemsPicker` and `TextCtrl` using the following code:

```
    def _DoLayout(self):
        sizer = wx.BoxSizer(wx.VERTICAL)
        sizer.Add(self.picker, 1, wx.EXPAND)
        sizer.Add(self.txt, 1, wx.EXPAND)
        self.Sizer = sizer
        self.SetInitialSize()
```

3. For the last step, we just need to define the event handler for when the selections change in the picker, as follows:

```
    def OnChange(self, event):
        msg = "Shopping List:\n\n"
        items = "\n".join(event.GetItems())
        self.txt.Value = msg + items
```

How it works...

The `ItemsPicker` control is a composite control made up of a panel with two `ListBox` controls and two buttons. The choices that are provided to the control's constructor are filled into the `ListBox` control on the left-hand side of the control. Then, any selected items can be moved to the selection's `ListBox` control on the right-hand side. The **Remove** button can be used to move selected items from the `ListBox` control on the right-hand side back to the unselected items on the left-hand side. Each time one of the control's buttons is clicked on, the control emits the `EVT_IP_SELECTION_CHANGED` event to notify the application of the changes in the state of the control. In this recipe, we used the event to update the shopping list in `TextCtrl` at the bottom of the window.

There's more...

The `ItemsPicker` control has a few optional style flags that can be applied to modify its behavior. Take a look at the following table:

Style flag	Description
IP_DEFAULT_STYLE	The items are inserted in the order that they are moved and copied from the choices box to the selected box in
IP_SORT_CHOICES	This sorts the items in the choice's `ListBox` control
IP_SORT_SELECTED	This sorts the items in the selected `ListBox` control
IP_REMOVE_FROM_CHOICES	This removes items from one box to another when the **Add** or **Remove** buttons are clicked on

See also

> ▶ Take a look at the next recipe in this chapter, *Retrieving multiple selections*, for another way to request and retrieve multiple choices from a user

Retrieving multiple selections

For a quick and ready-to-use way to pop up and retrieve multiple selections from a user, `MultiChoiceDialog` can be used to provide a simple and quick way for users to select multiple items by enabling checkboxes next to items in a list. The use of checkboxes provides a simple way for users to make selections without having to perform multiselections using the *Shift* or *Ctrl* keys when clicking on items in the list. So, in this recipe, we will use `MultiChoiceDialog` to request the user to provide a list of the bitmap resources that they would like to see displayed in the application.

How to do it...

Here are the steps that you need to perform:

1. First, let's make a simple panel that we will use to display the chosen bitmaps with, as follows:

```
class BitmapPanel(wx.Panel):
    def __init__(self, parent):
        super(BitmapPanel, self).__init__(parent)

        sizer = wx.WrapSizer(wx.HORIZONTAL)
        self.Sizer = sizer

    def AddBitmap(self, artID):
        bmp = wx.ArtProvider.GetBitmap(artID)
        sbmp = wx.StaticBitmap(self, bitmap=bmp)
        self.Sizer.Add(sbmp, 0, wx.ALL, 8)
        self.Layout()
```

2. Next, we will make a panel to contain `BitmapPanel` and a `Button` using the following code:

```
class MainPanel(wx.Panel):
    def __init__(self, parent):
        super(MainPanel, self).__init__(parent)

        sizer = wx.BoxSizer(wx.VERTICAL)
        self.panel = BitmapPanel(self)
        sizer.Add(self.panel, 1, wx.EXPAND)
        button = wx.Button(self, label="Pick Images")
        sizer.Add(button, 0, wx.ALIGN_CENTER_HORIZONTAL)
        button.Bind(wx.EVT_BUTTON, self.OnGetChoices)

        self.Sizer = sizer
```

3. Now, let's define the event handler to show `MuliChoiceDialog` and get the choices from the user through the following script:

```
    def OnGetChoices(self, event):
        msg = "Pick the are resources to view."
        ids = [ x for x in dir(wx)
                if x.startswith("ART_") ]
        dlg = wx.MultiChoiceDialog(self, msg,
                                   "Pick Images", ids)
        if (dlg.ShowModal() == wx.ID_OK):
            for selection in dlg.GetSelections():
```

```
            theId = getattr(wx, ids[selection])
            self.panel.AddBitmap(theId)
```

4. For the last step, let's wrap up `MainPanel` into a `Frame`:

```
class BitmapViewer(wx.Frame):
    def __init__(self, parent, title):
        super(BitmapViewer, self).__init__(parent,
                                           title=title)

        sizer = wx.BoxSizer(wx.VERTICAL)
        self.panel = MainPanel(self)
        sizer.Add(self.panel, 1, wx.EXPAND)

        self.Sizer = sizer
```

How it works...

`MultiChoiceDialog` takes a list of strings to display in a list. Each of the items in the list is displayed with a checkbox that can be clicked on to select it. In this recipe, we populated the dialog with all of the art resource IDs that are built into the wxPython library. When the dialog is displayed, the user can select the art resource that they would like to view in the main window of the application:

An important point to note is that it is necessary to keep a reference to the list of strings that were passed into the dialog, as was done in the `OnGetChoices` method. This is necessary as the `GetSelections` method of the dialog only returns the indexes of the selected items and not the actually selected values. So, after retrieving the selected indexes, we must use the indexes to get the values from the source's list of choices.

After getting all the selected art resource IDs, they are used to look up the bitmap resources from ArtProvider and then put them into the StaticBitmap controls to be displayed in the BitmapPanel class.

There's more...

Selections in the dialog can be preselected before showing the dialog using the dialog's SetSelections method. This method takes a list of index values to select. Each item in the list specifies the index of an item in the list of choices that should have its checkbox selected.

See also

▶ Refer to the *Showing MessageBox* recipe in *Chapter 6, Ways to Notify and Alert*, for a recipe about the standard MessageBox dialog

Using Print dialogs

Adding printing support to an application can be a difficult task, as there are a number of tasks that need to be handled. These include selecting and configuring a printer, translating your on-screen presentation to paper and ultimately sending the data to the printer.

In wxPython, there are three dialog classes related to printing: PageSetupDialog, PreviewFrame, and Printer. In addition to these, there are a number of supporting classes that must be used in conjunction with these dialogs in order to add printing support to an application. This recipe shows some of the basics of how to use the wxPython printing framework by creating a class that encapsulates the usage of the three printing dialogs and allows an application to print a bitmap.

How to do it...

Here are the steps to perform in this recipe:

1. First, we will make a subclass of wx.Printout. This object is used by the print framework to control how the printout is rendered to the media, as follows:

```
class BitmapPrintout(wx.Printout):
    def __init__(self, bmp, data):
        super(BitmapPrintout, self).__init__()

        self.bmp = bmp
        self.data = data
```

2. Next, there are some virtual methods that we need to override in `Printout`. These first two methods are used by the framework to query information about the print job. They are quite simple here as we will only support single-page printing in this recipe, as follows:

```
def GetPageInfo(self):
    # min, max, from, to
    return (1, 1, 1, 1)

def HasPage(self, page):
    return page == 1
```

3. Now, to finish up this class, we need to override the `OnPrint` method to render the page:

```
def OnPrintPage(self, page):
    dc = self.GetDC()
    bmpW, bmpH = self.bmp.GetSize()

    # Check if we need to scale the bitmap to fit
    self.MapScreenSizeToPageMargins(self.data)
    rect = self.GetLogicalPageRect()
    w, h = rect.width, rect.height
    if (bmpW > w) or (bmpH > h):
        # Image is large so apply some scaling
        self.FitThisSizeToPageMargins((bmpW, bmpH),
                                       self.data)
        x, y = 0, 0
    else:
        # try to center it
        x = (w - bmpW) / 2
        y = (h - bmpH) / 2

    # Draw the bitmap to DC
    dc.DrawBitmap(self.bmp, x, y)

    return True
```

4. With the `Printout` object defined, let's now make a helper class to manage the print dialogs and data:

```
class BitmapPrinter(object):
    def __init__(self, parent):
        super(BitmapPrinter, self).__init__()

        self.parent = parent
        self.print_data = wx.PrintData()
```

5. This next method is a helper method to create the `Printout` object for use by the print dialogs:

```
def CreatePrintout(self, bmp):
    assert bmp.IsOk(), "Invalid Bitmap!"
    data = wx.PageSetupDialogData(self.print_data)
    return BitmapPrintout(bmp, data)
```

6. Now, we can get to using `PageSetupDialog` through the following code:

```
def PageSetup(self):
    # Make a copy of our print data for the setup dialog
    dlg_data = wx.PageSetupDialogData(self.print_data)
    print_dlg = wx.PageSetupDialog(self.parent, dlg_data)
    if print_dlg.ShowModal() == wx.ID_OK:
        # Update the printer data
        newdata = dlg_data.GetPrintData()
        self.print_data = wx.PrintData(newdata)
        paperid = dlg_data.GetPaperId()
        self.print_data.SetPaperId(paperid)
    print_dlg.Destroy()
```

7. Next, let's add a function to show `PreviewFrame`, as follows:

```
def Preview(self, bmp):
    printout = self.CreatePrintout(bmp)
    printout2 = self.CreatePrintout(bmp)
    preview = wx.PrintPreview(printout, printout2,
                              self.print_data)
    preview.SetZoom(100)
    if preview.IsOk():
        pre_frame = wx.PreviewFrame(preview,
                                    self.parent,
                                    "Print Preview")
        # Default size of the preview frame needs help
        dsize = wx.GetDisplaySize()
        width = self.parent.GetSize()[0]
        height = dsize.GetHeight() - 100
        pre_frame.SetInitialSize((width, height))
        pre_frame.Initialize()
        pre_frame.Show()
    else:
        wx.MessageBox("Failed to create print preview",
                      "Print Error",
                      style=wx.ICON_ERROR|wx.OK)
```

8. The last part to wrap up this helper class is a method to show the `Print` dialog:

```
def Print(self, bmp):
    pdd = wx.PrintDialogData(self.print_data)
    printer = wx.Printer(pdd)
    printout = self.CreatePrintout(bmp)
    result = printer.Print(self.parent, printout)
    if result:
        # Store copy of print data for future use
        dlg_data = printer.GetPrintDialogData()
        newdata = dlg_data.GetPrintData()
        self.print_data = wx.PrintData(newdata)
    elif printer.GetLastError() == wx.PRINTER_ERROR:
        wx.MessageBox("Printer error detected.",
                      "Printer Error",
                      style=wx.ICON_ERROR|wx.OK)
    printout.Destroy()
```

How it works...

The `BitmapPrinter` class encapsulates the three main print-related tasks that an application may need to support: printer setup, print preview, and printing. This class is the interface that any application wanting to allow printing bitmaps would use for all of its printing needs. All that the application requires is a bitmap, and all that it needs to do is to use one of the three methods: `PageSetup`, `Preview`, and `Print`. So, let's take a look at how this class and these three methods work.

The constructor takes one argument for a parent window. This is used as the parent window for all the dialogs. This will typically be an application's main window. We will also create and store a reference to a `PrintData` object in the constructor. All print dialogs use `PrintData` in one form or another as a way to pass around and retrieve the settings to be used in the print job. This allows us to save any print configuration changes a user may make while using one of the dialogs.

The `PageSetup` method is used to create and show `PageSetupDialog`. To use `PageSetupDialog`, we will first create a `PageSetupDialogData` object by passing our `PrintData` object to its constructor, so it will use any settings that may already be persisted in our data object. We will then simply create the dialog by passing in the `PageSetupDialogData` object. If the dialog is closed by the **OK** button, we would then get `PrintData` from the dialog and make a copy of it to store. It is important to make a copy because when `PageSetupDialog` is destroyed, it will delete the data.

The `Preview` method creates a preview of what the printout will look like and shows it with `PreviewFrame`. `PreviewFrame` requires a `PrintPreview` object. To create the `PrintPreview` object, it must be passed two `Printout` objects and a `PrintData` object. A `Printout` object does the actual work of rendering what will be printed by the printer. We will come back to the details of how `printout` works when we get to our `BitmapPrintout` class. The first `Printout` object is used for `PreviewFrame`, and the second one is used for the actual printing if the user clicks on the **Print** button of `PreviewFrame`.

The `Print` method creates a `printer` object that will show the `printer` dialog when its `Print` method is called. As with the `Preview` object, the `printer` object is created with some `PrintData` and an instance of a `printout` object. When the `Print` dialog's **Print** button is clicked on, it uses the `printout` object to tell the physical printer what to draw on the paper.

The `BitmapPrintout` class implements a `printout` object that is used to print a single bitmap on a single sheet of paper at a time. The `printout` objects must always be subclassed in order to implement the application-specific requirements of the data that needs to be printed as the base class only provides an interface of virtual methods to be overriden in the subclass. In our class, we overrode three methods: `GetPageInfo`, `HasPage`, and `OnPrintPage`. The first two are used to return information about the number of pages that will be printed; as we are only supporting one page, these are quite trivial in this recipe. The `OnPrintPage` method does the actual drawing on the printer's device context. This method gets called to do the drawing of each page that will be printed.

The drawing of the `printout` object is done using the device context object returned by the call to `GetDC`. The use of device contexts is covered in detail in *Chapter 8*, *User Interface Primitives*; so, just to keep things simple, all we did here was set the scale of the canvas calculations to try and center the image on the paper and then use DC's `DrawBitmap` method to draw the bitmap to the device context. For an example of the `BitmapPrinter` class in action, refer to the sample code that accompanies this chapter.

There's more...

Take a look at the example code that comes with this chapter for an example that shows how to use `BitmapPrinter` in a sample application. Try and extend this example to support printing multiple pages by allowing more than one image to be selected and overriding some of the additional virtual methods in your `Printout` class. The `OnPreparePrinting` method can be overridden and used to calculate how many pages the job may have based on the contents.

See also

▶   Refer to *Chapter 8*, *User Interface Primitives*, for more information on how to use `DeviceContexts`

Guiding selections with Wizard

Sometimes, it is necessary to guide a user through a series of actions to complete some choices. Wizard provides a way to accomplish this task by chaining a number of panels together in a special dialog that guides users through a series of sequential choices. In this recipe, we will take a look at what it takes to put together a Wizard dialog in the wxPython framework.

How to do it...

Perform the following steps:

1. First, we need to import an extra submodule to get access to the Wizard classes, as follows:

```
import wx
import wx.wizard as WIZ
```

2. Next, let's make a base class to use for the pages in the custom `Wizard` class that we will make:

```
class PageBase(WIZ.WizardPageSimple):
    def __init__(self, parent, title):
        super(PageBase, self).__init__(parent)

        sizer = wx.BoxSizer(wx.VERTICAL)
        label = wx.StaticText(self, label=title)
        font = wx.Font(18, wx.SWISS, wx.NORMAL, wx.BOLD)
        label.SetFont(font)
        sizer.Add(label, 0, wx.ALIGN_CENTER)
        line = wx.StaticLine(self)
        sizer.Add(line, 0, wx.EXPAND|wx.ALL, 5)
        self.Sizer = sizer

    def IsValid(self):
        return True
```

3. Now, we will make one more page class that has an input field to capture the responses from the user:

```
class QuestionPage(PageBase):
    def __init__(self, parent, title):
        super(QuestionPage, self).__init__(parent, title)

        self.field = wx.TextCtrl(self)
        self.Sizer.Add(self.field, 0, wx.ALL|wx.EXPAND, 5)

    def IsValid(self):
        val = self.field.Value.lower()
```

```
if not val or " dont " in val:
    return False
return super(QuestionPage, self).IsValid()
```

4. The next step is to start defining our `Wizard` class, as follows:

```
class MyWizard(WIZ.Wizard):
    def __init__(self, parent, title):
        bmp = wx.Bitmap("Monty_python_foot.gif")
        super(MyWizard, self).__init__(parent,
                                        title=title,
                                        bitmap=bmp)
        self._pages = list()
        self._SetupPages()

        self.Bind(WIZ.EVT_WIZARD_PAGE_CHANGING,
                  self.OnChanging)
```

5. This next function sets up all the pages in `Wizard` and links them together:

```
def _SetupPages(self):
    page1 = QuestionPage(self, "What is your Name?")
    self._pages.append(page1)
    page2 = QuestionPage(self, "What is your Quest?")
    self._pages.append(page2)
    WIZ.WizardPageSimple.Chain(page1, page2)
    q3 = "What is your Favorite Color?"
    page3 = QuestionPage(self, q3)
    self._pages.append(page3)
    WIZ.WizardPageSimple.Chain(page2, page3)
```

6. This event handler is used to see whether the request on the current page has been successfully entered by the user:

```
def OnChanging(self, event):
    if not event.Page.IsValid():
        event.Veto()
        wx.MessageBox("Into the Volcano!", "Fail!")
        self.Close()

    elif event.Page.GetNext() is None:
        wx.MessageBox("Go on. Off you go.", "Success!")
```

7. For the last step, we will add a convenience method to start the `Wizard` by using the following code:

```
def Run(self):
    firstPage = self._pages[0]
    self.FitToPage(firstPage)
    return self.RunWizard(firstPage)
```

How it works...

As can be seen in the following screenshot, the pages are displayed in the area to the right of the bitmap and above the buttons. The rest of the area is a part of the `Wizard` dialog:

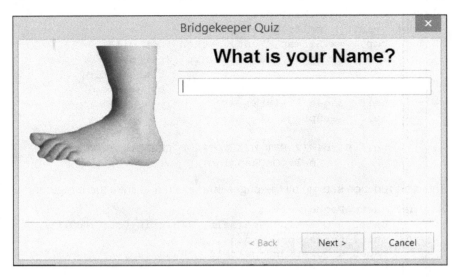

The `Wizard` dialog is initialized by being given a starting page to run from; each of the pages that it can navigate to are discovered through `GetNext`/`GetPrev` interface methods of `WizardPage`. When the `Wizard` dialog's **Next** or **Back** buttons are clicked on, it queries the current page to find which page should be navigated to. Once it finds the last page in the chain, the **Next** button becomes a **Finish** button to exit `Wizard`.

In our `PageBase` class, we added an additional `IsValid` interface method that our `OnPageChanging` method uses to check whether the user entered a valid answer to the question. If a valid answer is entered, then the page change is allowed to continue; otherwise, a failure message is displayed and `Wizard` is closed.

There's more...

If you find yourself needing more control over how the pages transition, such as allowing pages to be skipped or dynamically changing the content of the pages, you can derive your Wizard pages from `PyWizardPage`, which has virtual versions of the navigation methods that can be overridden to dynamically decide which pages are next or to modify the contents of the next page.

8
User Interface Primitives

In this chapter, we will cover:

- ▶ Painting in your UI
- ▶ Drawing basic shapes
- ▶ Customizing grid labels
- ▶ Drawing gradients with GraphicsContext
- ▶ Recreating native controls with RendererNative

Introduction

At times, you may find yourself running into needs in your application that cannot be solved in the way you want by any of the default controls provided by the library. Alternatively, there may be cases where the control works but doesn't fit the look and feel you wish to provide in your application. This is where the use of user interface primitives comes in; these primitives are the basic drawing routines that are used to draw and display all of the visible content of the graphical user interface on screen.

The wxPython library provides access to a number of classes that can be used to draw custom displays on screen. These functions include DeviceContexts, pens, brushes, colors, and a number of other high-level functions that allow you to create and draw whatever you like on a canvas or, in some cases, even provide custom renders to customize the existing controls. In this chapter, we will take an overview of how to use DeviceContexts to draw custom controls and graphics on screen.

Painting in your UI

All the controls that are visible on screen are created by being painted to DeviceContext. wxPython offers the `EVT_PAINT` event to allow user codes to paint their own custom displays on a canvas, such as a window, control, or panel. With this level of control on how the UI is painted, your imagination is the limit; however, in this recipe, we will start simple with just the basics of using `EVT_PAINT` and `PaintDC`. We will use these features to make a custom panel control that can use bitmaps as its background.

How to do it...

You need to perform the following steps:

1. First, let's start by defining the custom `Panel` class that will use a bitmap for the background, as follows:

```
class ImageBackground(wx.Panel):
    def __init__(self, parent, bitmap):
        super(ImageBackground, self).__init__(parent)

        self.bitmap = bitmap
        self.width = bitmap.Size.width
        self.height = bitmap.Size.height

        self.Bind(wx.EVT_PAINT, self.OnPaint)
```

2. Next, we will define the `OnPaint` event handler, which will draw the bitmap on the panel:

```
    def OnPaint(self, event):
        dc = wx.PaintDC(self)

        w, h = self.Size
        cols = (w / self.width) + 1
        rows = (h / self.height) + 1
        x = y = 0

        # Tile the image on the background
        for r in range(rows):
            for c in range(cols):
                dc.DrawBitmap(self.bitmap, x, y, True)
                x += self.width
            y += self.height
            x = 0
```

3. Now that we have the custom panel defined, let's put it to use by making a subclass of it:

```
class BinaryInput(ImageBackground):
    def __init__(self, parent, bmp):
        super(BinaryInput, self).__init__(parent, bmp)

        self._DoLayout()

        self.Bind(wx.EVT_BUTTON, self.OnButton)
```

4. Next, it's time to do the layout on the panel:

```
def _DoLayout(self):
    sizer = wx.BoxSizer(wx.VERTICAL)
    self.txt = wx.TextCtrl(self, style=wx.TE_MULTILINE)
    sizer.Add(self.txt, 0, wx.EXPAND|wx.ALL, 5)
    hsizer = wx.BoxSizer()
    hsizer.AddStretchSpacer()
    btn0 = wx.Button(self, label="0")
    btn1 = wx.Button(self, label="1")
    hsizer.AddMany([(btn0,), ((20, 20),), (btn1,)])
    hsizer.AddStretchSpacer()
    sizer.Add(hsizer, 0, wx.EXPAND)
    self.Sizer = sizer
```

5. Next, let's make an event handler for the button, as follows:

```
def OnButton(self, event):
    obj = event.EventObject
    lbl = obj.Label
    self.txt.AppendText(lbl)
```

6. For the last step, let's wrap the panel up in a frame and set it up with a bitmap to use for the background. Use the following code for this:

```
class MyFrame(wx.Frame):
    def __init__(self, parent, title):
        super(MyFrame, self).__init__(parent, title=title)

        sizer = wx.BoxSizer()
        bmp = wx.Bitmap("binary.png")
        self.panel = BinaryInput(self, bmp)
        sizer.Add(self.panel, 1, wx.EXPAND)

        self.Sizer = sizer
        self.SetInitialSize((400, 200))
```

How it works...

As can be seen in the following screenshot, a panel is displayed with a custom background that is created from a bitmap, which was given to the `ImageBackground` class that we made at the beginning of this recipe:

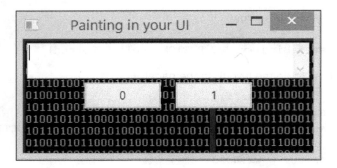

The important point to take note of in this recipe is the use of the `EVT_PAINT` event and the `OnPaint` function that we defined. When using `EVT_PAINT`, it is required to create `PaintDC` in the event handler that is bound to it. Failing to do so will result in an error on some platforms. Inside `OnPaint`, we do some simple calculations to see how many times we need to tile and repeat the image on the background to fill the space. Then, in the loop, we will use the `DrawBitmap` method of `PaintDC` to draw a bitmap at a given point on the panel.

The point is represented by an *x* and *y* coordinate system on the two-dimensional plane. This point is where the upper-left corner of the bitmap will be drawn from; using this, we can draw one column of the bitmap at a time by moving the *x* position over by the width of the bitmap, and it needs to be repeated each time. Then, we can continue down for each row the same way by moving the *y* position by the height of the bitmap.

The `OnPaint` event handler gets called automatically every time the framework detects that the screen should be redrawn. This happens, for example, every time the window is resized or something is dragged over the top of the window.

See also

▶ Refer to the next recipe in this chapter, *Drawing basic shapes*, for some more examples of the functionality a `DeviceContext` such as `PaintDC` can provide

Drawing basic shapes

The `DeviceContext` API in wxPython provides several methods to draw different kinds of shapes. These primitive shapes can be used as the basis for creating controls, animations, and anything else that you may want to draw on the screen. In this recipe, we will use several `DeviceContext` drawing routines in order to paint a little scene on a panel.

How to do it...

Here are the steps that you need to perform:

1. First, let's set up a panel to use as the canvas for the little scene that we will draw in this recipe, as follows:

```python
import wx

class Canvas(wx.Panel):
    def __init__(self, parent):
        super(Canvas, self).__init__(parent)

        self.Bind(wx.EVT_PAINT, self.OnPaint)
        self.Bind(wx.EVT_ERASE_BACKGROUND, self.OnBackground)
```

2. Now, we will define the `EVT_ERASE_BACKGROUND` handler to fill the background:

```python
    def OnBackground(self, event):
        sky = wx.TheColourDatabase.FindColour("SKY BLUE")
        event.DC.SetBrush(wx.Brush(sky))
        event.DC.DrawRectangleRect(self.Rect)
```

3. Next, we will define the `EVT_PAINT` handler to draw the shapes to make up the simple scene that we will draw in this recipe:

```python
    def OnPaint(self, event):
        dc = wx.PaintDC(self)
        w, h = self.Size

        self.DrawSun(dc, h, w)
        self.DrawGrass(dc, h, w)
        self.DrawStopSign(dc, h, w)
```

4. The `DrawSun` method here shows you how to draw a circle:

```python
    def DrawSun(self, dc, h, w):
        dc.SetBrush(wx.YELLOW_BRUSH)
        dc.SetPen(wx.RED_PEN)
        dc.DrawCircle(w - 55, 55, 50)
```

5. The `DrawGrass` method here uses a filled rectangle to represent the grass:

```
def DrawGrass(self, dc, h, w):
    dc.SetBrush(wx.GREEN_BRUSH)
    dc.SetPen(wx.GREEN_PEN)
    dc.DrawRectangle(0, h - 75, w, 75)
```

6. For the last step, we will draw a stop sign with the `DrawPolygon` method:

```
def DrawStopSign(self, dc, h, w):
    dc.SetBrush(wx.RED_BRUSH)
    dc.SetPen(wx.BLACK_PEN)
    dc.DrawPolygon([(70, 190), (70, 215), (85, 230),
                    (110, 230), (125, 215), (125, 190),
                    (110, 175), (85, 175)])
    dc.SetTextForeground(wx.WHITE)
    dc.DrawText("STOP", 80, 193)
    dc.DrawLine(97, 230, 97, h - 75)
```

How it works...

The `EVT_ERASE_BACKGROUND` event is fired when the `PaintDC` object is created in the `EVT_PAINT` handler. It allows the window to paint the background before the contents. We used `DrawRectangleRect` to fill the background with a light blue color.

Then, once `OnBackground` completes its work, the `OnPaint` method will continue to execute. In each of the methods, we can get a look at some of the ways to draw different shapes. Starting in `DrawSun`, we set `Brush` and `Pen` on the `PaintDC` object; `Brush` will be used to fill the shape, and `Pen` will be used to draw the outline. Using the built-in `DrawCircle` method, all that is required are the *x* and *y* coordinates for where the center of the circle should be placed on the panel and then to give the radius of the circle to draw it.

Moving on to `DrawGrass`, we changed which `Brush` and `Pen` were in use in order to draw a rectangle to represent the grass in the scene. Then, as a way to show how to draw more complex shapes, we used the `DrawPolygon` method to draw a stop sign in the `DrawStopSign` method. The `DrawPolygon` method takes a list of points in the (*x*, *y*) coordinate system and then draws a line to connect the points from the first to last. Finally, we used the `DrawText` and `DrawLine` methods to finish up the sign by adding the label and signpost.

There's more...

The `PaintDC` object has several other drawing methods that can be used to draw different shapes or effects. Take a look at the following table:

Method name	Description
DrawArc	This draws an arc of a circle centered on a point
DrawBitmap	This draws a bitmap with its upper-left corner at a given point
DrawCheckMark	This draws a check mark
DrawEllipse	This draws an ellipse
DrawImageLabel	This draws a bitmap and then a text label on top of it
DrawPoint	This draws a point (dot) at a given coordinate
DrawRotatedText	This draws text at a rotated angle
DrawRoundedRectangle	This draws a rectangle with rounded corners
DrawSpline	This draws a spline between a series of points

Customizing grid labels

Many owner-drawn controls, such as grid, allow client code to override or customize the look of the control by installing custom renderers. This is possible because the controls are owner drawn in the `wx` framework and not by the underlying system toolkit. Also, the `Grid` control itself provides a wide array of options for customization. In this recipe, we will take a look at the `GridWithLabelRendererMixin` class to discuss a convenient way to customize how row and column labels are rendered in the `Grid` control.

Getting ready

This recipe will assume that you are familiar with the basics of using a `DeviceContext`, so if you haven't already, you may want to take a quick review of the earlier recipes in this chapter.

How to do it...

Perform the following for this recipe:

1. First, let's look at the imports we need and define a grid class that uses the mixin. Run the following code:

    ```
    import wx
    import wx.grid as gridlib
    import wx.lib.mixins.gridlabelrenderer as glr

    class FancyGrid(gridlib.Grid, glr.GridWithLabelRenderersMixin):
    ```

```
        def __init__(self, parent):
            gridlib.Grid.__init__(self, parent)
            glr.GridWithLabelRenderersMixin.__init__(self)
```

2. Next, we will define a custom render to use on the row labels, as follows:

```
class FancyRowLabelRenderer(glr.GridLabelRenderer):
    def __init__(self, color):
        super(FancyRowLabelRenderer, self).__init__()
        self.color = color

    def Draw(self, grid, dc, rect, row):
        dc.SetBrush(wx.Brush(self.color))
        dc.DrawRoundedRectangleRect(rect, -0.4)
        text = grid.GetRowLabelValue(row)
        hAlign, vAlign = grid.GetRowLabelAlignment()
        self.DrawText(grid, dc, rect, text, hAlign, vAlign)
```

3. Similarly, we will also define a render to customize the column labels:

```
class FancyColLabelRenderer(glr.GridLabelRenderer):
    def __init__(self, color):
        super(FancyColLabelRenderer, self).__init__()
        self.color = color

    def Draw(self, grid, dc, rect, col):
        dc.SetBrush(wx.Brush(self.color))
        dc.DrawRoundedRectangleRect(rect, -0.4)
        text = grid.GetColLabelValue(col)
        hAlign, vAlign = grid.GetColLabelAlignment()
        self.DrawText(grid, dc, rect, text, hAlign, vAlign)
```

4. To finish up the renders, we will define one more to control how the corner cell is displayed, as follows:

```
class FancyCornerLabelRenderer(glr.GridLabelRenderer):
    def __init__(self, color):
        super(FancyCornerLabelRenderer, self).__init__()
        self.color = color

    def Draw(self, grid, dc, rect, rc):
        dc.SetBrush(wx.Brush(self.color))
        dc.DrawRectangleRect(rect)
        bmp = wx.ArtProvider.GetBitmap(wx.ART_HARDDISK)
        x = rect.left + (rect.width - bmp.Width) / 2
        y = rect.top + (rect.height - bmp.Height) / 2
        dc.DrawBitmap(bmp, x, y, True)
```

5. Now, for the last step, let's take a look at how to put it all together:

```python
class GridPanel(wx.Panel):
    def __init__(self, parent):
        super(GridPanel, self).__init__(parent)

        self.grid = FancyGrid(self)
        squareGrid = 5
        self.grid.CreateGrid(squareGrid, squareGrid)

        # Assign our custom corner renderer
        corRender = FancyCornerLabelRenderer("#FF6666")
        self.grid.SetCornerLabelRenderer(corRender)

        # Assign column and row renderers
        rowRender = FancyRowLabelRenderer("#6666FF")
        self.grid.SetDefaultRowLabelRenderer(rowRender)
        colRender = FancyColLabelRenderer("#66FF66")
        self.grid.SetDefaultColLabelRenderer(colRender)

        self.Sizer = wx.BoxSizer()
        self.Sizer.Add(self.grid, 1, wx.EXPAND)
```

How it works...

The `GridWithLabelRenderersMixin` class adds several methods to the grid to simplify the applying of renderers to the labels of the grid. It allows us to assign renderers to customize how the columns, rows, and corner headers of the grid look:

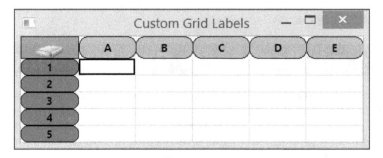

The mixin makes use of the objects derived from `GridLabelRender`. These objects have a virtual `Draw` method that needs to be overridden to customize the drawing of the headers. The `Draw` method is called with a reference to the grid that it's drawing on, a `DeviceContext` to draw in, the dimensions of the label, and the index of the row or column that is being drawn.

For each of the three regions, we created a separate renderer that customizes the display of each region. The renderers for the column and row headers are quite similar, in that they draw the labels as rounded rectangles filled with a specified color and then draw the label at the center of the rounded rectangle. For the corner cell, we instead opted to fill the rectangle with a specified color and draw a bitmap in the space, which in this example, is a generic image of a hard disk retrieved from the system art provider.

Finally, to put it all together, we created an instance of each renderer and used them as the default renderers for different areas. This way, a single renderer can be applied to all columns or rows in the grid with no further interaction needed from our application.

There's more...

If there is a need to add a special indicator or to show some rows or columns differently, then each can row or column can optionally be assigned its own specific renderer instance to further customize how it is displayed. This is achieved using either the `SetRowLabelRenderer` or `SetColLabelRenderer` methods that are added to the grid by the mixin used in this recipe. These methods each take an index to specify which row or column and `GridLabelRenderer` instance to use for this column.

See also

> ▶ For an additional example of the uses of grid, refer to the recipes found in *Chapter 5, Data Displays and Grids*

Drawing gradients with GraphicsContext

`GraphicsContext` is another drawing utility class, similar to a `DeviceContext`, which provides some higher-level or advanced functionality for drawing on screen. The `GraphicsContext` is a new feature that was added back in wxPython 2.8, which can be used to access some of the platform's higher-level drawing functionality-supporting features, such as antialiasing, a floating point precision coordinate system, alpha blending, gradient brushes, and a handful of other advanced methods. In this recipe, we will make use of some of these features, most notably the gradient brush, to draw a custom control that uses gradient shading to give more depth to the control's appearance.

How to do it...

Here are the steps you need to perform:

1. First, we will start by deriving a class from `PyControl` to use it as a custom StaticText-like control, as follows:

```
class PodLabel(wx.PyControl):
    def __init__(self, parent, label, color):
        super(PodLabel, self).__init__(parent,
                                        style=wx.NO_BORDER)
        self._label = label
        self._color = color

        self.Bind(wx.EVT_PAINT, self.OnPaint)
```

2. Next, we need to override a virtual method to determine the best size for the control based on the specified label:

```
    def DoGetBestSize(self):
        txtsz = self.GetTextExtent(self._label)
        size = wx.Size(txtsz[0] + 10, txtsz[1] + 6)
        return size
```

3. Next, we will implement the `EVT_PAINT` event handler to draw the control:

```
    def OnPaint(self, event):
        gcdc = wx.GCDC(wx.PaintDC(self))
        gc = gcdc.GetGraphicsContext()

        # Get the working rectangle we can draw in
        rect = self.GetClientRect()

        # Setup the GraphicsContext
        pen = gc.CreatePen(wx.TRANSPARENT_PEN)
        gc.SetPen(pen)
        rgb = self._color.Get(False)
        alpha = self._color.Alpha() *.2 # fade to transparent
        color2 = wx.Colour(*rgb, alpha=alpha)
        x1, y1 = rect.x, rect.y
        y2 = y1 + rect.height
        gradbrush = gc.CreateLinearGradientBrush(x1, y1,
                                                 x1, y2,
                                                 self._color,
                                                 color2)

        gc.SetBrush(gradbrush)
```

```
# Draw the background
gc.DrawRoundedRectangle(rect.x, rect.y,
                             rect.width, rect.height,
                             rect.height/2)

# Use the GCDC to help draw the aa text
gcdc.DrawLabel(self._label, rect, wx.ALIGN_CENTER)
```

4. For the last step, we will create a few instances of the preceding custom control to show an example of how to use it:

```
class MyPanel(wx.Panel):
    def __init__(self, parent):
        super(MyPanel, self).__init__(parent)

        vsizer = wx.BoxSizer(wx.VERTICAL)
        for color in (wx.RED, wx.GREEN, wx.BLUE):
            hsizer = wx.BoxSizer(wx.HORIZONTAL)
            label = PodLabel(self, "Label String", color)
            hsizer.Add(label, 0, wx.ALIGN_CENTER_VERTICAL)
            hsizer.Add(wx.TextCtrl(self), 1,
                        wx.EXPAND|wx.ALIGN_CENTER_VERTICAL)
            vsizer.Add(hsizer, 0, wx.EXPAND|wx.ALL, 5)
        self.Sizer = vsizer
```

How it works...

In this recipe, we created a custom StaticText-like control that has a rounded appearance and gradient-filled background, which is shown in the following screenshot:

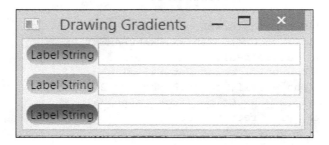

There are two important points to take from this recipe. The first is the overriding of the `DoGetBestSize` method, which is used to return the suggested "best" size that the control should be sized to when it is contained in a sizer-controlled layout. We used this method to set the size of the control to be just a little wider and taller than the space needed for the label to be displayed. This method is an important override to provide when making custom controls such as this.

The second point and the main focus of this recipe is the use of `GraphicsContext` in the `OnPaint` method. We indirectly created `GraphicsContext` using the required `PaintDC` class to create GCDC. This object wraps the `DeviceContext` and provides a DC, such as an API, while using `GraphicsContext` internally.

Here, we used GCDC primarily to get access to `GraphicsContext` to create `GraphicsBrush` that is capable of drawing a blended gradient when it is used to fill the background of the control. The brush is created by specifying the points that specify the rectangle of a gradient pattern that will be used to fill the background and the colors to start and end the gradient with. The brush we created is to specify the size of the rectangle for our `PodLabel` so that one smooth gradient is drawn from the top to the bottom of the control.

There's more...

The `GraphicsContext`, in addition to the linear gradient brush, also supports a radial gradient brush through its `CreateRadialGradientBrush` method, which results in creating a brush that draws a gradient in a circular pattern radiating from the center outward.

Take this chance to play with the sample, and switch the brush type or adjust the parameters on the gradient brush used in this recipe to see how adjusting these parameters affects the way the background gets filled.

Recreating native controls with RendererNative

The `RendererNative` class is a drawing class that encapsulates and exposes routines for drawing parts of the native system's UI components. It provides high-level drawing functions that allow you to draw items such as a `Button` or `CheckBox` control in a DeviceContext without needing to know any of the details of how it is done. This is a powerful feature that can allow you to create your own custom widgets that still maintain a native look. In this recipe, we will recreate the `CheckBox` control to add support to align the label below the `CheckBox` control.

How to do it...

Perform the following:

1. First, we will start with the constructor for our custom `CheckBox` control:

```
class CustomCheckBox(wx.PyControl):
    def __init__(self, parent, label, style=0):
        style |= wx.NO_BORDER
        super(CustomCheckBox, self).__init__(parent,
                                             style=style)
```

```
                    self.Label = label
                    self._value = False
                    self._style = style
                    self._clickIn = False

                    self.Bind(wx.EVT_PAINT, self.OnPaint)
                    self.Bind(wx.EVT_LEFT_DOWN, self.OnLeftDown)
                    self.Bind(wx.EVT_LEFT_UP, self.OnLeftUp)
                    self.Bind(wx.EVT_ENTER_WINDOW,
                              lambda event: self.Refresh())
                    self.Bind(wx.EVT_LEAVE_WINDOW,
                              lambda event: self.Refresh())
```

2. Next, we need to add a few methods to help match the CheckBox API to get and set its value:

```
          def GetValue(self):
              return self._value

          def SetValue(self, value):
              self._value = value

          Value = property(GetValue, SetValue)
```

3. Next, we will define the event handlers to catch when the user clicks on the control:

```
          def OnLeftDown(self, event):
              self._clickIn = True

          def OnLeftUp(self, event):
              if self._clickIn:
                  self.Value = not self.Value
              self._clickIn = False

              # generate a checkbox event
              etype = wx.wxEVT_COMMAND_CHECKBOX_CLICKED
              event = wx.CommandEvent(etype)
              event.EventObject = self
              event.Checked = self.Value
              self.ProcessEvent(event)

              self.Refresh()
```

4. Next, we will override DoGetBestSize to calculate the size needed for the control, as follows:

```
          def DoGetBestSize(self):
              txtsz = self.GetTextExtent(self.Label)
```

```
        cboxsz = (16, 16)
        size = None
        if self._style & wx.ALIGN_BOTTOM:
            size = wx.Size(txtsz[0] + 4,
                           txtsz[1] + cboxsz[1] + 6)
        else:
            size = wx.Size(txtsz[0] + cboxsz[0] + 6,
                           max(txtsz[1], cboxsz[1]) + 4)
        return size
```

5. This next method is a helper method that we will use to help determine how to draw the `CheckBox` control depending on what state it is currently in. These flags are passed to `RendererNative` when drawing the control:

```
def GetFlags(self):
    flag = 0
    pt = self.ScreenToClient(wx.GetMousePosition())
    hitResult = self.HitTest(pt)

    if not self.Enabled:
        flag |= wx.CONTROL_DISABLED
    elif hitResult == wx.HT_WINDOW_INSIDE:
        flag |= wx.CONTROL_CURRENT

    if self.Value:
        flag |= wx.CONTROL_CHECKED
    return flag
```

6. For the final step, we just need to define the `OnPaint` handler and draw the control based on the style flags and current state of the control:

```
def OnPaint(self, event):
    dc = wx.GCDC(wx.PaintDC(self))
    renderer = wx.RendererNative.Get()
    txtsz = dc.GetTextExtent(self.Label)
    cboxsz = (16, 16)

    cx, cy, lx, ly = 2, 2, 2, 2
    if self._style & wx.ALIGN_BOTTOM:
        cx += (self.Rect.Width / 2) - (cboxsz[0] / 2)
        ly += (2 + cboxsz[1])
    else:
        cy += (self.Rect.Height / 2) - (cboxsz[1] / 2)
        lx += (2 + cboxsz[0])
        ly += (self.Rect.Height / 2) - (txtsz[1] / 2)
```

```
cboxRect = wx.Rect(cx, cy, cboxsz[0], cboxsz[1])
flag = self.GetFlags()
renderer.DrawCheckBox(self, dc, cboxRect, flag)

dc.DrawText(self.Label, lx, ly)
```

How it works...

The default wxPython `CheckBox` control allows the label to be either to its right or left. In this recipe, we created a new `CheckBox` control that looks similar to the native one provided by the system but is completely owner-drawn and supports having the label to the right of or below the control.

We recreated this custom `CheckBox` control by handling a few mouse events and `EVT_PAINT` to draw the control. The cursor enters and leaves window events are used to tell the control to refresh so that `OnPaint` is called to update the control with any hover-over highlighting that needs to be drawn. The left-click events are used to capture and toggle the state of the control to update its value from `True` to `False`, and vice versa, as well as to emit a `CheckBox` event so that users of the control can get `EVT_CHECKBOX` events when the value changes.

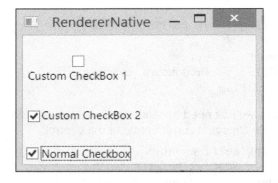

In order to draw this control, we had to do some calculations to determine the necessary space to reserve for the control in `DoGetBestSize`. Then, in `OnPaint`, we get a reference to the renderer using the static `Get` method of the `RendererNative` class. Then, calling the renderer's `DrawCheckBox` method will draw a `CheckBox` control of the given size and position defined by `Rect` passed to the method using the provided DC. The use of the flag mask that is determined in `GetFlags` is used to tell the renderer what state to draw the control in.

The `GetFlags` method checks a few things about the current state of the control in order to ensure that it is drawn with an expected appearance. The current position of the mouse cursor is checked to see whether it's over the control to apply the hover-over affect if it is supported by the system. If the control is currently not enabled, the `CONTROL_DISABLED` flag is applied. Finally, the current value of the control is checked to see whether the `CheckBox` control should be drawn in a checked state or not.

There's more...

The `RendererNative` class is capable of drawing several other common UI components as well; included here is a list some of the available methods:

Method	Description
DrawChoice	This draws a `Choice` control.
DrawComboBox	This draws a `ComboBox` control.
DrawComboBoxDropButton	This draws the button of a `ComboBox` control.
DrawDropArrow	This draws a drop arrow such as on the `ComboBox` button but with a transparent background.
DrawFocusRect	This draws a focus rectangle. This is the rectangle drawn around some controls when they have the focus.
DrawHeaderButton	This draws the header button as is found in `ListCtrl`.
DrawPushButton	This draws a normal button, such as `wx.Button`.
DrawRadioButton	This draws a `RadioButton` control.
DrawTextCtrl	This draws `TextCtrl`.
DrawTreeItemButton	This draws a button that is the same as what is used to expand/contract nodes in a `TreeCtrl`.

As we discussed with `DrawCheckBox`, the renderer's `Draw` method takes flags to draw the controls in different states. The following table contains a list of flags that can be applied to get different effects out of what is drawn by the renderer:

Flag	Description
CONTROL_CHECKABLE	An item can be checked
CONTROL_CHECKED	`CheckBox` or `RadioButton` is checked
CONTROL_CURRENT	The mouse is currently over the control
CONTROL_DISABLED	The control is disabled
CONTROL_EXPANDED	`TreeItemButton` is expanded
CONTROL_FLAT	This draws `CheckBox` with a flat border
CONTROL_FOCUSED	The control has a keyboard focus
CONTROL_ISDEFAULT	The draws a button as default button
CONTROL_PRESSED	The draws a button in a pressed state
CONTROL_UNDETERMINED	`CheckBox` in an undetermined state

9
Creating and Customizing Components

In this chapter, we will cover:

- ▶ Making your own dialog
- ▶ Validating user input
- ▶ Interacting with StatusBar
- ▶ Providing your own information window
- ▶ Creating a managed layout
- ▶ Drawing your own list control
- ▶ Implementing highlighting in StyledTextCtrl
- ▶ Creating a composite control
- ▶ Designing an owner-drawn control

Introduction

Throughout the earlier chapters of this book, we looked at many individual components and features provided by the wxPython library. There is a large amount of functionalities provided through the standard components of the library; however, as your applications and skills mature, you will undoubtedly begin to recognize the need for additional functionalities or behaviors to enhance your applications.

In this chapter, we will explore some approaches to building new advanced controls from existing components as well as creating our own new components from scratch in order to handle new use cases and provide additional features in our applications that wxPython does not provide out of the box.

Making your own dialog

Even though wxPython provides a large number of dialog options that can be used for most standard actions that any general application may need to perform, there will almost certainly come a time when you need to make your own custom dialog. There are many actions that can be better customized for a given application through their own dialogs. For example, wxPython provides `PasswordEntryDialog`, but this dialog only has one field for a password; if your application requires a login dialog, this likely won't meet your needs. So, in this recipe, we will take a look at how to create custom dialogs by making a user login dialog.

How to do it...

For this recipe, perform the following steps:

1. First, let's begin by defining the dialog subclass and its major parts using the following code:

```python
class LoginDialog(wx.Dialog):
    def __init__(self, parent, title="Login"):
        super(LoginDialog, self).__init__(parent, title=title)

        self._user = wx.TextCtrl(self)
        self._pass = wx.TextCtrl(self, style=wx.TE_PASSWORD)

        self.__DoLayout()
        self.SetInitialSize((350, -1))
```

2. Next, we will finish building the UI by performing the layout, as follows:

```python
    def __DoLayout(self):
        sizer = wx.BoxSizer(wx.VERTICAL)

        fieldSz = wx.FlexGridSizer(2, 2, 5, 8)
        fieldSz.AddGrowableCol(1, 1)
        userLbl = wx.StaticText(self, label="Username:")
        fieldSz.Add(userLbl, 0, wx.ALIGN_CENTER_VERTICAL)
        fieldSz.Add(self._user, 1, wx.EXPAND)
        passLbl = wx.StaticText(self, label="Password:")
        fieldSz.Add(passLbl, 0, wx.ALIGN_CENTER_VERTICAL)
```

```
fieldSz.Add(self._pass, 1, wx.EXPAND)

sizer.Add((10, 10))
sizer.Add(fieldSz, 1, wx.ALL|wx.EXPAND, 5)
btnSz = self.CreateButtonSizer(wx.OK|wx.CANCEL)
sizer.Add(btnSz, 0, wx.EXPAND|wx.BOTTOM|wx.TOP, 5)

self.Sizer = sizer
```

3. For the last step, we just need to define a couple of properties to give access to the dialog's data:

```
@property
def Username(self):
    return self._user.Value

@property
def Password(self):
    return self._pass.Value
```

How it works...

The `wx.Dialog` class is quite well equipped to make it an easy task for you to build your own custom dialogs. It has built-in handling to generate return codes from `ShowModal` based on the affirmative or escape buttons on the dialog. In this recipe, we created **OK** and **Cancel** buttons using the built-in `CreateButtonSizer` method of the dialog, which creates `StdDialogButtonSizer` that contains the requested buttons and does the proper platform-dependent layout.

With the built-in handling of the buttons, the dialog is dismissed when the user clicks on the **OK** or **Cancel** button. This choice determines the return value from `ShowModal`, which will be either `ID_OK` or `ID_CANCEL`. After the dialog is closed, the controlling application can retrieve the user's entries through the two properties that were provided to verify that the credentials were correctly entered.

There's more...

The `Dialog` class also provides means to hook custom buttons into the default handling of nonstandard buttons. The `SetAffirmativeId` method can be used to associate a user-defined button ID with the **OK** button, which will invoke any dialog validation as well as exit the dialog with the affirmative ID. Likewise, `SetEscapeId` can be used to associate a user-defined button as the **Cancel** button for the dialog.

If you want to handle exiting the dialog yourself in your event handler, you can call `EndModal` to end the modal state of the dialog and set the desired return code.

See also

▶ Take a look at the *Using the standard dialog button sizer* recipe in *Chapter 3, UI Layout and Organization*, for more details on StdDialogButtonSizer

▶ Also, check out the *Making dialog layout easy* recipe in *Chapter 3, UI Layout and Organization*, for another way to make a custom dialog

Validating user input

There may be times where you need to validate the input of a field before accepting a value from users. This validation could be done manually in the close handler for the dialog, but this leads to lots of duplicated and specialized code that would need to be copied to other dialogs. In order to help avoid this and provide a common way of validating user input, the wxPython library provides a Validator API that allows you to create custom Validator objects that can be assigned to controls. When a dialog's Validate method is called, all child controls of the dialog have their validation methods called as well to validate the input. In this recipe, we will discuss how to make a custom validator that can be used in TextCtrl.

How to do it...

Perform the following steps:

1. First, we will create a subclass of wx.PyValidator to implement our field-checking logic:

```
class InputValidator(wx.PyValidator):
    def __init__(self, checker = lambda s: s):
        super(InputValidator, self).__init__()
        assert callable(checker), "Checker must be callable"
        self._checker = checker
```

2. Next, it is necessary to provide a Clone method as the validator needs to be copied in some cases by the framework:

```
    def Clone(self):
        return InputValidator(self._checker)
```

3. Now, the next method is a required override to perform the validation of the data:

```
    def Validate(self, win):
        ok = False
        txt = self.GetWindow();
        if self._checker(txt.Value):
            txt.BackgroundColour = wx.NullColour
            txt.ForegroundColour = wx.NullColour
            ok = True
```

```
    else:
        # Indicate the invalid field
        txt.BackgroundColour = wx.RED
        txt.ForegroundColour = wx.WHITE
    txt.Refresh()
    return ok
```

4. For the last step, there are two additional required overrides that we will just provide default implementations for as we don't need to use this functionality:

```
def TransferToWindow(self):
    return True

def TransferFromWindow(self):
    return True
```

How it works...

The validator class we created in this recipe is intended for use with `TextCtrl`. The `TextCtrl` constructor can optionally refer to a `Validator` object, as shown in the following snippet. In this example, we will use `InputValidator` to add some simple sanity checks to the two fields. The `Username` field uses the validator to ensure that the field is not empty, while the `Password` field verifies that at least three characters are input:

```
class LoginDialog(wx.Dialog):
    def __init__(self, parent, title="Login"):
        super(LoginDialog, self).__init__(parent, title=title)

        self._user = wx.TextCtrl(self,
                                 validator=InputValidator(),
                                 name="Username")
        pvalid = InputValidator(lambda pw: pw and len(pw) > 2)
        self._pass = wx.TextCtrl(self,
                                 validator=pvalid,
                                 style=wx.TE_PASSWORD,
                                 name="Password")

        self.__DoLayout()
        self.SetInitialSize((350, -1))
```

When a `Dialog` constructor that has control on it is dismissed with its affirmative button, it calls the `Validate` method on itself. This results in the `Validate` method being called on the validators of each of its child controls. Our implementation of `Validate`, as used by `TextCtrl`, will turn the field red and return `False` when the input does not meet the criteria set by the optional `checker` method. The `checker` method's default implementation returns `True` when there is any text in the field, but it returns `False` when a field is left empty. When a `Validate` method returns `False`, the validation for the dialog fails and prevents the dialog from being dismissed.

There's more...

The `TransferToWindow` and `TransferFromWindow` methods can be implemented to transfer data to a control from a data structure and from the control back to the data structure, providing a way to collect data from the dialog.

For example, if your dialog provides a data property that was a dictionary mapping field name to value, then during `TransferToWindow`, which is called when a dialog is initialized, validator can populate the field with its initial value. In this case, during `TransferFromWindow`, which is called after a successful `Validate` method, the current value from the field can be copied back to the data dictionary. This can be a useful feature to implement for dialogs that have many fields or complex data structures that need to be returned to the caller.

Interacting with StatusBar

The `StatusBar` area is a common component to display information messages at the bottom of a frame. In its default form, it is really just a specialized panel that allows us to create separate regions for the displaying of read-only text fields. Normally, this control is a static control that the user cannot interact with; however, with a little customization, it is possible to add controls and other ways for users to interact with the `StatusBar` area. In this recipe, we will discuss how to add clickable area to `StatusBar` and use it to show a pop-up menu.

How to do it...

Here are the steps to be performed:

1. First, let's define the constructor to set up our custom `StatusBar` subclass, as follows:

    ```
    import wx
    CSB_MSG = 0
    CSB_ICON = 1

    class CustomStatusBar(wx.StatusBar):
        def __init__(self, parent):
    ```

```
        super(CustomStatusBar, self).__init__(parent)

        self.err, self.info = self._GetIcons()
        self.img = wx.StaticBitmap(self)
        self.menu = wx.Menu()
        self.menu.Append(wx.ID_COPY)

        self.SetFieldsCount(2)
        self.SetStatusWidths([-1, 24])

        self.Bind(wx.EVT_LEFT_UP, self.OnLeftUp)
        self.Bind(wx.EVT_MENU, self.OnMenu)
        self.Bind(wx.EVT_SIZE, self.OnSize)
```

2. Next is a simple helper function to get some bitmaps from `ArtProvider`:

```
    def _GetIcons(self):
        errBmp = wx.ArtProvider.GetBitmap(wx.ART_ERROR,
                                          wx.ART_MENU,
                                          (16,16))
        infoBmp = wx.ArtProvider.GetBitmap(wx.ART_INFORMATION,
                                           wx.ART_MENU,
                                           (16,16))
        return errBmp, infoBmp
```

3. This next method is the event handler for when the mouse's left button is clicked. We will use it to check and decide whether to show a pop-up menu or not:

```
    def OnLeftUp(self, event):
        pt = event.GetPosition()
        if self.GetFieldRect(CSB_MSG).Contains(pt):
            rect = self.GetFieldRect(CSB_MSG)
            self.PopupMenu(self.menu, (rect.x, rect.Bottom))
```

4. When the menu item in the pop-up menu is selected, it will be handled by the following event handler:

```
    def OnMenu(self, event):
        if event.Id == wx.ID_COPY:
            msg = self.GetStatusText()
            if wx.TheClipboard.Open():
                data = wx.TextDataObject(msg)
                wx.TheClipboard.SetData(data)
```

5. In order to support the positioning of `StaticBitmap` on `StatusBar`, we must manually respond to the `EVT_SIZE` events and update the position of `StaticBitmap` as the size of `StatusBar` changes:

```
def OnSize(self, event):
    rect = self.GetFieldRect(CSB_ICON)
    w, h = self.img.Size
    xpad = (rect.width - w) / 2
    ypad = (rect.height - h) / 2
    self.img.SetPosition((rect.x + xpad, rect.y + ypad))
    event.Skip()
```

6. For the final step, we just need to add a couple methods to put different types of messages in `StatusBar`, which will update the indicator bitmap according to the message's type. For this, we will use the following code:

```
def PushInfoMsg(self, msg):
    self.img.SetBitmap(self.info)
    self.img.Show()
    self.PushStatusText(msg)

def PushErrorMsg(self, msg):
    self.img.SetBitmap(self.err)
    self.img.Show()
    self.PushStatusText(msg)
```

How it works...

In this recipe, we created a `StatusBar` area that supports a context menu as a way to show how users can interact with this area of the UI as well as how to place a child control on `StatusBar`.

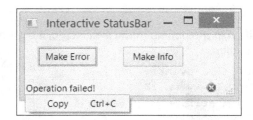

In order to show the menu, we bound to the `EVT_LEFT_UP` event, which will be fired when the left mouse button is clicked on the `StatusBar` area. The handler for this shows how you can determine which of the status fields was clicked in. This can be useful if you have multiple fields and want to invoke different actions depending on the portion of the control that is clicked on.

In order to support `StaticBitmap` being displayed in `StatusBar`, we had to bind to `EVT_SIZE`. This event will be fired every time `StatusBar` changes size. When the size of the control changes, we need to recalculate where `StaticBitmap` should be positioned, and reset its position so that it still shows up in the correct relative location.

Finally, we added a couple of new methods to use to push text to `StatusBar`; these methods allow specifying whether the message is an error or just information and provide additional feedback to users by switching between an error and information icon so as to indicate the severity of the message.

There's more...

The same strategy for control placement can be used to place almost any control in `StatusBar`. For example, if you wanted to add a `Gauge` control to show the progress feedback of a long-running task, the steps would be very similar to what was done with the status indicator of `StaticBitmap` in this recipe. You just need to create a status field and then use the size event to adjust the position and size of the `Gauge` control.

Providing your own information window

When the screen's real estate is at a premium or you just need to show some additional information that may not fit in with your main user interface, a floating `MiniFrame` or tool window can be a nice way to show this information while giving the user the ability to place it where they like or to dismiss it entirely when it is no longer needed. In this recipe, we will use a `MiniFrame` to make a file information window that shows detailed information about a file selected from the user's hard drive.

How to do it...

Here are the steps that you need to perform:

1. First, we need to import some additional modules from Python's standard library, as follows:

```
import os
from time import asctime, localtime
import stat
import mimetypes
import wx
```

2. Next, we will define a subclass of `MiniFrame` to wrap a panel that we will use to display the file's information:

```
class FileInfoDlg(wx.MiniFrame):
    def __init__(self, parent, fname):
```

```
                    style = wx.DEFAULT_DIALOG_STYLE
                    super(FileInfoDlg, self).__init__(parent,
                                                     style=style)

                    sizer = wx.BoxSizer()
                    panel = FileInfoPanel(self, fname)
                    sizer.Add(panel, 1, wx.EXPAND)
                    self.Sizer = sizer

                    self.Title = panel.Label
                    self.Fit()

                    self.Bind(wx.EVT_CLOSE, self.OnClose)

                def OnClose(self, event):
                    self.Destroy()
                    event.Skip()
```

3. Next, we need to define the constructor for the display panel:

```
class FileInfoPanel(wx.Panel):
    def __init__(self, parent, fname):
            super(FileInfoPanel, self).__init__(parent)

            self._file = fname
            self.Label = os.path.basename(fname)

            self._DoLayout()
```

4. Now, we can create the controls and lay out the panel using the following function:

```
            def _DoLayout(self):
                sizer = wx.BoxSizer(wx.VERTICAL)

                bmp = wx.ArtProvider.GetBitmap(wx.ART_INFORMATION,
                                               wx.ART_CMN_DIALOG)
                staticBmp = wx.StaticBitmap(self, bitmap=bmp)
                sizer.Add(staticBmp, 0, wx.ALIGN_CENTER_HORIZONTAL)

                info = self._GetInfo()
                isize = wx.FlexGridSizer(len(info), 2, 3, 5)
                for k,v in info:
                    label = wx.StaticText(self, label="%s:" % k)
                    isize.Add(label, 0, wx.ALIGN_RIGHT)
                    isize.Add(wx.StaticText(self, label=v), 0)

                sizer.Add(isize, 0, wx.EXPAND|wx.ALL, 5)
                self.Sizer = sizer
```

5. The following is a helper function used to get detailed information about the file:

```
def _GetInfo(self):
    fstat = os.stat(self._file)
    info = [
    ("Kind", GetFileType(self._file)),
    ("Size", GetSizeLabel(fstat[stat.ST_SIZE])),
    ("Created", asctime(localtime(fstat[stat.ST_CTIME]))),
    ("Modified", asctime(localtime(fstat[stat.ST_MTIME])))
    ]
    return info
```

6. For the last step, we will define a couple of utility methods to format the information on display, as follows:

```
def GetSizeLabel(bits):
    val = ('bytes', 'KB', 'MB', 'GB', 'TB')
    ind = 0
    while bits > 1024 and ind < len(val) - 1:
        bits = float(bits) / 1024.0
        ind += 1

    rval = "%.2f" % bits
    rval = rval.rstrip('.0')
    if not rval:
        rval = '0'
    rval = "%s %s" % (rval, val[min(ind, 4)])
    return rval


def GetFileType(fname):
    if os.path.isdir(fname):
        return "Folder"

    mtype = mimetypes.guess_type(fname)[0]
    if mtype is not None:
        return mtype
    else:
        return "Unknown"
```

How it works...

The usage of `MiniFrame` is nearly the same as that of `Frame`, except that it provides a slightly more compact top-level window that stays at the top of its parent window—it is similar to a dialog, except that it is not modal. This means that it can be displayed, and users can still continue to use the main window while `MiniFrame` is shown.

In this recipe, we used `MiniFrame` as a container to display some detailed information about a file. `FileInfoDlg` takes the path to a file as an argument to its constructor, and then performs a file stat operation to gather details about the file. Then, some basic formatting is applied to the data to change it into a more human readable representation, which is then displayed in the dialog using the `StaticText` controls.

See also

- ▶ Refer to the *Selecting files with FileDialog* recipe in *Chapter 7, Requesting and Retrieving Information*, for more options on working with files

Creating a managed layout

Though the wxPython `Sizer` API provides a relatively convenient way to handle programmatically laying out controls, you may find yourself repeating common layout patterns in your application. If your application has some common layout patterns that can be reused in many places, it can be convenient to encapsulate and hide some of the layout in some reusable `Panel` classes that manage specific ways of presenting the controls. In this recipe, we will create a managed layout panel that supports displaying a main content pane as well as a specialized function panel, which can be used to create and display application-defined buttons.

How to do it...

Perform the following steps:

1. First, we will define a class to be used as the layout manager and container for the function bar, as follows:

```
class FunctionPanel(wx.Panel):
    def __init__(self, parent):
        super(FunctionPanel, self).__init__(parent)

        self._pane = None
        self._bar = FunctionBar(self)
        self.Sizer = wx.BoxSizer(wx.VERTICAL)
        self.Sizer.Add(self._bar, 0, wx.EXPAND)

        self.Bind(wx.EVT_BUTTON, self.OnButton)
```

2. Next, we need to define the button handler to allow hiding FunctionBar:

```
    def OnButton(self, event):
        if event.Id == wx.ID_CLOSE:
            self.ShowFunctionBar(False)
        else:
            event.Skip()
```

3. The next two methods are used to access and manage the main content area of the FunctionPanel:

```
    @property
    def ContentPane(self):
        return self._pane

    def SetContentPane(self, pane):
        if self._pane == None:
            self.Sizer.Insert(0, pane, 1, wx.EXPAND)
        else:
            self.Sizer.Replace(self._pane, pane)
            self._pane.Destroy()
        self._pane = pane
        self.Layout()
```

4. For the last three methods of this class, we will add some API to manage FunctionBar, which is owned by FunctionPanel, as follows:

```
    def AddFunctionButton(self, id, label=wx.EmptyString):
        self._bar.AddFunctionButton(id, label)
```

```
def IsBarShown(self):
    return self._bar.IsShown()

def ShowFunctionBar(self, show=True):
    self._bar.Show(show)
    self.Layout()
```

5. For the last step of this recipe, we will define the `FunctionBar` class, which is a simple panel-based class that has a close button and can manage the layout of a number of user-defined buttons. Execute the following code:

```
class FunctionBar(wx.PyPanel):
    def __init__(self, parent):
        super(FunctionBar, self).__init__(parent)

        cbmp = wx.ArtProvider.GetBitmap(wx.ART_CLOSE,
                                        wx.ART_MENU)
        self._close = wx.BitmapButton(self, wx.ID_CLOSE, cbmp)
        self.Sizer = wx.BoxSizer(wx.HORIZONTAL)
        self.Sizer.Add(self._close, 0, wx.ALL, 5)

    def AddFunctionButton(self, id, label=wx.EmptyString):
        button = wx.Button(self, id, label)
        self.Sizer.Add(button, 0, wx.ALL, 5)
```

How it works...

`FunctionPanel` acts as the main container that can be used to display an application-defined content panel as its main display area. When `SetContentPane` is called, the panel that is passed in is inserted into the sizer-based layout in position zero. `FunctionBar` is kept at position one in the sizer, which keeps it below the main `ContentPane`.

During construction of `FunctionPanel`, an empty `FunctionBar` is created and placed in the layout of `FunctionPanel`. Any application's code using `FunctionPanel` must call its `AddFunctionButton` method to add application-defined buttons to the layout. The user, or the application code, can also control whether `FunctionBar` is visible or not by either clicking on its close button or by invoking its `ShowFunctionBar` method to toggle its visible states.

With these two classes, we can now create and reuse a common layout that has multiple controls and views without having to directly interact with the Sizers that are managed internally by each of the controls.

Drawing your own list control

If you need to display a list of some data but would like more control over how it looks, the `VListBox` control provides an interface to create an owner-drawn ListBox-like control. This control works by providing a number of pure virtual callback methods that you must override in your subclass in order to draw the list of items on demand. In this recipe, we will see how to create our own custom list of controls using `VListBox`.

How to do it...

Here are the steps that you need to perform:

1. First, we will start by creating a simple little data class to hold information about the custom list of items that we will create a display for, as follows:

```
import wx

class UserInfo(object):
    def __init__(self, name, email):
        super(UserInfo, self).__init__()

        self.name = name
        self.email = email
```

2. Next, we will start declaring our custom list box control that will be used to display this data using the following code:

```
class UserListBox(wx.VListBox):
    def __init__(self, parent, users):
        super(UserListBox, self).__init__(parent)

        self.bmp = wx.Bitmap("system-users.png",
                             wx.BITMAP_TYPE_PNG)
        self.bh = self.bmp.GetHeight()
        self.users = users

        self.SetItemCount(len(self.users))
```

3. This next method is a required override that is called to allow the subclass to provide the measured height of each item:

```
def OnMeasureItem(self, index):
    bmpHeight = self.bh + 4
    nsize = self.GetTextExtent(self.users[index].name)
    esize = self.GetTextExtent(self.users[index].email)
    return max(bmpHeight, nsize[1] + esize[1] + 6)
```

4. The following override is used to draw the separator between items in the list:

```
def OnDrawSeparator(self, dc, rect, index):
    oldpen = dc.GetPen()
    dc.SetPen(wx.Pen(wx.BLACK))
    dc.DrawLine(rect.x, rect.y,
                rect.x + rect.width,
                rect.y)
    rect.Deflate(0, 2)
    dc.SetPen(oldpen)
```

5. Now, this last override draws an individual row item in the list itself:

```
def OnDrawItem(self, dc, rect, index):
    # Draw the bitmap
    dc.DrawBitmap(self.bmp, rect.x + 2,
                  ((rect.height - self.bh) / 2) + rect.y)
    # Draw the name label to the right of the bitmap
    textx = rect.x + 2 + self.bh + 2
    lblrect = wx.Rect(textx, rect.y,
                      rect.width - textx,
                      rect.height)
    user = self.users[index]
    dc.DrawLabel(user.name, lblrect,
                 wx.ALIGN_LEFT|wx.ALIGN_TOP)
    dc.DrawLabel(user.email, lblrect,
                 wx.ALIGN_LEFT|wx.ALIGN_BOTTOM)
```

6. To finish it up, we will add a few methods to allow adding, removing, and accessing the control's data after it was created:

```
def AddItem(self, user):
    self.users.append(user)
    self.SetItemCount(len(self.users))

def GetItem(self, index):
    return self.users[index]

def RemoveItem(self, index):
    self.users.remove(index)
    self.SetItemCount(len(self.users))
```

How it works...

This new `UserListBox` control is specialized to display a list of users and their e-mail addresses along with a bitmap:

This control works based on a few pieces of information that we give to the base class about our data. In the constructor, we tell the base class how many items are initially in the control by calling `SetItemCount`. This lets the control know how many times it needs to call `OnMeasureItem`, which is used to calculate the height of each item in the control The returned heights are used to calculate the virtual space and scrollbar dimensions as well as to build the `Rect` objects that are later passed to `OnDrawSeparator` and `OnDrawItem`, which are used to draw the item and its data in the list box.

There's more...

There are a couple of additional methods that can be useful when implementing `VListBox`. Take a look at the following table:

Method	Description
`OnDrawItemBackground`	This method can be overridden to customize how the background of an item is drawn. The default base class implementation does the reasonable thing of drawing the background with the default color as well as of handling.
`IsSelected`	This method can be used to check whether an item is currently the selected item. We can check this in `OnDrawItem` if we want to add different effects, such as bolding the text in a selected item.

Implementing highlighting in StyledTextCtrl

The `StyledTextCtrl` provides a vast number of built-in lexers to provide syntax highlighting of various types of programming languages. Its API also allows us to extend these capabilities by providing our own custom styling of text in the buffer. This can be useful to create a text editor for your own custom markup or for special text formatting. In this recipe, we will take a look at how to implement custom text styling in `StyledTextCtrl`.

Getting ready

If you haven't already, you may want to jump back and take a look at the other `StyledTextCtrl` recipes in *Chapter 4, Containers and Advanced Controls*, to get some familiarity with `StyledTextCtrl` prior to continuing with this recipe.

How to do it...

Here are the steps for this recipe:

1. First, we need to import the `wx.stc` submodule and define a couple of IDs to use for our custom lexer's different styles, as follows:

```
import wx
import wx.stc as stc

# Style IDs for the KeywordLexer
STC_STYLE_KW_DEFAULT, \
STC_STYLE_KW_KEYWORD = range(2)
```

2. Next, we will define a new class to manage the styling of the text in `StyledTextCtrl`:

```
class KeywordLexer(object):
    def __init__(self):
        super(KeywordLexer, self).__init__()
        self._kw = list()

    def SetKeywords(self, kws):
        self._kw = kws
```

3. This next method will perform custom highlighting on `StyledTextCtrl` and allow us to specify and do the highlighting of user-assigned keywords:

```
def StyleText(self, event):
    buffer = event.EventObject
    lastStyled = buffer.GetEndStyled()
    startPos = buffer.PositionFromLine(lastStyled)
```

```
            startPos = max(startPos, 0)
            endPos = event.GetPosition()

            curWord = ""
            while startPos < endPos:
                c = chr(buffer.GetCharAt(startPos))
                curWord += c
                if c.isspace():
                    curWord = curWord.strip()
                    if curWord in self._kw:
                        style = STC_STYLE_KW_KEYWORD
                    else:
                        style = STC_STYLE_KW_DEFAULT

                    wordStart = max(0, startPos - (len(curWord)))
                    buffer.StartStyling(wordStart, 0x1f)
                    buffer.SetStyling(len(curWord), style)
                    buffer.SetStyling(1, STC_STYLE_KW_DEFAULT)
                    curWord = ""
                startPos += 1
```

4. Now, we will make a simple subclass of `StyledTextCtrl` that can make use of the `KeywordLexer` class, as follows:

```
class KeywordSTC(stc.StyledTextCtrl):
    def __init__(self, parent):
        super(KeywordSTC, self).__init__(parent)

        self._lexer = None

        self.Bind(stc.EVT_STC_STYLENEEDED, self.OnStyle)

    def OnStyle(self, event):
        if self._lexer:
            self._lexer.StyleText(event)
        else:
            event.Skip()
```

5. To finish up this subclass, we will override a couple of methods to inject the usage of `KeywordLexer` into `StyledTextCtrl`:

```
    def SetKeyWords(self, idx, keywords):
        if self._lexer:
            self._lexer.SetKeywords(keywords.split())
        else:
            super(KeywordSTC, self).SetKeyWords(idx, keywords)
```

```
def SetLexer(self, lexerID):
    if lexerID == stc.STC_LEX_CONTAINER:
        self._lexer = KeywordLexer()
    super(KeywordSTC, self).SetLexer(lexerID)
```

6. For the final step, we will show how to use this new class by putting it inside a simple frame:

```
class MyFrame(wx.Frame):
    def __init__(self, parent, title):
        super(MyFrame, self).__init__(parent, title=title)

        sizer = wx.BoxSizer()
        self.stc = KeywordSTC(self)
        sizer.Add(self.stc, 1, wx.EXPAND)

        self.stc.SetLexer(stc.STC_LEX_CONTAINER)
        self.stc.SetKeyWords(0, "Hello World Highlight Me")
        self.stc.StyleSetSpec(STC_STYLE_KW_DEFAULT,
                              "fore:#0000FF,back:#FFFFFF")
        self.stc.StyleSetSpec(STC_STYLE_KW_KEYWORD,
                              "fore:#FF0000,bold")
        self.Sizer = sizer
        self.SetInitialSize((400, 300))
```

How it works...

The EVT_STC_STYLEDNEEDED event is fired by StyledTextCtrl every time there is a change in the buffer that requires the styling to be updated. StyledTextCtrl only raises this event when the current lexer is set to STC_LEX_CONTAINER, which specifies that the container window is to provide the styling of the text.

We created KeywordLexer as a separate object that StyledTextCtrl delegates the handling of its styling to in the OnStyle event handler. The StyleText method of KeywordLexer first uses some information from the text control and event to determine the line in the text control that requires styling. It then looks through each character in the line until it finds a word. Once a word is found, the keyword list is checked to see whether it is one of the keywords that the keyword style should be applied to. If not, it uses the default style ID. The StartStyling is called to set the current styling position to the beginning of the word, followed by two calls to SetStyling to style the word with the selected style and then the space character using the default style.

As per the example usage shown in the MyFrame class, the text buffer displays all normal text in blue and any of the keywords *Hello*, *World*, *Highlight*, or *Me* in bold red text as they are typed into the buffer.

See also

▶ Take a look at the *Styling text in StyledTextCtrl* recipe in *Chapter 4, Containers and Advanced Controls*, for an example of using a built-in lexer

▶ Refer to the *Annotating StyledTextCtrl* recipe in *Chapter 4, Containers and Advanced Controls*, for some tips on using additional features of `StyledTextCtrl`

Creating a composite control

Sometimes, there are already controls that provide some functionalities that can meet most of your application's needs but maybe just not in the right way, or you find that you are missing some basic fundamental need that can be provided by another control. If you find yourself in this situation, it can be convenient to encapsulate the functionality of multiple controls into a single composite control that provides the combined functionality that is needed from both controls. In this recipe, we will make a composite control that is made up of the `TextCtrl` and `ColourSelect` controls, which provides both a visual and textual representation of the color on screen.

How to do it...

Perform the following steps:

1. First, we will start by deriving a class from `PyPanel` to use as the base container for our composite control, as follows:

```python
import wx
import wx.lib.colourselect as CSEL

class ColourEntry(wx.Panel):
    def __init__(self, parent, colour=wx.NullColour):
        super(ColourEntry, self).__init__(parent)

        self._cs = CSEL.ColourSelect(self, colour=colour)
        self._txt = wx.TextCtrl(self, style=wx.TE_READONLY)
        self._Synch()

        self.__DoLayout()

        self.Bind(CSEL.EVT_COLOURSELECT, self.OnCSel)
```

2. Next, we need to do the layout to group the individual controls into a single composite control:

```python
    def __DoLayout(self):
        self.Sizer = wx.BoxSizer(wx.HORIZONTAL)
```

```
self.Sizer.Add(self._txt, 0, wx.EXPAND|wx.ALL, 3)
tsize = self._txt.Size
self._cs.SetMinSize((tsize[1], tsize[1]))
self.Sizer.Add(self._cs, 0, wx.EXPAND|wx.ALL, 3)
```

3. This next method is used internally by the control to keep the `TextCtrl` display value in sync with `ColourSelect` control:

```
def _Synch(self):
    c = self.Colour
    self._txt.Value = c.GetAsString(wx.C2S_HTML_SYNTAX)
```

4. For the next step, we will intercept `ColourSelectEvent` to resync the text control as well as change the source of the event from `ColourSelect` to our composite control, as follows:

```
def OnCSel(self, event):
    self._Synch()
    # Reassign object to the ColourEntry instance
    event.SetEventObject(self)
    event.Skip() # allow propagation
```

5. For the last step, we will add some properties to extend the `PyPanel` API and give access to the values of the composite control via the following properties:

```
@property
def Colour(self):
    return self._cs.GetColour()

@Colour.setter
def Colour(self, colour):
    self._cs.SetColour(colour)
    self._Synch()

@property
def ColourCode(self):
    return self._txt.Value
```

How it works...

A `PyPanel` API is used to group the `TextCtrl` and `ColourSelect` controls into a single composite control that provides both a way to select a color as well as one to display the hex code for the color. The use of `TextCtrl` also means that the user can copy the hex value of the control to paste elsewhere if they would like to do so:

For simplicity and convenience, we reused `ColourSelectEvent`, which is emitted by the `ColourSelect` control for this custom control. However, in order to provide access to the `ColourCode` property of the new `ColourEntry` control, we switched out `EventObject` to refer to the `ColourEntry` control instead of `ColourSelect`. When this event is raised, it means the user has selected a different color from `ColourSelect`, so we also used this opportunity to synchronize `TextCtrl` to show the new hex code for the currently selected color.

See also

▸ Take a look at the *Laying out controls with Sizers* recipe in *Chapter 3, UI Layout and Organization*, where the concept of Sizer-based layouts is introduced

▸ Refer to the *Controlling the propagation of events* recipe in *Chapter 1, wxPython Starting Points*, for more information on the propagation of events and how to make custom event objects

Designing an owner-drawn control

If you find a need in your UI that can't be filled in just the right way by the controls provided in the wxPython library, you may find that you need to make your own. In the previous chapters of this book, we covered many of the building blocks that we can now look at for ways to leverage and combine to build our own controls. In this recipe, we will build our own container control that has a custom-drawn border and appearance.

Getting ready

Ensure that you have taken a look at *Chapter 8, User Interface Primitives*, before continuing with this recipe. This recipe will combine the use of `DeviceContext` and `Sizer` to create a custom control.

How to do it...

1. First, we will start by defining a subclass of `PyPanel` to derive our new control from, as follows:

```
class CaptionBox(wx.PyPanel):
    def __init__(self, parent, caption, flag=wx.VERTICAL):
        super(CaptionBox, self).__init__(parent,
                                         style=wx.NO_BORDER)
        self.Label = caption
        self._csizer = wx.BoxSizer(flag)

        self.__DoLayout()

        self.Bind(wx.EVT_PAINT, self.OnPaint)
```

2. In this next method, we will set up the internal Sizer layout of the control to reserve some space at the top, where we will draw the header box and caption:

```
def __DoLayout(self):
    msizer = wx.BoxSizer(wx.VERTICAL)
    tsize = self.GetTextExtent(self.Label)
    msizer.AddSpacer(tsize[1] + 3) # extra space for caption
    msizer.Add(self._csizer, 0, wx.EXPAND|wx.ALL, 8)
    self.SetSizer(msizer)
```

3. The `DoGetBestSize` method is a virtual one exposed by `PyPanel` in our implementation. We will use the base method but adjust the width to ensure that the caption can fit in cases when the caption is larger than the controls:

```
def DoGetBestSize(self):
    size = super(CaptionBox, self).DoGetBestSize()
    # Make sure there is room for the label
    tsize = self.GetTextExtent(self.Label)
    size.SetWidth(max(size.width, tsize[0]+20))
    return size
```

4. This next method can be called by the user code to add child controls into `CaptionBox`:

```
def AddItem(self, item):
    self._csizer.Add(item, 0, wx.ALL, 5)
```

5. Now, in `OnPaint`, we will draw the custom portions of the control, which includes a border and a small caption label at the top, as follows:

```
def OnPaint(self, event):
    dc = wx.PaintDC(self)
    rect = self.ClientRect

    # Get the system color to draw the caption
    ss = wx.SystemSettings
    color = ss.GetColour(wx.SYS_COLOUR_ACTIVECAPTION)
    txtcolor = ss.GetColour(wx.SYS_COLOUR_CAPTIONTEXT)
    dc.SetTextForeground(txtcolor)

    # Draw the border
    self.OnDrawBorder(dc, color, rect)

    # Add the Caption
    self.OnDrawCaption(dc, color, rect)
```

6. The next two methods are called during `OnPaint` to draw the border and caption section. They were extracted so that user-defined subclasses could override them to provide additional custom behavior if desired:

```
def OnDrawBorder(self, dc, color, rect):
    rect.Inflate(-2, -2)
    dc.SetPen(wx.Pen(color))
    dc.SetBrush(wx.TRANSPARENT_BRUSH)
    dc.DrawRectangleRect(rect)

def OnDrawCaption(self, dc, color, rect):
    tsize = dc.GetTextExtent(self.Label)
    rect = wx.Rect(rect.x, rect.y,
                   rect.width, tsize[1] + 3)
    dc.SetBrush(wx.Brush(color))
    dc.DrawRectangleRect(rect)
    rect.Inflate(-5, 0)
    dc.SetFont(self.GetFont())
    dc.DrawLabel(self.Label, rect, wx.ALIGN_LEFT)
```

How it works

The `CaptionBox` class that we created in this recipe can be used much in the same way as `StaticBox`. It supports a `VERTICAL` or `HORIZONTAL` layout as well as a caption label to be displayed at the top of the box. The `CaptionBox` class is a custom control that can be used as a container for other controls, as is shown in the following screenshot:

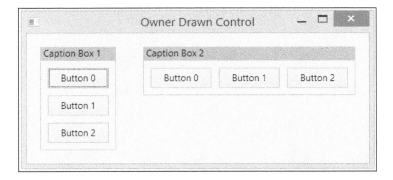

This control works using a `PyPanel` API and `Sizer` to control the space and size of the control. A `PyPanel` API is functionally equivalent to a normal panel, except that it provides additional access to the protected virtual methods of the underlying C++ control. We overrode one of these methods, `DoGetBestSize`, in order to measure the size of the label. The measurement is used to increase the overall size of the control to accommodate the header caption area in addition to the.

During `OnPaint`, the control's rectangle is used to define where the border should be drawn, and then, the space that was reserved at the top of the control is filled in with the caption bar and label. After this, the control is managed through its `AddItem` method, which allows users to place other controls inside of the `CaptionBox` class.

See also

▶ Refer to the *Recreating native controls with RendererNative* recipe in *Chapter 8, User Interface Primitives*, for another example of creating an owner-drawn control

10
Getting Your
Application Ready
for Release

In this chapter, we will cover:

- ► Storing your configuration with StandardPaths
- ► Saving the application's state
- ► Supporting internationalization
- ► Optimizing for OS X
- ► Handling errors gracefully
- ► Embedding your resources
- ► Distributing an application
- ► Updating your software

Introduction

Once you master how to build user interfaces for your Python applications using wxPython, the last important step is learning how to build the application and its supporting features. This includes managing user configuration, error handling, translations, and the building of an installer. In this chapter, we will explore all of these important aspects of putting together an application for release. Each recipe will provide you with detailed steps and explanations on how to make use of the features available in the wxPython framework to build your application's infrastructure in order to make your application ready to be released to your users.

Storing your configuration with StandardPaths

You have built your cross platform application, but in order to run your application on multiple platforms, you also need a standard way to access external resources, such as icons and user configuration data. Luckily, wxPython also has a cross platform way to access standard system paths. There are the platform-specific locations where applications store their user configuration data, which can be accessed through the `StandardPaths` singleton. In this recipe, we will take a look at how to set up and access application configuration data using `StandardPaths`.

How to do it...

Perform the following steps:

1. First, we will start by defining a class to help manage the configuration of an application:

```python
import os
import json
import wx

class AppConfig(object):
    _instance = None
    def __init__(self):
        super(AppConfig, self).__init__()

        # create base dir if it doesnt exist
        if not os.path.exists(self.UserConfigDir):
            os.mkdir(self.UserConfigDir)

        self.data = dict()
        if os.path.exists(self.ConfigFile):
            with open(self.ConfigFile) as dataFile:
                self.data = json.load(dataFile)
```

2. Next, we will define a couple of properties to give easy access to where the configuration is stored, as follows:

```python
@property
def UserConfigDir(self):
    return wx.StandardPaths_Get().GetUserDataDir()

@property
def ConfigFile(self):
```

```
appName = wx.GetApp().AppName
return os.path.join(self.UserConfigDir,
                    "%s.json" % appName)
```

3. These next two methods can be used to access or create application-defined configuration files or additional resources:

```
def GetConfigFile(self, relPath):
    return os.path.join(self.UserConfigDir, relPath)

def ConfigFileExists(self, relPath):
    path = self.GetConfigFile(relPath)
    return os.path.exists(path)
```

4. The following group of methods allow us to access, update, and add configuration data to the managed configuration data object, which is stored as the main application's configuration:

```
def GetValue(self, key, default=None):
    return self.data.get(key, default)

def WriteValue(self, key, value):
    self.data[key] = value

def SaveConfig(self):
    with open(self.ConfigFile, 'w') as configFile:
        json.dump(self.data, configFile)
```

5. To finish up this class, we will add a static singleton accessor method to ensure that the application can use a shared instance of the common configuration data, as follows:

```
@staticmethod
def Instance():
    if AppConfig._instance is None:
        AppConfig._instance = AppConfig()
    return AppConfig._instance
```

How it works...

When an instance of the AppConfig class is created, such as when the Instance method is accessed, the application's configuration folder is checked for and created in the proper location. The name of the folder and the configuration file is based on the Name property of the wx.App object that is created. This object stores data in a dictionary in memory during runtime using a simple key-to-value mapping. Then, when the SaveConfig method is called, the data is dumped into a JSON file in UserConfigDir that is named the same way as App.

The application can get and store its configuration values to `AppConfig` using the `GetValue` and `WriteValue` methods. For example, to get a stored configuration value from the `AppConfig` object, we just need to call its `GetValue` method with the key and optional default value to return when value is not set in the configuration file. Here's the code we executed for this:

```
cb1 = wx.CheckBox(self, label="Option 1", name="opt1")
cb1.Value = AppConfig.Instance().GetValue(cb1.Name, False)
```

Then, to store a value related to a control such as this for `AppConfig` to persist, the application would call the `WriteValue` method, as in the following example snippet:

```
def OnCheck(self, event):
    obj = event.EventObject
    AppConfig.Instance().WriteValue(obj.Name, obj.Value)
    event.Skip()
```

There's more...

The `wx.StandardPaths` object provides several other additional methods to access common configuration, installation, and system paths. The following table lists some of the additional methods available:

Method	Description
GetConfigDir	This lets us access the parent directory for system configuration files.
GetDataDir	This lets us access the application's global data directory.
GetUserConfigDir	This lets us access users' parent configuration directory. This is usually the home directory for the user.
GetUserLocalDataDir	This is the same as GetUserDataDir, except that on Windows, it returns the one under local settings.
GetAppDocumentsDir	This lets us access the document directory for the application under GetDocumentsDir.
GetDocumentsDir	This lets us access the current users' document directory.
GetExecutablePath	This gets us the absolute path to the running executable.
GetInstallPrefix	This gets us the program installation prefix; it only has any meaning on Linux.
GetLocalDataDir	This is the same as GetDataDir, except that on Unix, it returns the app-specific directory under /etc/.
GetLocalizedResourcesDir	This gets us access to the location where localized resources should be stored or located for the application.
GetPluginDir	This gets us the path to where plugins or loadable resources are located.

Method	Description
GetResourcesDir	This lets us access the location where auxiliary resource files should be located.
GetTempDir	This gets us the location of the system temp directory.

Saving the application's state

Many applications provide some functionality that remembers the window size, location, and other visual settings that a user may have left the UI in during its last usage. Adding such a feature can be accomplished in different ways. The wx.lib package provides a PersistentControls library that can be used to store the state of a window and its child controls to a file and can then restore the state to the controls at the next launch of the application. In this recipe, we will take a look at how to integrate PersistentControls into an application.

How to do it...

Here are the steps that you need to perform:

1. First, we will define our app's App object and set AppName:

```
import wx
import wx.lib.agw.persist as PERSIST


class MyApp(wx.App):
    def OnInit(self):
        self.SetAppName("PersistControls")
        self.frame = MyFrame(None, title="Save State")
        self.frame.Show()
        return True
```

2. Next, we will make a Panel for the app's main window that has a couple of CheckBox controls on it, as follows:

```
class MyPanel(wx.Panel):
    def __init__(self, parent):
        super(MyPanel, self).__init__(parent)

        sizer = wx.BoxSizer(wx.VERTICAL)
        cb1 = wx.CheckBox(self, label="Option 1", name="opt1")
        cb2 = wx.CheckBox(self, label="Option 2", name="opt2")
        sizer.AddMany([(cb1, 0, wx.ALL, 10),
                       (cb2, 0, wx.ALL, 10)])
        self.Sizer = sizer
```

3. Now, we will start to define our main window class using the following code:

```
class MyFrame(wx.Frame):
    def __init__(self, parent, title):
        super(MyFrame, self).__init__(parent, title=title,
                                      name="MyAppsFrame")
        sizer = wx.BoxSizer()
        sizer.Add(MyPanel(self), 1, wx.EXPAND)
        self.Sizer = sizer

        self.Register(self)

        self.Bind(wx.EVT_CLOSE, self.OnExit)
```

4. Next is the `Register` method, which we will use to register our named controls with `PersistenceManager`, as follows:

```
def Register(self, win):
    mgr = PERSIST.PersistenceManager.Get()
    if win and win.Name not in PERSIST.BAD_DEFAULT_NAMES:
        mgr.RegisterAndRestore(win)

    for child in win.Children:
        self.Register(child)
```

5. For the last step, we need to tell `PersistenceManager` when our windows are being destroyed so that it can save their state:

```
def OnExit(self, event):
    mgr = PERSIST.PersistenceManager.Get()
    mgr.SaveAndUnregister()
    event.Skip()
```

How it works...

`PersistenceManager` works by managing the properties of named windows and controls in an application. To use `PersistenceManager`, each window instance that is managed must have a unique name. In this recipe, we added a `Register` method to our `Frame` class to handle registering all the windows and controls that are contained within the frame with `PersistenceManager`. This is accomplished by recursively calling `Register` on each child window of the frame until all are registered.

When the frame's `EVT_CLOSE` event is fired, the `OnExit` event handler calls `SaveAndUnregister` on `PersistenceManager` to tell it to save the current state of all the registered controls to the application's data directory. This will result in the current position and size of the frame being saved as well as the current value of each of the two named `CheckBox` controls owned by `Panel`.

Then, the next time the application is started, these persisted values will be restored to each of the controls during the same `RegisterAndRestore` call that is used to register the window with the manager.

See also

 ▶ Take a look at the *Advancing your UI with AuiManager* recipe in *Chapter 3, UI Layout and Organization*, for another way to persist the state of a user interface that uses AUI components

Supporting internationalization

If you are creating an app for more than just yourself, you should consider building in support for internationalization into your UIs. Adding in the appropriate hooks for supporting interface translations in wxPython is quite simple if you plan ahead and do it from the beginning of your application's development. In this recipe, we will look at how to make use of and enable support for translations in your wxPython application.

How to do it...

Here are the steps to be performed for this recipe:

1. First, we will set up the imports and create a function alias through the following lines of code:

```
import wx
import os

# Function alias
_ = wx.GetTranslation
```

2. Next, we will define our app's subclass to set up the application's `locale` object based on user-configured settings:

```
class TranslatableApp(wx.App):
    def OnInit(self):
        self.SetAppName("I18NTestApp")

        # Get user configured language if set
        config = wx.Config()
        lang = config.Read('lang', 'LANGUAGE_DEFAULT')

        # Setup the Local
        self.locale = wx.Locale(getattr(wx, lang))
        path = os.path.abspath('./locale') + os.path.sep
```

```
        self.locale.AddCatalogLookupPathPrefix(path)
        self.locale.AddCatalog(self.AppName)

        self.frame = TestFrame(None, title=_("Sample App"))
        self.frame.Show()
        return True
```

3. For the next couple of steps, we will create a simple UI to demonstrate how to make use of translations. Take a look at the following:

```
class TestFrame(wx.Frame):
    def __init__(self, parent, title=""):
        super(TestFrame, self).__init__(parent, title=title)

        self.panel = TestPanel(self)

        sizer = wx.BoxSizer(wx.VERTICAL)
        sizer.Add(self.panel, 1, wx.EXPAND)
        self.Sizer = sizer
        self.SetInitialSize((350, 200))

        self.Bind(wx.EVT_BUTTON, self.OnButton)

    def OnButton(self, event):
        if event.Id == wx.ID_CLOSE:
            self.Close()
```

4. Next, we will make the `Panel` class that will hold the controls to allow the user to select a different language to use, as follows:

```
class TestPanel(wx.Panel):
    def __init__(self, parent):
        super(TestPanel, self).__init__(parent)

        self.closebtn = wx.Button(self, wx.ID_CLOSE)
        self.langch = wx.Choice(self,
                                choices=[_("English"),
                                         _("Japanese")])
        self.__DoLayout()
        self.Bind(wx.EVT_CHOICE, self.OnChoice)
```

5. Next, we will do the layout for `Panel` via the following code:

```
    def __DoLayout(self):
        sizer = wx.BoxSizer(wx.VERTICAL)

        greeting = wx.StaticText(self, label=_("Hello"))
        sizer.Add(greeting, 0, wx.ALIGN_CENTER_HORIZONTAL)
```

```
langsz = wx.BoxSizer(wx.HORIZONTAL)
langlbl = wx.StaticText(self, label=_("Language"))
langsz.Add(langlbl, 0,
           wx.ALL|wx.ALIGN_CENTER_VERTICAL, 5)
langsz.Add(self.langch, 1,
           wx.ALIGN_CENTER_VERTICAL|wx.EXPAND)
sizer.Add(langsz, 0, wx.ALL|wx.EXPAND, 5)

sizer.Add(self.closebtn, 0,
          wx.ALIGN_RIGHT|wx.RIGHT, 5)
self.Sizer = sizer
```

6. For the final step, we will define the `OnChoice` handler to do some simple configuration setting changes for the selected language:

```
def OnChoice(self, event):
    if self.langch.Selection == 0:
        val = 'LANGUAGE_ENGLISH'
    else:
        val = 'LANGUAGE_JAPANESE'
    config = wx.Config()
    config.Write('lang', val)
```

How it works...

One of the main points to take note of in this application is how we wrapped all the strings that appear in the UI to the user with the `wx.GetTranslation` function. This function uses the application's current `locale` object to check whether any language catalogues are registered for the application. In the catalogues, it looks for a match to the passed in string and returns the translated version of the string instead.

Next, in the `OnInit` method of our application, we created a `locale` object and added a lookup path that points to the directory that our application keeps its translations in. This enables `GetTranslation` to locate any translations for catalogs that are found on the path for the `locale` object's currently set language.

When this sample application starts, it uses the default locale as the `Config` object has no stored setting in it. Once a language is selected in the choice control and the application is restarted, you can see how the display strings are now translated from English on the left to Japanese on the right in the preceding image.

There's more...

The wxPython translation system uses `gettext` formatted files to load translated resource strings from. There are two files for each translation: the `.po` file (**Portable Object**) and the `.mo` file (**Machine Object**). The Portable Object file is the source file that is edited to create the mapping of the default string to the translated version. The Machine Object file is a compiled version of the `.po` file. To compile a `.po` file with a `.mo` file, you need to use either msgfmt or Poedit, both of which are free tools available on any platform that has wxPython.

See also

▶ Refer to the *Enhancing ComboBox with bitmaps* recipe in *Chapter 4, Containers and Advanced Controls*, for an example of a custom control that can be used to select a language

Optimizing for OS X

Even though wxPython is a native cross platform user interface library, it can still leave gaps on some platforms due to various reasons. Historically, the support in wxPython for Windows and Linux (GTK) has been fairly complete and consistent; however, for OS X, due to its different conventions, available features, as well as user expectations, it requires special attention when developing your application. In this recipe, we will look at some of the important small details to keep in mind when developing a wxPython application that may be deployed on OS X.

How to do it...

Perform the following steps:

1. First, let's add some code to our app's `OnInit` method to enable `wx.SystemOption`, as follows:

```
class OSXApp(wx.App):
    def OnInit(self):
        if wx.Platform == '__WXMAC__':
            spellcheck = "mac.textcontrol-use-spell-checker"
            wx.SystemOptions.SetOptionInt(spellcheck, 1)
            self.SetMacHelpMenuTitleName("&Help")
        self.frame = OSXFrame(None, "Optimize for OSX")
```

```
            self.frame.Show()
            return True

        def MacReopenApp(self):
            self.GetTopWindow().Raise()
```

2. Next, we will create a `Frame` class with `TextCtrl` to show how `SystemOption` from step one affects `TextCtrl` via the following class:

```
class OSXFrame(wx.Frame):
    def __init__(self, parent, title):
        super(OSXFrame, self).__init__(parent, title=title)

        self._SetupMenus()

        self.text = wx.TextCtrl(self, style=wx.TE_MULTILINE)
        sizer = wx.BoxSizer()
        sizer.Add(self.text, 1, wx.EXPAND)
        self.Sizer = sizer
        self.SetInitialSize((350, 200))
```

3. Now, we will create a number of standard menus using the stock IDs by executing the following code:

```
        def _SetupMenus(self):
            mb = wx.MenuBar()
            fmenu = wx.Menu()
            fmenu.Append(wx.ID_OPEN)
            fmenu.Append(wx.ID_EXIT)
            mb.Append(fmenu, "&File")
            emenu = wx.Menu()
            emenu.Append(wx.ID_COPY)
            emenu.Append(wx.ID_PREFERENCES)
            mb.Append(emenu, "&Edit")
            hmenu = wx.Menu()
            hmenu.Append(wx.NewId(), "&Online help...")
            hmenu.Append(wx.ID_ABOUT, "&About...")
            mb.Append(hmenu, "&Help")
            self.MenuBar = mb
```

How it works...

We did several small things in this recipe to highlight some things to take note of when developing an application that will be run on a Macintosh system.

First, we enabled `SystemOption` to turn on the native spell checking that is available in `TextCtrl` on OS X 10.4 or higher. Next, we called `SetMacHelpMenuTitleName` to inform the application which menu is our **Help** menu. We needed to do this because all OS X applications by default have a **Help** menu, and as we used an accelerator character (`&`) in the title to allow keyboard shortcuts in our application on Windows and Linux, the menu title text does not match the default name **Help**. Not calling `SetMacHelpMenuTitleName` in this case could result in two **Help** menus being displayed as the framework would not recognize our menu as the **Help** menu.

Some additional things to note about the other standard menu items that were created in `_SetupMenus` is that items such as **Preferences**, **Exit**, and **About** will be automatically moved to the app menu. This happens because all OS X applications have these standard items located there, and to help make your application appear similar to a native OS X application, the framework will make these modifications for you.

There's more...

There are some other additional Macintosh-specific methods that belong to the `wx.App` object that can be used to customize the handling for three special menu items. These methods are a no-op when called from other platforms. Take a look at the following table:

Method	Description
`SetMacAboutMenuItemId`	This changes the ID used to identify the **About** menu item from `ID_ABOUT` to a custom value
`SetMacExitMenuItemId`	This changes the ID used to identify the **Exit** menu item from `ID_EXIT` to a custom value
`SetMacPreferencesMenuItemId`	This changes the ID used to identify the **Preferences** menu item from `ID_PREFERENCES` to a custom value
`SetMacSupportPCMenuShortcuts`	This enables the use of menu mnemonics on OS X
`SetMacHelpMenuTitleName`	This sets a custom title text for the **Help** menu

ToolBars

When using a ToolBar in your application on OS X, there are a couple special things to take note of to ensure that it works well when your application is run on OS X:

1. Firstly, the order in which the `ToolBar` is created and attached to the frame matters on OS X. The ToolBar should be created and attached to the frame, and then we should call `Realize` in that order, as shown here:

```
class MyFrame(wx.Frame):
def __init__(self, parent):
    super(MyFrame, self).__init__(parent)
```

```
toolbar = wx.ToolBar(self)
# add icons to the toolbar here…
self.SetToolBar(toolbar)
toolbar.Realize()
```

2. Secondly, applications on OS X tend to use 32x32-pixel-sized tool icons on the toolbar as a standard. So, if you are using custom icons in your application's toolbar, you should keep at least two sizes—16x16 for Windows and 32x32 for OS X—and load the appropriate one depending upon which platform the application is running on. Not doing this would result in the small icons being stretched on OS X, leading to fuzzy-looking icons.

See also

- ▸ Take a look at the *Handling AppleEvents* recipe in *Chapter 1, wxPython Starting Points*, for another OS X-specific recipe for handling special system events on OS X
- ▸ Refer to *Starting with the easy button* recipe in *Chapter 2, Common User Controls*, for more details about using stock IDs in controls

Handling errors gracefully

In even simple applications, it can be difficult to know or account for all the possible error conditions that could occur during the execution of a program. So, it is important to build in a way to catch all the errors that slip by normal handling and provide as graceful a handling of them as possible. This can be the difference between your users thinking your application is buggy or doesn't work and continuing to give it another chance. In this recipe, we will discuss how to install an exception hook to give feedback to users when an unexpected error occurs.

How to do it...

Here are the steps that you need to perform:

1. First, we need to start by importing a few extra modules to help out with this recipe, as follows:

```
import sys
import traceback
import wx
import wx.lib.dialogs as DIA
```

2. Next, let's define an app object that can deal with unhandled exceptions through the following code:

```
class ErrorHandlingApp(wx.App):
    def OnInit(self):
```

```
        sys.excepthook = self.ExceptionHook

        self.frame = TestFrame(None, "Unhandled error")
        self.frame.Show()

        return True
```

3. Next, we will define our custom exception hook function, as follows:

```
    def ExceptionHook(self, errType, value, trace):
        err = traceback.format_exception(errType,
                                         value, trace)
        errTxt = "\n".join(err)
        msg = "An unexpected error has occurred:\n%s" % errTxt
        if self and wx.Thread_IsMain() \
                and self.IsMainLoopRunning():
            # only use UI notification if APP is running
            if not self.HandleError(value):
                DIA.scrolledMessageDialog(None, msg,
                                          "Unexpected Error")
                self.Exit()
        else:
            sys.stderr.write(msg)
```

4. With the exception hook in place we will use the following script to also add an overridable method that subclasses can use to provide custom error handling or ignore certain exceptions:

```
    def HandleError(self, error):
        """Override in subclass to handle errors
        @return: True to allow program to continue running
        """
        return False
```

5. For the final step, we will just create a sample `Frame` class that has a button, which causes an unhandled exception to be thrown:

```
class TestFrame(wx.Frame):
    def __init__(self, parent, title):
        super(TestFrame, self).__init__(parent, title=title)

        panel = wx.Panel(self)
        psz = wx.BoxSizer()
        btn = wx.Button(panel, wx.NewId(), "Cause Error")
        psz.Add(btn, 0, wx.ALIGN_CENTER|wx.ALL, 100)
        panel.Sizer = psz
```

```
        sizer = wx.BoxSizer()
        sizer.Add(panel, 1, wx.EXPAND)
        self.Sizer = sizer
        self.SetInitialSize()

        self.Bind(wx.EVT_BUTTON, self.OnError, btn)

    def OnError(self, event):
        # cause an unhandled exception
        x = 1 / 0
```

How it works...

This application object installs an exception hook to replace `sys.excepthook`. Whenever Python encounters an unhandled exception thrown by an application, it invokes the exception hook. You can make use of this functionality, as we did in this example application, to catch the error and provide the user with some sort of error message or information to let them know that the application needs to be shut down. It also gives you an opportunity to log the error and save any state that your application may need to be in during a normal shutdown. For this application, we just provided a simple interface that allows subclasses to do a special handling and even suppress errors by overriding the `HandleError` method. When the error remains unhandled by `HandleError`, a simple notification dialog is shown to display the stack trace of the error, and the application is finally exited after it's dismissed.

Embedding your resources

Though it's relatively easy to load bitmap resources from files local to your scripts on your development machine, this task can add complexity and fail points to your application when it is deployed in different environments or locations that you may not have accounted for. Luckily, wxPython also has some additional tools built in that allow you to embed images into Python code modules, so you can reference them in your application as with any other variable. In this recipe, we will show you how to make a module that has embedded images as well as how to use these embedded images in an application.

How to do it...

Perform the following steps:

1. First, we need to import some extra modules to help out in this recipe, as follows:

```
import sys
import os
import glob
import wx.tools.img2py as img2py
```

2. This next function is used to enumerate all the PNG files in a directory, and then `img2py` is used to embed them in a module:

```
def generateIconModule(sourcePath, outModule):
    search = os.path.join(sourcePath, "*.png")
    lst = glob.glob(search)
    splitext = os.path.splitext
    basename = os.path.basename
    i = 0
    for i, png in enumerate(lst):
        name = splitext(basename(png))[0]
        name = name.replace('-', ' ').title()
        name = name.replace(' ', '')
        img2py.img2py(png, outModule, i > 0, imgName=name)
    return i
```

3. The last step is the main section for the execution of our little utility script:

```
def printHelp():
    print("PNG image file embedder")
    print("embedded.py imgDirectory resource.py")


if __name__ == '__main__':
    if len(sys.argv) != 3:
        printHelp()
        sys.exit()
    dName = sys.argv[1]
    print("Locating PNG images in %s" % dName)
    modName = sys.argv[2]
    n = generateIconModule(dName, modName)
    print("%d images embedded in %s" % (n, modName))
```

How it works...

The `img2py` function in the `img2py` module reads in the raw image data and then uses Base64 to encode it into a string that can be stored as a resource in the module as with any other Python string. This string is then stored into a `PyEmbeddedImage` object and assigned to a global variable in the specified output module. The output module can then be imported into any Python script and used to provide access to the bitmaps. Take a look at the following code:

```
class ImagePanel(wx.Panel):
    def __init__(self, parent):
        super(ImagePanel, self).__init__(parent)

        sz = wx.BoxSizer()
```

```
sb = wx.StaticBitmap(self,
                        bitmap=resource.FaceGlasses.Bitmap)
sz.Add(sb, 0, wx.ALIGN_CENTER|wx.ALL, 100)
self.Sizer = sz
```

The preceding code snippet shows how bitmap resources can be accessed from a resource module. The `PyEmbeddedImage` object provides a bitmap, an icon, and image properties to give the application access to the image data in all the three formats that can be used by different application components.

There's more...

The `img2py` module itself can be run from the command line to embed images into a module. This recipe just made another wrapper script to help simplify generating and regenerating a resource module from a directory of images. When executed as a script, this module can take several optional arguments on how to generate the resource data for the image. Consider the following table:

Command line option	Description
-a	This appends the image data to the output file.
-n	This expects a value argument along with it that specifies the image's variable name to use.
-m	This specifies a mask color for the image using a value argument that is the hex color code value of the mask color.
-i	This generates a function that returns an icon version of the image. This only applies when we use the compatibility mode.
-c	This generates a catalog in the output module. This is a global-level dictionary that gives access to the embedded images by name.
-f	This generates a module interface compatible with the old `img2py` formatting.
-F	This uses the new style embedded resource module that uses `PyEmbeddedImage` objects and no module-level get functions.

See also

▸ Refer to the *Using bitmaps* recipe in *Chapter 1*, *wxPython Starting Points*, for a recipe showing how to load bitmaps from normal image files

Distributing an application

Once you reach the point of being ready to share your application with others, you will need a way to package it up and ship it out. wxPython applications can be distributed in a similar way to any other Python application or script—by creating a `setup.py` script and using the `distutils` module's setup function. However, this recipe focuses on how to build standalone executables for Windows and OS X so that your users don't need to install all the dependencies that your application has from your development environment. This can be accomplished using `py2exe` on Windows and `py2app` on OS X. So, in this recipe, we will consider how to make a `setup.py` script to leverage these tools and generate standalone executables.

Getting ready

This recipe requires that you have installed the appropriate extension module for your target platform. So, if you haven't already installed either `py2exe` or `py2app` for the version of Python and wxPython you are using, do so now.

How to do it...

Perform the following steps for this recipe:

1. First, we will import the needed modules and define some constants that will be used for either platform's build:

```
import wx
import sys
import platform

APP = "EditorApp.py"
NAME = "FileEditor"
VERSION = "1.0"
AUTHOR = "Author Name"
AUTHOR_EMAIL = "authorname@someplace.com"
URL = "http://fileeditor_webpage.foo"
LICENSE = "wxWidgets"
YEAR = "2015"
```

2. Next, we will make a function to encapsulate building our standalone application using `py2exe`:

```
def BuildPy2Exe():
    from distutils.core import setup
    try:
        import py2exe
    except ImportError:
```

```
        print "\n!! You dont have py2exe installed. !!\n"
        exit()

    archDat = platform.architecture()
    is32 = "32bit" in archDat
    bundle = 2 if is32 else 3
    OPTS = {"py2exe" : {"compressed" : 1,
            "optimize" : 1,
            "bundle_files" : bundle,
            "includes" : ["fileEditor", "EditorApp"],
            "excludes" : ["Tkinter",],
            "dll_excludes": ["MSVCP90.dll"]}}

    setup(name = NAME,
          version = VERSION,
          options = OPTS,
          windows = [{"script": APP,
                      "icon_resources": [(1, "Icon.ico")],
          }],
          description = NAME,
          author = AUTHOR,
          author_email = AUTHOR_EMAIL,
          license = LICENSE,
          url = URL,
          )
```

3. Next is the definition to build an OS X app using `py2app`. Take a look at the following code:

```
def BuildOSXApp():
    """Build the OSX Applet"""
    from setuptools import setup

    copyright = "Copyright %s %s" % (AUTHOR, YEAR)
    appid = "com.%s.%s" % (NAME, NAME)
    PLIST = dict(CFBundleName = NAME,
                 CFBundleIconFile = 'Icon.icns',
                 CFBundleShortVersionString = VERSION,
                 CFBundleGetInfoString = NAME + " " + VERSION,
                 CFBundleExecutable = NAME,
                 CFBundleIdentifier = appid,
                 CFBundleTypeMIMETypes = ['text/plain',],
                 CFBundleDevelopmentRegion = 'English',
                 NSHumanReadableCopyright = copyright
    )
```

```
PY2APP_OPTS = dict(iconfile = "Icon.icns",
                    argv_emulation = True,
                    optimize = True,
                    plist = PLIST)
setup(app = [APP,],
      version = VERSION,
      options = dict( py2app = PY2APP_OPTS),
      description = NAME,
      author = AUTHOR,
      author_email = AUTHOR_EMAIL,
      license = LICENSE,
      url = URL,
      setup_requires = ['py2app'],
      )
```

4. The last step is to check the platform when this `setup.py` script is run and delegated to the appropriate setup function. We can do this via the following:

```
if __name__ == '__main__':
    if wx.Platform == '__WXMSW__':
        # Windows
        BuildPy2Exe()
    elif wx.Platform == '__WXMAC__':
        # OSX
        BuildOSXApp()
    else:
        print "Unsupported platform: %s" % wx.Platform
```

How it works...

With this `setup.py` script, we can build either an executable for Windows or an applet for OS X out of the text editor application that we built through the earlier chapters in this book. After building the application with this script, all the items needed to run it will be bundled together in the `dist` directory that is created by the setup method.

To build the `py2exe` version of the application, the script must be run as follows:

```
python setup.py py2exe
```

When this is run on Windows, it invokes our `BuildPy2exe` method, which builds up the list of options needed to build the application. The first of these options that we set is the `bundle_files` option, which is used to bundle files into `library.zip`. The lower the number, the more the files that will be bundled in. We did a check for whether the system is 32-bits as `bundle_files` with values less than three does not work on 64-bit systems currently.

Building the `py2app` version of the application can be done in a similar way by running the following command:

```
python setup.py py2app
```

When the script is executed with this command on a Macintosh operating system, the `BuildOSXApp` method is executed to build up the applet. To build the OS X app, we constructed a dictionary that `py2app` will use to convert the application's `PList`. This is similar to a manifest on Windows and contains several bits of information that help the application be integrated into the system. Specifically for this text editor application, we can specify file types to the `CFBundleTypeMIMETypes` argument, which will tell the OS that this application is capable of opening and working with the specified types of files. The rest of the arguments to the setup method are quite similar to building the `py2exe` executable.

There's more...

When using `py2exe`, it may not include all the needed DLLs when it builds your application. The DLLs that were excluded will be listed when the setup script finishes running; most that are listed are usually system DLLs that can be ignored and don't need to be included. There are however some DLLs that are needed by Python or wxPython to enable your standalone application to run. It is sometimes necessary to either include some additional DLLs (`gdiplus.dll`, `msvcrXX.dll`) with your application or instruct your users to install the freely available Visual Studio redistributable package when trying to run it on other systems.

Also, if you are targeting installs on older versions of Windows, such as Windows XP, you may also need to modify the setup script used here to include an appropriate manifest in the executable. This is necessary in some cases in order to make the user interface use the modern styling over the older Windows 2000-style UI.

See also

▶ Take a look at the *Searching text with FindReplaceDialog* recipe in *Chapter 7, Requesting and Retrieving Information*, for the code that this recipe's `setup.py` script builds an app for

Updating your software

No matter what you do to try and make your first release perfect and defect-free, there will always be something that will come up and raise the need to make an update to your application. Notifying your users of the update and making it easy for them to install it is an important step toward ensuring that they have the latest patched versions with all the newest features you add. Starting in wxPython 2.9.2.2, an extension module was added that provides a convenient mixin class for `wx.App` called `SoftwareUpdate`, which integrates the update features of the Esky (`https://pypi.python.org/pypi/esky`) auto-update framework into a wxPython application. In this recipe, you will learn how to bundle an Esky package for your wxPython application as well as how make use of the `SoftwareUpdate` mixin.

Getting ready

For this recipe, you will need to ensure that you review the previous recipe about building an application for distribution.

We will also need to install some extension packages for this recipe as well, so ensure that you install the Esky package. If you are on Windows, also ensure that you have the `pywin32` extension modules installed as well.

How to do it...

You need to perform the following steps:

1. First, we need to rework the `setup.py` file that was developed in the previous recipe in order to build an Esky compatible bundle. In this first section, the important changes have been highlighted:

```
import wx
import sys
from esky import bdist_esky
from setuptools import setup
import version

APP = "EditorApp.py"
NAME = "FileEditor"
VERSION = version.VERSION
AUTHOR = "Author Name"
AUTHOR_EMAIL = "authorname@someplace.com"
URL = "http://fileeditor_webpage.foo"
LICENSE = "wxWidgets"
YEAR = "2015"
```

2. Next, the `BuildPy2Exe` method has to be reworked to build up a set of options to pass the Esky build:

```
def BuildPy2Exe():
    import py2exe
    opts = dict(compressed = 0,
                optimize = 0,
                bundle_files = 3,
                includes = ["fileEditor", "EditorApp"],
                excludes = ["Tkinter",],
                dll_excludes = ["MSVCP90.dll"])
    icon = "Icon.ico"
    BundleEsky("py2exe", opts, icon)
```

3. Similarly, the `BuildOSXApp` method also needs to be updated to pass the `py2app` options to the Esky build:

```
def BuildOSXApp():
    """Build the OSX Applet"""
    copyright = "Copyright %s %s" % (AUTHOR, YEAR)
    appid = "com.%s.%s" % (NAME, NAME)
    plist = dict(CFBundleName = NAME,
                CFBundleIconFile = 'Icon.icns',
                CFBundleShortVersionString = VERSION,
                CFBundleGetInfoString = NAME + " " + VERSION,
                CFBundleExecutable = NAME,
                CFBundleIdentifier = appid,
                CFBundleTypeMIMETypes = ['text/plain',],
                CFBundleDevelopmentRegion = 'English',
                NSHumanReadableCopyright = copyright
    )
    icon = "Icon.icns"
    opts = dict(iconfile = icon,
                argv_emulation = True,
                optimize = True,
                plist = plist)

    BundleEsky("py2app", opts, icon)
```

4. Finally, the `BundleEsky` method takes the appropriate platform options and builds the `esky` bundle, as follows:

```
def BundleEsky(freezer, options, icon):
    app = [bdist_esky.Executable(APP, gui_only=True,
                                 icon=icon),]
    eskyOps = dict(freezer_module = freezer,
                   freezer_options = options,
```

```
                        enable_appdata_dir = True,
                        bundle_msvcrt = True)

        data = [ icon, ]

        setup(name = NAME,
              scripts = app,
              version = VERSION,
              author = AUTHOR,
              author_email = AUTHOR_EMAIL,
              license = LICENSE,
              url = URL,
              data_files = data,
              options = dict(bdist_esky = eskyOps))
```

5. Now, with the setup file updated, to build an Esky-compatible bundle we need to make a small update to our `App` object to have it check for updates at startup. The parts that are important for the `SoftwareUpdate` mixin are highlighted in the following code:

```
import wx.lib.softwareupdate as UPDATE

class MyApp(wx.App, UPDATE.SoftwareUpdate):
    def OnInit(self):
        self.SetAppDisplayName("Cookbook Text Editor")
        # Use local host as update url for example
        url = "http://127.0.0.1:8000"
        self.InitUpdates(url)
        self.CheckForUpdate(True)

        name = "TextEditor %s" % version.VERSION
        self.frame = TextEditorWithFind(None, title=name)
        self.frame.Show();
        return True
```

How it works...

The `SoftwareUpdate` mixin class only works with frozen Esky-compatible application bundles. So, the first thing we did was make a `setup.py` script that can use Esky to bundle a `py2exe` or `py2app` build version of the application. When built, this will bundle the application into a special ZIP file, which will have its name formatted with some platform and version information. This file can then be deployed to a web server to automatically make updates available to users of the application.

The SoftwareUpdate mixin makes using the auto-update features of Esky quite simple to do. All that is needed is to mix in the class with the application's App object. Then, use it to check for updates, such as in OnInit or in a check for updates action somewhere else in the application. In order to check for and download any updates, all that needs to be done is call two methods that the SoftwareUpdate mixin adds to the App object:

- ▶ The first is to call InitUpdates with the URL to the path that contains the uploaded application bundle.

- ▶ The second is to call CheckForUpdate to have Esky check the URL for newer versions of the application. If one is found, a dialog will pop up asking the user if he/she would like to update to the new version.

If the user chooses to accept the update, the framework will automatically download and deploy the update to the system.

There's more...

To make use of this recipe for your application, you will need to have a web server setup to distribute your updates from. The example code in OnInit uses a localhost with a server running on port 8000 as the update server. Take a look at the README_FIRST file in the example code that comes with this recipe for how to set up a simple HTTP server on this address on your computer to try and test out this recipe.

See also

- ▶ Refer to the *Distributing an application recipe* earlier in this chapter for more details about using py2exe and py2app with a wxPython application

Index

Symbols

.mo file (Machine Object) 222
.po file (Portable Object) 222

A

AboutBox
  used, for displaying app information 145-147
AboutDialogInfo class, parameters
  SetArtists 147
  SetDevelopers 147
  SetDocWriters 147
  SetIcon 147
  SetLicense 148
  SetTranslators 148
  SetWebsite 148
AddTool method, values
  wx.ITEM_CHECK 42
  wx.ITEM_DROPDOWN 42
  wx.ITEM_NORMAL 42
  wx.ITEM_RADIO 42
AppleEvents
  handling 17, 18
application
  distributing 230-233
  state, saving with PersistentControls
      library 217, 218
  web browser, surfing 97-100
application object
  creating 2, 3
AuiManager
  used, for advancing UI 66-69
  window's state, restoring 69
  window's state, saving 69
AuiPaneInfo
  CloseButton(bool) property 69

MaximizeButton(bool) property 69
MinimizeButton(bool) property 69
PinButton(bool) property 69
automatic wrapping layout
  creating 54

B

basic shapes
  drawing 173, 174
bitmaps
  used, for enhancing ComboBox 74, 75
  using 6, 7
buttons
  implementing 22-24
  using 20, 21

C

CalendarCtrl 33
callback functions
  binding, to events 7-9
CheckBoxes
  options 25, 26
clipboard
  accessing 13, 14
ComboBox
  enhancing, with bitmaps 74, 75
command line option
  -a 229
  -c 229
  -f 229
  -F 229
  -i 229
  -m 229
  -n 229

Thank you for buying
wxPython Application
Development Cookbook

About Packt Publishing

Packt, pronounced 'packed', published its first book, *Mastering phpMyAdmin for Effective MySQL Management*, in April 2004, and subsequently continued to specialize in publishing highly focused books on specific technologies and solutions.

Our books and publications share the experiences of your fellow IT professionals in adapting and customizing today's systems, applications, and frameworks. Our solution-based books give you the knowledge and power to customize the software and technologies you're using to get the job done. Packt books are more specific and less general than the IT books you have seen in the past. Our unique business model allows us to bring you more focused information, giving you more of what you need to know, and less of what you don't.

Packt is a modern yet unique publishing company that focuses on producing quality, cutting-edge books for communities of developers, administrators, and newbies alike. For more information, please visit our website at www.packtpub.com.

About Packt Open Source

In 2010, Packt launched two new brands, Packt Open Source and Packt Enterprise, in order to continue its focus on specialization. This book is part of the Packt open source brand, home to books published on software built around open source licenses, and offering information to anybody from advanced developers to budding web designers. The Open Source brand also runs Packt's open source Royalty Scheme, by which Packt gives a royalty to each open source project about whose software a book is sold.

Writing for Packt

We welcome all inquiries from people who are interested in authoring. Book proposals should be sent to author@packtpub.com. If your book idea is still at an early stage and you would like to discuss it first before writing a formal book proposal, then please contact us; one of our commissioning editors will get in touch with you.

We're not just looking for published authors; if you have strong technical skills but no writing experience, our experienced editors can help you develop a writing career, or simply get some additional reward for your expertise.

Python Parallel Programming Cookbook

ISBN: 978-1-78528-958-3   Paperback: 286 pages

Master efficient parallel programming to build powerful applications using Python

1. Design and implement efficient parallel software.

2. Master new programming techniques to address and solve complex programming problems.

3. Explore the world of parallel programming with this book, which is a go-to resource for different kinds of parallel computing tasks in Python, using examples and topics covered in great depth.

Python 3 Object-oriented Programming

Second Edition

ISBN: 978-1-78439-878-1   Paperback: 460 pages

Unleash the power of Python 3 objects

1. Stop writing scripts and start architecting programs.

2. Learn the latest Python syntax and libraries.

3. A practical, hands-on tutorial that teaches you all about abstract design patterns and how to implement them in Python 3.

Please check **www.PacktPub.com** for information on our titles